AS ICT for OCR

GLEN MILLBERY
SONIA STUART
ALAN WILKES
MAGGIE BANKS

Published in 2005 by:
Nelson Thornes Ltd
Delta Place
27 Bath Road
CHELTENHAM
GL53 7TH
United Kingdom

05 06 07 08 09 / 10 9 8 7 6 5 4 3 2 1

A catalogue record for this book is available from the British Library

ISBN 0 7487 9116 7

Page make-up & Illustrations by Pantek Arts Ltd, Maidstone, Kent

Printed and bound in Great Britain by Scotprint

Acknowledgements

The authors and publishers are grateful to the following for permission to reproduce photographs:
p10 Bladerunner poster – Ladd Company/Ronald Grant Archive; p25 Computer/tower unit – Photodisc 43 (NT); p26 Software, paper, ink cartridges – iStockphoto.com; p37 CPU – Photodisc 55 (NT); p41 Qwerty keyboard – Photodisc 44B (NT); p42 Concept keyboard – iStockphoto.com; p43 Lottery ticket – Stuart Sweatmore; p43 Bar code – Elektravision 1 (NT); p47 Drum plotter – iStockphoto.com; p70 Telephone directory – Stuart Sweatmore.

Contents

Introduction

AS ICT for OCR is a new book that has been written by principal examiners specifically for use by students studying for the OCR Advanced Subsidiary GCE in Information and Communication Technology qualification. The content has been carefully mapped to the specification so it is relevant and concise. The clear structure and layout make this text easily accessible whilst taking you through everything you require in manageable portions. Using this text will enable you to achieve your best results in the theory papers.

The structure of the book

The content of the text covers modules 2512: Information, Systems and Communications (chapters 1-6) and 2514: Practical Applications of ICT using Standard/Generic Applications Software (chapters 7-13). Chapter 15 covers examination techniques, which will help you perform at your best in the theory papers. Chapter 14 also provides guidance of carrying out and presenting your coursework for Module 2513.

Making the most of the features in the book

Objectives

You will find objectives panels at the beginning of each chapter that outline what will be covered and what you should have learnt after studying the chapter. Read these panels carefully before you start the chapter as they will help you pull out important points from the text whilst you study. You may also like to refer back to these panels at the end of each chapter to check you have learnt everything you need to and/or at the end of the course during your revision.

Key words

Key terms are provided in the margins and define essential vocabulary alongside the main text. It is essential that you understand what these words mean and that you can use them confidently when communicating your ideas in class, in your coursework and in your exam answers. These terms are compiled into a glossary at the end of the book that can be used for quick reference.

Short questions and activities

You will find short-answer questions and activities throughout the text. Make sure you complete these as they will help you understand and engage with the content of the chapter and will encourage you to start taking notes that you can use during your revision.

Examination-style practice questions

At the end of each chapter you will find a number of examination-style practice questions. Your teacher may ask you to complete these questions for homework but you could also practise answering them before you start revising to highlight areas on which you need to concentrate.

Data, information, knowledge and processing

Objectives

Your objectives for this chapter are to:

◎ know what is meant by, and the difference between, data, information and knowledge

◎ understand different methods of representing information and the difference between syntactic and semantic information

◎ describe different data types and know when they should be used

◎ know different sources of data

◎ understand how the quality of the data source affects information

◎ discuss the problems and benefits of coding data

◎ know the purpose of test plans

◎ understand the difference between verification and validation and methods of achieving these

◎ discuss the costs of producing information and understand the value of information

◎ know about expert systems

◎ understand input, output, storage, processing and feedback.

Keep these objectives in mind as you work through the chapter.

What is data?

Everything is made up of data. Anything that is written or spoken is made up of data. If you break any words down you eventually, at the bottom of the pile, find data.

It is important to understand that data itself has no meaning. For example:

● 23edfr32
● 12ws43fr

The above are examples of data. There is no way to tell what they mean, they are just a random series of numbers and letters.

Remember:

● data is a range of alphanumeric characters (letters, numbers, sound and graphics)
● data is raw facts before they have been processed
● data has no meaning.

> ✱ **Data** is the raw facts and figures before they have been processed.

> **hint** If you have to give an example of data, make sure that it is just a set of random numbers and letters and that there is no meaning to it.

Questions

1 Using an example, define what is meant by the term 'data'.
2 Identify **two** characteristics of data.

What is information?

Information is the result of taking the data and processing it. This involves giving the data meaning. Processing is performing some action on the data. This might be sorting, searching, saving or editing.

There is a formula that you need to know that shows how data can become information:

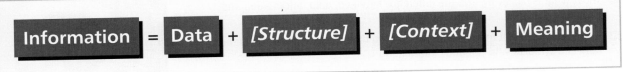

Information = **Data** + *[Structure]* + *[Context]* + **Meaning**

Figure 1.1
The formula showing how data becomes information

In some cases, the data does not need to have a structure and a context in order to become information. However, it is always best to know the complete formula.

Figure 1.2 Examples of converting data into information

Data	Structure	Context	Meaning
12102005	12/10/2005	UK date	Date of hotel room booking
31 32 34 32 31	Numbers	Celsius	Temperature over 5 days in the Maldives
TRBL34	First 2 letters – type of garment Second 2 letters – colour Last 2 numbers – waist size	A shop stock code	A pair of blue trousers, size 34"
1	Selected from a scale of 1-4	How enjoyable was the film? 1 = good 4 = bad	The film was good

Information is the result of taking data and processing it.

Structure is how the data is presented – are the numbers actually numbers or should they be read as text? Should the data be organised in a particular way – grouped by numbers of characters? What, if any, coding system has been used?

Context is taking the data and giving it an environment where our prior knowledge and understanding can make sense of it.

Meaning is putting the data into the correct structure and placing it within the context.

Activity

Complete the following table, showing how data can be turned into information. Use the scenarios given at the top of the table.

Scenario:	Estate agents	Removal company	School
Data			
Structure			
Context			
Meaning			

hint You will need to be able to give an example of information. The example you give **must** be relevant to the context of the question being asked in the examination – if the question is about hotels, give an example to do with hotels.

Questions

1 Give a definition of information.
2 Within the definition of information, what is meant by structure?
3 Within the definition of information, what is meant by context?
4 Within the definition of information, what is meant by meaning?
5 Using a bank as the scenario, show how data can become information.

Representation methods to convey meaning

For people to be able to use information they must be able to extract it and pass it on. If information is only known by one person then its value is limited.

Ideally, information should be available in many different formats. However, there are restrictions. Some information needs to be kept secure and if it became known then it could cause problems – this includes:

- secret service intelligence
- business information.

Another restriction is the language barrier. If information is presented in one particular language then how can someone who does not understand that language acquire the information?

People who are disabled have restrictions – for example, people who have visual (seeing) or aural (hearing) disabilities may have problems acquiring information if it is in the wrong format for them.

It can be difficult to select and justify different methods (known as representation methods) of conveying information for different situations. The three main ones are:

- text (including writing)
- graphics (including pictures)
- sound (including voice).

Each one has its advantages and disadvantages. However, the user must be considered when selecting a representation method.

General examples of the advantages and disadvantages of each of the three representation methods are given in Figure 1.3 overleaf:

Activity

Make a copy of the table below. Look around the room and complete your table. Add as many rows as required. Identify the type of representation (text, sound, picture, light); a description of the representation; how it is used and the intended audience. The first one has been done for you.

Type of representation	Description	Use	Audience
Light	LED on the Keyboard	To show when the Caps Lock key has been pressed	All users of the keyboard who can see

Figure 1.3 Advantages and disadvantages of each of the three representation methods

	Text	Graphics	Sound
Advantages	• Clear to understand • Lots of detail	• Multilingual – do not need language to understand an image – e.g. male and female signs • Can match your understanding to what you see – physical shapes	• No fixed position • No line of sight required
Disadvantages	• Need to be able to read • Need to understand the language • Can be confusing – level of language	• Can be confusing if you do not know the symbols – does everyone know what road signs mean? • May not know • Some symbols do not mean the same thing in different countries • Need to be able to see	• No good in large areas – distortion of sound • Usually language based the sound – e.g. different alarms have different sounds • Need to be able to hear

The context in which the information is being used needs to be considered:

● User manuals are commonly provided as text and graphics, not sound.
● Fire alarms are sound rather than text-based.
● Electronic tills are text and sound-based.
● Early learning toys are sound, picture and text-based.

hint These are only examples. User manuals might be computerised and include sound. Fire alarm systems can include arrows pointing to the exit.

Questions

1 Identify **three** different representation methods.
2 What are the advantages of using graphics instead of sound in a software user manual?
3 Give **three** situations where the use of sound to convey information would be appropriate.
4 Give **three** situations where the use of sound to convey information would not be appropriate.
5 Explain, using examples, why it might be advantageous for an electronic till to use graphics as well as sound and text.
6 Why do road signs have symbols and not text?

Semantic and syntactic representations of information

Being able to interpret the meaning of the data is very difficult. It not only requires the correct representation method – text, graphics or sound – but it also requires the individual who is presenting the information to have the syntax and semantics correct.

The difference between syntactic and semantic representation is very simple:

- **Semantic** is the **meaning** of the sentence. The words and relationship of the words within the sentence give a meaning.
- **Syntax** or **syntactics** is the **rules** of the sentence. Each sentence or item of information has rules to follow – the rules make up the syntax.

It is usually through an understanding of the syntax of a sentence that we can understand the semantics. For example:

'The cat chased the mouse.' 'The mouse chased the cat.'

The two sentences contain the same words yet they do not mean the same thing.

The syntax of the sentence – the context, order of words and rules of language – allows us to understand the meaning.

There are two aspects to processing a sentence: meaning and structure or, more technically, semantics and syntax.

Semantic

Semantic representation is about taking the different possible meanings of words or expressions and, with knowledge of sentence structure, working out what the whole sentence means.

Most of the time we can read a sentence and understand its meaning. This is usually because we do not read individual sentences but paragraphs and pages and we can see the meaning of an individual phrase or sentence within this context.

The problem arises when we just have a sentence and no surrounding context. For example:

- fruit flies like a banana
- John went to the bank.

These are both examples that can have more than one meaning. We do not know which meaning is correct because we do not have a context.

Syntactic

Syntactic representation is about the rules of sentences. It is about word order and being able to apply known rules to work out the meaning.

Examples of syntax include:

- dd/mm/yyyy as opposed to: mm/dd/yyyy (UK dates instead of US dates)
- sentences beginning with a capital letter and ending with a full stop.

This understanding of the rules allows us to work out the semantics of the sentence.

Questions

1 Using an example, describe what is meant by semantic representation of data.

2 Using an example, describe what is meant by syntactic representation of data.

3 What is the difference between semantic and syntactic representations of data?

Knowledge and how to distinguish between knowledge and information

Data is meaningless. When we add context, structure and meaning to data we get information. Knowledge is the use and application of that information.

For example:

Data:	60
Information:	UMS marks awarded for 2513
Knowledge:	This means that I need to get 60/180 UMS marks in the two theory papers to pass the AS.

It is easiest to think of knowledge as being the action that you need to take or a general rule you can determine from the information.

For example:

'I know what I need to get to pass my AS.'
'How do you know?'
'Because of what I got in 2513 and the pass mark.'

This is taking information and applying it to acquire knowledge.

Information is processed data. **Knowledge** is the application of information.

Figure 1.4 Taking information and applying it to acquire knowledge

Data	Information	Knowledge
2 and 4	2 kilograms of ice cream sold in January, 4 kilograms of ice cream sold in July	More ice cream is sold in July – the hotter the temperature the more ice cream is sold
101	BBC1 channel number	Sky TV number to input to get BBC 1

Information is based on certainties – there is a formula that allows us to determine where the information has come from and how it is derived. It has a context, a structure and raw data. If we take all of these we can associate a meaning to the data – then it becomes information.

Certainties are things that will appear the same every single time, or mean the same thing every single time. They do not change or alter.

Knowledge can change. It does not mean that it will change every time, but it can change. More information can be added to our knowledge and as we add more information we revise our knowledge.

Figure 1.5

If you are driving towards a junction for the first time and you see traffic lights turn from green to amber (the light turning amber is the data), the information is that you need to stop (the light will turn from amber to red and red means to stop in the context of traffic lights on roads in the UK). The knowledge is how to stop the vehicle you are driving and when you need to start braking in order to stop the vehicle in time.

As you approach the traffic lights you will need to be aware of conditions that determine your knowledge of the situation. For example, the proximity of traffic behind you will affect your decision to brake or not. The road conditions, tyre grip and the weather will also affect your knowledge of the situation. These individual pieces of information will affect the knowledge that we have of a current situation and the action that we take.

Questions

1 What is the difference between information and knowledge?
2 Using an example, show how data can be turned into knowledge.
3 What is meant by the term 'knowledge'?
4 Within the context of using online banking, show how a user can adapt their knowledge as they are given additional information.

Different data types and their uses

Knowledge is based on information; information is based on data. Data is meaningless facts and figures.

These facts and figures are made up of alphanumeric characters. An alphanumeric character is any character that can be displayed on a computer screen. It could be a letter, number or symbol.

Alphanumeric characters can be grouped into different data types. There are five data types that you need to be aware of:

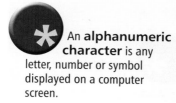
An **alphanumeric character** is any letter, number or symbol displayed on a computer screen.

- Boolean
- real
- integer
- text/string
- date/time.

Boolean

The Boolean data type is one that can contain one of only two values:

0/1
male/female
yes/no

Boolean data can contain one of only two values.

It is used to hold data where the response can only be one of two values:

- Is the motorway open yet?
- Does the property have a garden?

Real

This data type contains numbers that have decimals.

45.78
123.0323

It is used to hold numbers where precision is important:

- measurements in a house/building (2.7m wide)
- prices of goods (£1.75)
- height and weight of people (1.82m).

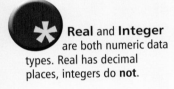

Real and **Integer** are both numeric data types. Real has decimal places, integers do **not**.

Integer

The integer data type contains whole numbers with **NO** decimal places.

45
125
1250

It is used where accuracy may not be of vital importance or the value allocated is specifically a whole number:

- number of miles from London to Birmingham
- large amounts of money – house prices
- coding responses – 1–4.

Currency may be a real or an integer. If it is a small amount of currency then it will be a real, for example, £16.99. However if the amount is large (house prices) then it is an integer - £175,000. In general the units used may influence whether a number is represented as a real or an integer. A price in pence may be an integer – 75p, in pounds a real – £0.75.

Text/string

This is any alphanumeric character. It includes numbers, text and symbols:

12345
Examination
123GD56
8ΛΘ∀

Text/String can hold any alphanumeric character.

Text is used to convey basic information, for example, on labels:

- forename of a person
- postcode – B17 4BH

Text/string is also used to hold telephone numbers. In a computer, telephone numbers are stored as text. This is because a telephone number contains a leading 0, spaces and, most importantly, no mathematical calculations are performed on telephone numbers, so there is no need to store them as numbers.

Date/time

This contains numbers and letters, which, depending on the format used, display the date or the time to different degrees of accuracy:

12:45:45

1995

24 January 2003

Officially, the date is actually worked out from a number. A predetermined date, 1 January 1900 is given a value – 1. Every date is then calculated numerically.

Figure 1.6 Definitions and examples of the five data types

	Boolean	Real	Integer	Text/string	Date/time
Definition	One of only two values	Numbers with decimals	Whole numbers	Alphanumeric characters	Numbers and letters
Example	M/F	123.32	87	Hello	12/12/2004 17:04

Activity

Using the table below, give an example of how each of the data types could be used within the three scenarios.

Scenario	Estate agents	Removal company	School
Boolean			
Real			
Integer			
Text/string			
Date/time			

Why is it important to allocate the correct data type to the data?

Various processes are carried out on data, including sorting, searching and mathematical processes – addition, subtraction, etc.

Some of these processes can only be carried out on some data types.

Date/time data holds dates or times in a variety of formats.

For example:

- Text can only be added together to form a longer string such as 'hello' + 'there' = 'hellothere'. This is called concatenation.
- Boolean could not store the results of a survey with many choices.

Questions

1 Using an example, describe the Boolean data type.

2 Give **three** examples where the use of an integer data type would be more appropriate than a real data type.

3 Give **two** reasons why a telephone number is stored as text.

All data has to come from somewhere. This is known as the **source.**

Where does data come from?

Data has to come from somewhere – it does not just appear. If you need some data, you must consider where to get it.

If you have been given the task of creating a leaflet for a local cinema, you will need to find some data to go into the leaflet. Where this data comes from is known as the source.

Figure 1.7 A film poster is made up of data

Direct data has been collected from an original source.

Direct and indirect data

Direct data is data that has been collected from an original source. It is easiest to think of direct data as data that has been physically collected by you.

Indirect data has two interpretations:

1 The data is used for a purpose different to that for which it was originally collected. For example, collecting data on how many tickets have been sold for a film to make sure it has not oversold, and then using the data to find the most popular film.

2 The people/companies involved in collecting the data are different from those using the data. Typically this might be organisations that conduct market surveys and then sell the results to other companies who use it in advertising.

Two other sources of data are the by-product of processing an original set of data and stored archives (see below).

> **Indirect data** is either used for a different purpose than that for which it was originally collected **or** is collected by a different person/company than those using the data.

Activity

Using the scenario given in the table below, identify four direct sources of information and four indirect sources of information for producing leaflets.

Scenario:	Estate agents	Removal company
Direct		
Indirect		

By-product of processing

The by-product of the processing is not the results of the processing. It is using the results of the processing (calculation, sorting, searching, comparison, etc).

In the cinema example above, the total price of all the customer's tickets is direct data used to charge the customer. This bill is indirect data when it is used to offer vouchers off future screenings because the customer has spent so much money.

The totals of all ticket sales could be collated and averaged on a daily basis to give sales trends; this would be a by-product of processing the original set of data.

> The **by-product of processing** is using the result of processing for something for which the process was not originally intended.

Archives

Archived data is data that is not online or readily accessible (in other words it is off-line).

The data is not deleted as it may be needed at some future date. Archived data might be the sales figures of a film from many years ago – perhaps to compare a remake with the original ('The Italian Job', for example).

> **Archived data** can still be accessed – just not immediately. It needs to be loaded onto the system.

Questions

1 What is the difference between direct and indirect sources of data?

2 Give an example where the archives would need to be accessed to find data.

3 Information on the numbers of girls who play football in a town is required. Describe **one** direct and **one** indirect method of collecting this information.

How does the quality of data affect the information produced?

Factors affecting the quality of information

If you put incorrect data into a system you will get incorrect information out of it.

There are six factors that determine how good the data is:

1 accuracy
2 relevance
3 age
4 completeness
5 presentation
6 level of detail.

Different factors are applicable to different scenarios. These six factors are explained below and an estate agent is used as an example.

Accuracy

The information needs to be accurate. If it is not accurate, you cannot rely on it.

Validation and verification techniques do not ensure accuracy. They can remove information that is outside set boundaries, unreasonable and not sensible but cannot ensure correctness.

If you ask for the price of a house and you are given an incorrect figure, the information is worthless.

Relevance

The information must be relevant. If you have the information but it does not relate to the topic it is worthless. Having information that is not relevant can be a disadvantage. It increases the volume of data and reading through it can waste precious time.

If you ask for the distance of a property from different places within town, to be told how far it is from a bus stop on the other side of town, is not relevant because this is not a place you are likely to need.

Age

The information might be too old. Information can change over time. If you have obtained the information from an old source it may not still be relevant or accurate.

If you ask for the price of a house, to be given a figure that is five years old is of no value.

Completeness

If you only have part of the information then it is worthless. Think back to the formula for information – data requires a context, structure, and meaning for it to have value and be useful.

If you want to view a house and are only given the house number but no road name, or the hour of the viewing but not the minutes then the information is worthless.

Presentation

If the information is not presented in such a way that you can understand it or find what you want, it loses value. The presentation might be improved by sorting, or by using a different method of representation, for example, a picture or graph instead of text.

Pictures of a property make brochures easier to digest. Also, house brochures are presented in an organised way – as if you were walking through the house. This consistent presentation makes it easier to compare properties.

Level of detail

You can be given too much or too little information. The volume of data determines whether you have enough or too much to make a decision. If you have too much it can be difficult to find what you require.

If you are buying a house, having every minor alteration and samples of each colour scheme used in the house is too much information. On the other hand, being told how many bedrooms there are but no other details is too little.

There is a balance between too much and too little information and it can be difficult to get it right.

The six factors are not usually relevant in isolation. For example, level of detail is linked to completeness, and presentation can be linked to age.

Activity

Within the scenarios given in the table below, give examples of how the six factors can affect the quality of information produced.

Scenario	Removal company	Exam results
Accuracy		
Relevance		
Age		
Completeness		
Presentation		
Level of detail		

Questions

1 Describe the **six** factors affecting the quality of information.
2 For each factor, give an example of how it affects the quality of information produced.
3 Demonstrate, using examples, how **one** factor can have a knock-on effect and influence other factors.

The problems and benefits associated with coding data

Coding data

We need to collect data for a purpose. If the data that has been collected cannot be organised in such a way that it can be used for the original purpose, then it is worthless.

There needs to be some method of standardising the information so that it fulfils its purpose and is organised. One method is known as encoding data (putting data into code or short-hand data). This is nothing to do with secret messages, which are commonly called codes but should be called ciphers.

The coding of data involves taking the original data and storing it in a different representation. What is stored is not the actual data but a representation of it. An everyday example of this is using a postcode to represent an address or part of an address.

The following are examples of representations of data. It is easy to work out what the codes stand for:

- Mon, Tue, Wed, Thur
- Jan, Feb, Mar, Apr.

Other codes are not so easy to understand:

- BLTR36
- RDSK16.

It is not possible to interpret this data unless you have the key:

- BL = Blue, RD = Red
- TR = Trouser, SK = Skirt
- last two digits = size.

> The **coding of data** involves original data being stored in a different representation to standardise and organise it.

Activity

Create **three** different sets of codes. Hand them to another student and ask them to try to understand what the codes represent and how they work.

Problems of coding data

The precision of the data entered is coarsened when it is coded. This means that the data entered into the computer is not as accurate as the data originally given.

Imagine you are conducting a survey on hair colour and the options that you give people are:

- black
- red
- blonde
- grey
- brown.

These may cover the majority of hair colours, but most people do not categorise their hair in these precise terms. They may think of themselves as chestnut brown or strawberry blonde.

This will mean that the actual data entered into the computer is inaccurate. If the data is seen to be inaccurate then the integrity of the system will be questioned – how can the results be believed if the data is not correct?

If you were to ask a question, the response that you are given is unlikely to fit exactly into any coding system you try to come up with. This is why so many surveys ask you to give marks on a scale instead of allowing you to comment freely.

However, if you were to try to use code-free comments you would need to make some value judgements. Value judgements are where an absolute value is mapped onto some vague text. Different people will apply different value judgements to the same text.

Imagine you are carrying out a survey outside a cinema about the film that has just finished. You ask the people coming out of the cinema: 'Did you enjoy the film?'

Responses include:

- Yes, it was great.
- It was OK.
- Some of it was excellent, but bits were rubbish.
- It was rubbish, except for the end.

If you have a scale of 1–4 (1 being excellent, 4 being rubbish) how do you code these statements? Different people will give the same statement a different mark on the scale.

There are some other disadvantages to coding data. If the user does not know how the codes are being used, they will not be able to code any new data or be able to interpret the data that is currently held on computer.

Suppose that a coding system is devised that uses a system of numbers and letters to identify objects, for example:

BL36TR meaning Black Trousers 36" waist

Eventually, the number of codes will be used up and a new coding system developed. This will of course mean recoding all of the existing data.

Once a survey has been completed and all the information coded and entered into the computer it is unlikely that the computer operator will have access to the original survey forms. This means that they have to accept what is on the computer. If there are errors, value judgements that are incorrect or codes that have been input incorrectly, they will not know. This means that any information that is extracted will be taken as being correct.

Activity

a) Create a coding system to code people's facial features – hair colour, eye colour, skin tone, etc.

b) Try out the coding system. What are the advantages and disadvantages of the system you have created?

c) Is your coding system easy to understand and use? Why?

d) Investigate the Dewey Decimal system of coding for libraries. Is it easy to follow? Can it be improved?

Benefits of coding

There are some advantages to data coding.

The memory requirements are a lot less. Instead of storing Black Trousers 36" waist, you would only need to store BL36TR. This may not seem a lot, but when you have thousands of records, the space saving is considerable. This means you do not need as large a hard drive or backup capability and this in turn costs less money.

It can be quicker to enter a code into the computer than to type in the full details. Of course, with new users, there is a delay while they work out the codes.

Hopefully, there will be fewer errors. As the codes follow a set pattern, it is possible to apply validation to the different parts of the code, for example:

BL36TR

- The first two letters must match a colour code in the database.
- The second two numbers must be between two values.
- The final two letters must match an item code in the database.

This cannot ensure that the data is correct, but does ensure that it matches the codes. Fewer errors will occur than with free-text data entry.

Data that has been coded takes on a very precise structure. It is easier to sort and search the data if it is organised. It is also possible to analyse and graph data if it is tightly structured.

Figure 1.8 Summary of coding

Advantages of coded data	Disadvantages of coded data
Less memory requirement: Storing less information therefore less memory is required.	*Precision of data coarsened:* For example, 'light blue' coded as 'blue'.
Security: If the codes are not apparent then it is difficult to guess and understand them.	*Coding of value judgements:* For example, 'Was the film good?' to be coded as a judgement of 1–4. This will be coded differently by different people and makes comparisons difficult.
Speed of input: The codes take less time to enter, therefore it is quicker to input large amounts of data.	*The user needs to know the codes used:* If the user does not know the codes, they cannot use them.
Data validation: Since the codes follow a strict set of numbers and letters they are easy to validate.	*Limited number of codes:* If codes are made up of a range of letters and numbers eventually codes will run out.
Organisation of data: If the data is in a standardised format then it can be compared and organised.	*Difficult to track errors:* Validation will ensure the code is entered correctly but the nature of the code will make it difficult to see if the code is actually correct.

Questions

1 What is meant by 'coding of data'?
2 Describe **three** disadvantages of coding data.
3 Describe **three** advantages of coding data.
4 Explain, using an example, how data can be coded.
5 Give **two** situations where the coding of data is appropriate. For each situation, explain why the data needs to be coded.

How important is testing and what is test data?

Testing

Once any system has been designed and constructed there are set procedures to follow to ensure that it works. These procedures are grouped together to form a test plan.

Testing is important and required to:

- make sure that the program meets the design specification
- make sure that it returns the correct results – that it actually works
- give confidence to the end users – they will have more faith and confidence in the new system if it has passed the testing.

When talking about testing, it is important to understand the difference between an error and a fault. An error is a human action that produces an incorrect result. A fault is a manifestation of an error in software (also known as a defect or bug). If a fault is encountered it may cause a failure. A failure is a deviation of the software from what is expected.

A key term in testing is reliability. Reliability is the probability that the software will not cause the failure of a system for a specified time under specified conditions. Testing is about ensuring that software is reliable.

Errors occur because humans are not perfect and, even if we were, we are working under constraints such as delivery deadlines and cost deadlines and these contraints can cause mistakes to occur.

The amount of testing that needs to be done depends on the risks involved. The greater the risk, for example with safety-critical systems, the more testing is required.

Test data

The data that is selected for the test is important. It should cover:

- normal data
- extreme data
- erroneous data.

Normal data

This is data that is used everyday. It is data that is correct and should not generate any errors on data entry.

Extreme data

This is data that is also correct but is at the boundaries (upper and lower) of tolerance. As extreme data is also normal data, it should not generate any errors on data entry.

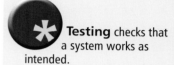

Testing checks that a system works as intended.

Errors are human actions that produce incorrect results, but **faults** are manifestations of defects in the software.

Reliability is the probability that software will not cause system failure under specified conditions.

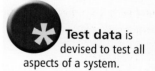

Test data is devised to test all aspects of a system.

Normal data is correct and should not generate errors.

Extreme data is data at the boundaries (upper and lower) of tolerance.

17

Erroneous data

This is data that is incorrect. It may be outside of the boundaries of tolerance or of the wrong data type.

A test plan is a formal description of what to test. It describes the data used, where it was input and the expected results. Once a test plan has been run, the actual results are included and any discrepancies explained.

Activity

You are to create a test plan for a simple computer program for the Head of ICT. It has three inputs: A, B and C.

A and C are numbers between 0 and 90.

B is a number between 0 and 120.

The three numbers are added together to give a total out of 300.

Complete the following test table:

Test no.	Type	Description	Inputs	Outputs

Test no. = a sequential number starting from 1.

Type = normal, erroneous or extreme.

Description = what the test is.

Inputs = all the inputs to be used.

Outputs = the expected outputs generated from using the given inputs.

Exhaustive testing (testing everything with every variable) would, in most cases, require a lot of resources – time and people – and is therefore usually impractical.

Testing is about trying to identify faults. The removal of the faults identified increases the reliability of the software and this in turn increases its quality.

Other factors that may determine the testing performed may be contractual requirements (part of the handover process of the software), or legal requirements (these may be industry specific requirements). It is difficult to determine how much testing is enough. It is unlikely that all faults will be found. Software manufacturers release patches to correct faults in their software.

The test plan is used to run the original tests again to ensure that any changes to the program do not create additional faults. When patches are created, the test plan will be changed and new tests added.

Questions

1 What is the purpose of a test plan?

2 When should a test plan be used?

3 Under what circumstances would a test plan be changed?

4 Identify the **three** types of test data.

5 Describe, with examples, the differences between the **three** types of test data.

Verification and validation methods and their purpose

In order for data to be useful within a computer system, it needs to be entered into the system. The point of data entry into the system is an area where errors can occur.

It is impossible to eradicate errors completely. There is NO method that can ensure complete accuracy. However, verification and validation methods can ensure that the information entered is:

- reasonable
- sensible
- complete
- within acceptable boundaries.

Verification

If you have collected some information on paper, at some point it will need to be entered into the computer.

Once you have entered it into the computer you have two copies, the original paper-based copy and the copy stored in the computer.

Verification
checks what is entered against the original.

Figure 1.9 Paper-based and computer-based copies

- The paper-based copy is known as the source document.
- The copy in the computer is known as the object document.

Verification is making sure that the information on the source document is the same as the information on the object document.

There are two main methods of verification:

- double entry.
- manual verification.

Double entry

This involves entering the data twice. The computer then compares the two sets of data and if it finds any differences, it informs the user.

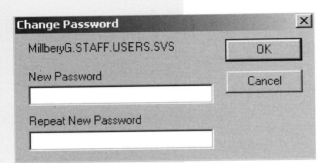

One method of double entry that you will have come across is passwords. When you are asked to enter a password twice this is called verification.

The double entry could be by the same person or by different people.

The main problem with double entry is that if the same error is made both times, then the computer will not find a difference.

Figure 1.10
An example of verification

Manual verification

This involves the entry on the paper being manually compared with the entry typed into the computer.

Unfortunately, this is not a very reliable method. It is very difficult to transfer attention between paper and screen and to keep track of where you are on the paper and on the screen.

Questions

1 Describe **two** methods of verification.
2 Give **two** disadvantages of double entry.
3 Give **one** advantage of manual verification.
4 Explain why verification cannot ensure that the data is accurate.

Validation checks data entered against a set of rules.

Validation

Validation is a check that is performed by the computer. It is done as the data is being entered and tries to prevent any data that does not conform to pre-set rules being entered.

There are lots of different rules that can be created. However, these will not stop incorrect data being entered.

The rules that can be applied fall into several categories:

- range checks
- type checks
- presence checks
- length checks
- picture checks
- check digit.

Range checks

A range check sets an upper and a lower boundary for the data. The data entered must lie between these two values.

For example, in a secondary school a pupil can be in Years 7–13. A lower boundary of 7 and an upper boundary of 13 can be set.

Type checks

This makes sure that the data entered is of the correct type. Types of data include: numeric, string, Boolean and date/time.

Type checks will not allow you to enter the wrong data type – if you try to enter text into a numeric field it will be rejected, for example.

Presence checks

These are also called existence checks. Not every field or question in data necessarily needs to be answered. However, there will be some that must have an answer and be filled in. By applying a presence check, the computer will insist that a value is entered for that field.

For example, if you are storing details about a student, you need to know their name and address. These are vital pieces of information. You may not need to store a telephone number in every case as not everyone has a telephone.

Length checks

When any data is entered into a computer it has a length. A single character has a length of 1, 'Hello' has a length of 5.

It is possible to apply a type of range check to the data – making sure that the length of the data entered is of a minimum length and within a maximum length.

Picture checks

This is also known as a format check. Some data entries might be a combination of numbers and letters. Therefore, you cannot apply a type check. However, the location of the numbers and letters within the data might be in the same place every time.

For example, an order number might look like:

RT678H

FD634K

The first two entries are letters.

The next three entries are numbers.

The last entry is a letter.

This would allow a format check to be applied to the field. L is letter, N is number:

LLNNNL

This makes sure that only letters can be entered for the first two and the last values and only numbers for the middle three.

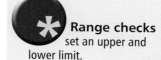

Range checks set an upper and lower limit.

Type checks confirm correct data type.

Presence checks confirm that required data has been entered.

Length checks check that the number of characters entered is correct.

Picture checks confirm that data is entered in the correct format.

Activity

You are recording information on a new student at your school.

a) List all the pieces of information you need to collect about the student.

b) For each piece of information, describe the validation methods that can be used. Each piece of information can have more than one validation method.

Check digit

A check digit is calculated using a set of numbers and then added to the end of them.

When the code is created, the check digit is created and added to the code. Before the code is processed, the check digit is recalculated and compared with the one in the code. If they are the same, processing continues. If they are different, an error has occurred and the code value needs to be re-entered.

Check digits are commonly used when data is transmitted. Corruption can occur during transmission of data and the check digit is used to ensure that the data received is the same as that sent.

The unique number on the back of books – the ISBN (International Standard Book Number) – has a check digit. The number is used to uniquely identify the book. The check digit is calculated using Modulus 11.

The following example shows how to use Modulus 11 to calculate a check digit. The ISBN number is: 0-7487-9116-7

Step 1:

Remove the last digit from the ISBN number:

0-7487-9116

Step 2:

Write out the remaining numbers. Starting from the right hand number, put a 2 under it. Put a 3 under the next one and so on.

Number	0	7	4	8	7	9	1	1	6
Code	10	9	8	7	6	5	4	3	2

Multiply the number by the code:

Number	0	7	4	8	7	9	1	1	6
Code	10	9	8	7	6	5	4	3	2
Result	0	63	32	56	42	45	4	3	12

Add the results together:

0+63+32+56+42+45+4+3+12 = 257

Step 3:

Divide the total by 11. You need to write down the remainder.

23 remainder 4

Step 4:

Take the remainder away from 11. The value that is left is the check digit.

$11 - 4 = 7$

The check digit is 7.

This is compared with the original check digit – if they are the same then the data has been transmitted correctly.

If the remainder is 0 then the check digit is 0

If the remainder is 1 then the check digit is X

This check digit calculation is very good for finding transposition errors. If two numbers were swapped around then they would have different weightings and the check digit would be different.

Activity

a) Use the Modulus 11 calculation to work out which of the following ISBN numbers have been copied down correctly.

i) 1-854-87918-9

ii) 0-552-77109-X

iii) 0-330-28414-3

iv) 0-330-34742-X

v) 0-330-35183-3

b) Use a spreadsheet to create a routine that will tell the user whether a check digit is correct or not.

Batch, control and hash totals

Batch, hash and control totals are another form of validation and verification. They involve a mathematical calculation and can be used to check that the data has been entered correctly.

A batch total is used to check that none of the records have been missed. It is a total of the number of records entered.

A control total is formed by adding up one field from each of the records entered. For example, if you were entering a set of invoices into a computer system, each invoice has a total value. The control total could be the total value of all of the invoices.

A hash total is similar to a control total but it does not have any meaning attached to it. See Figure 1.11.

Common errors

The two most common errors caused when entering data into a computer are transcription errors and transposition errors.

Transcription errors are where you have made a mistake copying the data, for example striking the wrong key or hitting two keys at once.

Figure 1.11 Hash and control totals

Figure 1.12 Examples of transcription errors

	Wrong	Correct
Postcode	TN18 7TH	TN28 7TH
Surname	Stuaet	Stuart
Date	25 March, 2004	26 March, 2004

Transposition errors are where you have reversed two numbers or letters.

Figure 1.13 Examples of transposition errors

	Wrong	Correct
Postcode	TN82 7TH	TN28 7TH
Surname	Staurt	Stuart
Date	26 March, 2040	26 March, 2004

Verification methods cannot make sure that the data entered is accurate, just whether it is the same as what was written down.

For example, imagine that on a data-capture form the individual has written down that their birth date was 26 February 1965.

If their birth date was actually 16 February 1965, then verification methods would not pick up the error.

Questions

1 Why is validation used?
2 Describe **three** different validation methods.
3 When is it appropriate to use range validation? Give examples of its use.

4 Describe how validation and verification methods could be used when collecting details from a prospective house purchaser in an estate agent's office.

5 Describe the difference between a control total and a hash total.

6 Explain where the use of batch, hash and control totals is appropriate.

7 Describe two types of error and explain methods that can be used to prevent them.

The cost of producing information

Information needs to be produced. It does not just appear. Information is not free; it costs money to produce. It takes time to collect, input and process data and produce an output that meets the required purpose.

There are four main areas where costs are incurred during the production of information:

- hardware
- software
- consumables
- manpower.

Figure 1.14 Example of hardware

Hardware

The initial costs of the hardware are expensive but these can be offset by the length of time it is in use, and that once it has been acquired it can be used for other tasks.

Ongoing hardware costs include repair and maintenance costs as well as upgrade costs. It is necessary to keep the hardware in good working order and the organisation needs to have either a maintenance contract or have the equipment repaired when required.

As time progresses, the storage requirements of the organisation will increase. If, for example, they are producing a newsletter, they will want to keep all back issues on computer. This will have an implication for disk space requirement and they may need to increase the capacity of the hard drive. This in turn has a knock-on effect on back-up – the larger the hard-disk drive, the greater the required capacity of the back-up.

Software

Figure 1.15 Example of software

The software needs to be purchased. This will include the operating system, utilities and the software used to produce the information. This can be purchased through a one-off cost or licensed year-to-year.

The software may also require a technical support agreement. When there are difficulties, third-party support is required to solve the problems.

There may be training costs associated with the software – courses that the users will need to attend in order to operate it correctly. They may also require manuals for reference.

Over time, the software may need to be upgraded, which will incur additional cost. However, it may be possible to acquire the new version at a lower cost. There are also potential costs involved in transferring data from the old system to the new system.

Consumables

Paper and toner are the two main consumables used in producing information.

Figure 1.16 Paper and ink cartridges

Manpower

Manpower costs relate to people working in the organisation. People may need to be hired to produce the information. This is a long-term cost. They may be required to collect, collate, enter, process and output the information.

If the time usually taken to produce a magazine is two weeks, when new staff first begin it is likely that it will take longer than this. They will need some time to get used to the system and software. Over a few months, as they get used to procedures and software, the time will reduce until they are able to meet the deadlines. This 'bedding in' time needs to be built into the costs.

When the people using the software go on training courses there may be costs associated with covering their job while they are away.

The manpower costs are likely to be the most expensive costs in producing information.

Activity

Imagine that you are producing a leaflet for a new pizza delivery service. Using the four headings:

- Hardware
- Software
- Consumables
- Manpower

list all the costs associated with producing the leaflet and give a cost to each item.

Questions

1 Describe the **four** main areas of costs associated with producing information.
2 Describe the hardware items required to collect and input data required for a fashion magazine.
3 Explain why an organisation might need to upgrade the software it uses to produce information.
4 Explain the manpower costs to an organisation of producing a leaflet from scratch.

How valuable is information?

All information is a commodity. A commodity is something that has a value, and because it has a value it can be bought and sold.

It is important to remember that the value of information might not just be financial. Information about concerts, for example, is given away for free. The information is valuable, as without it you would not know who is performing when. The information is given away so that you can use it to purchase tickets.

The value of information is related to several issues. The quality of the information is a large factor that affects how much the information is worth.

The six factors that affect the quality of information are:

1 accuracy
2 relevance
3 age
4 completeness

5 presentation

6 level of detail.

Another factor to consider is the intended use of the information. This is determined by the person who is buying the information.

The person buying the information may place different emphasis on one or more of the factors listed above. For example, the age of the information might outweigh the presentation. To have accurate information that is minutes old but is not presented in a neat fashion might not be of concern. The fact that it is not very old could be the main factor affecting the value in this case.

Not all information will be of value to everyone. For example, a business person, making the journey from Birmingham to Exeter, will want to know the train times but may not worry about the cost of tickets. The information on cost is not as important or relevant to them.

Activity

Look at the following information and explain how it has a value and to whom. Some may have value to more than one person.

a) A table of GCSE results from a school.

b) An online database of telephone numbers in the UK.

c) A list of people who have gone overdrawn on their store cards.

d) Train times from London to Paris.

Questions

1 If information has value why is it sometimes given away for free?

2 How can the value of information be calculated?

3 Giving examples, explain how the **six** factors affecting the quality of information can affect the value of information.

Expert systems

Expert systems are computer programs that analyse information about a specific type of problem.

We, as humans, begin with data, which we turn into information and then into knowledge. The knowledge helps us to make decisions.

Expert systems are computer programs that are made up of a set of rules that analyse information about a specific type of problem. They can also provide a recommended course of action in order to solve the problem. They attempt to reproduce the decision-making process.

The range of an expert system is very narrow. Each expert system concentrates on a specific area only. Expert systems are designed to replace the 'human expert' – they will attempt to ask similar questions and give the same response as you would get from a human with expertise in that area.

An expert system is made up of two main parts:

● the knowledge base

● the reasoning, or inference engine.

There is also the user interface – the method by which the user communicates with the expert system.

The knowledge base of expert systems contains both factual and heuristic knowledge.

- Factual knowledge is that knowledge of the specific area that is widely shared, typically found in textbooks or journals.
- Heuristic knowledge is the knowledge that is acquired through experience and reasoning. It is the knowledge that underpins the 'art of good guessing'.

The inference engine asks the end-user questions and, based on the answer received, will follow lines of logic. This may lead to more questions and ultimately to an answer.

The inference engine is based on rules. A rule consists of an IF part and a THEN part (also called a condition and an action).

The IF part lists a set of conditions. If the IF part of the rule is satisfied, the THEN part can be concluded. This may be the answer or a new set of rules.

At a basic level the inference engine can be seen as a tree:

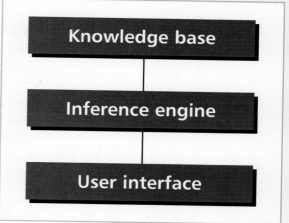

Figure 1.17 Components of an expert system

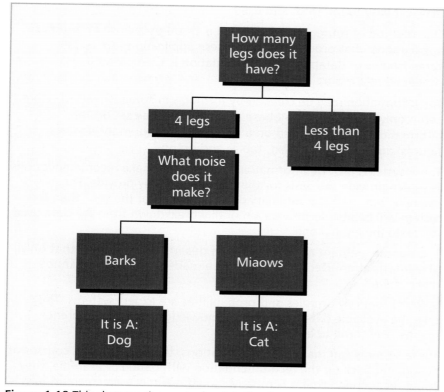

Figure 1.18 This shows a tiny part of a classification expert system

Activity

a) Look at the structure of Figure 1.18 and describe the problems that might cause a dog to be misclassified.

b) Enhance the structure to give a better classification system for a dog.

Cont...

c) Using a tree structure, design rules to work out the grade that you are likely to achieve in AS ICT.

Questions

1 What are the components of an expert system?
2 Describe the function of each of the components of an expert system.
3 Explain how the rules of an expert system work.
4 Using an example, explain how an expert system can deal with uncertain knowledge.
5 What are the advantages of being able to explain the reasoning behind a decision?

How do business applications and rule-based systems differ?

Information is only worth having if it is useful. Part of the usefulness of information depends on its accessibility. Within a business the information must be available when it is required in a format that makes it easy to interpret and use.

One method of retrieving information is through the use of 'business applications' that produce reports. These applications are usually spreadsheets or databases. The information is then collated and produced as a report.

The information may be collated by formulas in spreadsheets or, more commonly, queries in a database. Templates can be set up for information that is required on a regular basis (e.g. monthly sales figures) and can contain text, tables and graphs.

These systems provide information. They do not make recommendations. They can provide the basis for the information they provide. For example, if a chart is a summary of sales figures for the year, then the system will be able to provide a monthly breakdown from the data used to create the annual one.

The human element is essential when dealing with systems that only give information. Decisions have to be made – the system cannot make them.

Systems that rely on rules and probabilities are expert systems. They take the available data and, using a knowledge base and inference engine, will come to a conclusion.

These systems can make recommendations; they can suggest courses of action and back up the recommendation with data. For example, they could recommend that a company should buy more ice cream in July. This could be based on sales figures for previous years and meteorological data.

Although recommendations can be made, they should not be immediately accepted. There always needs to be some human element in the checking. Program trading was partly responsible for the stock market crash of 1987. When the prices of a stock fell below a preset price, a computer automatically sold the stock. Within one second, a computer would finalise 60 transactions. Other computers noticed the trend and started selling, causing the market to fall.

Rules are a set of procedures that must be followed.

Probabilities are the likelihood of events occurring.

If there had been human checks, then it is unlikely that such a large fall in stock prices would have occurred.

Human beings bring instinct and random knowledge to the decision-making process.

Questions

1 What are the advantages of a system that can make recommendations?
2 What are the disadvantages of a system that implements its recommendations without human intervention?
3 What are the similarities between the two types of systems?
4 What are the differences between the two types of systems?

Input, processing, output, storage and feedback

Any ICT system can be broken down into:

- input
- processing
- output
- storage
- feedback.

This can be represented as a diagram:

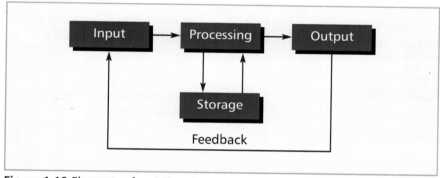

Figure 1.19 Elements of an ICT system

The elements within the diagram relate to any system. They do not necessarily relate to a computerised system. Some of the elements may be manual.

Input

This is taking information external to the system and entering it into the system. This may be manual input (for example, a keyboard) or automated input (for example, OMR). Information may also be input by electronic means via a network or disk/CD.

Processing

This is an action performed on the data. Processing can include sorting, searching or performing calculations on the data.

Input is the data that is put into a system.

Processing is performing an action on the data.

31

Output is the result of processing data.

Storage is where data is held while still within the system.

Feedback is output that is looped back to become input.

Output

This is taking information in the system and outputting it. The method used may result in printed output, output on screen, or electronic output on disk/CD.

There is always a problem when looking at input, storage and output. Where do CDs and disks fit in? In themselves, they are storage devices. However, if the data stored on them is being entered into the system via the storage device then they are input and if the data on them is being taken outside the system they are output.

Storage

This is where data is held. It may include the data that has been input, data required during processing or the results of processing. This is data that is still within the system.

Feedback

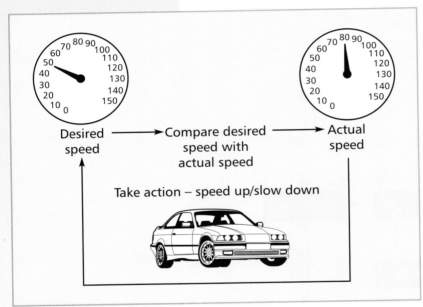

Figure 1.20 Diagram of cruise control including feedback

This is where the output from the system forms part of the input to the system. Feedback is usually applied to real-time situations. If the response to the feedback is automatic then the process is a closed loop. If there is an operator involved then the process is an open loop.

A feedback example is a cruise-control system in a vehicle.

The input data is how fast you want the vehicle to go. The processing is whether to speed up or slow down. The output is how much to speed up by or slow down by. Once the action has taken place, the new speed is fed into the system as an input.

Activity

Using the scenario below, describe the terms input, processing, output, storage and feedback.

A school trip is being booked to the Lake District. Letters are sent each week to all parents whose children are going, stating how much they still need to pay. If they send money in during the week, the records are altered. Once they have paid the full amount no more letters are sent to the parents.

Turnaround documents

In some systems a turnaround document is used. This is a document that has gone through the system and is output. It is printed by the computer. Additional data is recorded on the document and this is then input into the system at a later date.

Turnaround documents are used by utility companies. They allow the homeowner to record their own meter readings. The document has the name, address and account number of the homeowner already entered on it. The homeowner adds the meter reading and sends it back.

This is an example of feedback – the document is output from the system and forms part of the input at a later date.

Questions

1 Describe the terms: input; storage; processing; output; and feedback.
2 Using the school registration system, use a diagram to show the input, storage, processing, output and feedback.
3 What is the difference between a closed and an open loop?
4 What are the advantages of using a turnaround document?

End of Chapter 1 tests

Test 1

A Football Supporters' Club holds data on its members.

1 Describe the term data and give an example of data. [2]

2 Using an example from the Football Supporters' Club, show how data can become information. [3]

3 The Football Supporters' Club is producing a leaflet for its members.

Identify **two** different methods of representing information that they could use. [2]

4 Describe **three** costs the Football Supporters' Club would incur if they decided to produce the leaflet in-house? [6]

5 The Football Supporters' Club is setting up a database to hold details of its members. The data needs to be coded before it is entered into the database.

Describe **three** advantages of coding data. [6]

6 Describe and give examples of **three** different methods of validation the database could use. [6]

7 Data is input into the system, processed, stored and output from the system.

Draw a diagram to show how the terms input, process, storage, and output are related. [4]

Test 2

A small company writes books on how to use different pieces of software.

1 The manuals contain semantic and syntactic aspects of information.

   Using examples, describe semantic and syntactic aspects of information. [4]

2 The manuals are designed to give the reader information that they can turn into knowledge.

   Describe the difference between information and knowledge. [4]

3 The manuals will only sell if the quality of the information contained within them is high.

   Identify **three** factors that affect the quality of information and, for each, use an example to describe how it could affect the information in the book. [6]

4 The books need to be tested before they are published.

   (i) Why is it important to test the books? [1]
   (ii) A test plan is written prior to testing the books. Explain the importance of having a test plan. [3]

5 The information in the book has value.

   Explain under what circumstances the book may lose its value. [2]

6 The company has created an expert system to answer software problems.

   Describe, with examples, the components of an expert system. [6]

7 Describe what feedback the company could receive on its books and how it could use the feedback to improve future books. [4]

Components of an information system

Objectives

Your objectives for this chapter are to:

◎ know the difference between hardware and software

◎ understand how standardisation affects hardware and software

◎ know the function of the main components of a general purpose computer

◎ understand the factors affecting the speed of a computer

◎ describe a range of input, storage and output devices

◎ describe devices for physically disabled users

◎ know the difference between the backing up and archiving of data

◎ understand the difference between a range of types of software.

Keep these objectives in mind as you work through the chapter.

Hardware and software

Hardware is things you can touch. It is the physical components that make up the computer. Examples include a mouse, keyboard and a monitor.

Software is the programming code that makes the computer work. There are two main types of software:

● System software (operating systems), which control the workings of the computer.

● Applications, such as word-processing programs, spreadsheets, and databases.

Parts of the computer you can touch – monitor, keyboard, mouse – are **hardware.**

Software is programming code that makes a computer work.

Questions

1 Using an example, define what is meant by the term 'hardware'.

2 Using an example, define what is meant by the term 'software'.

3 What is the difference between hardware and software?

How does the lack of standardisation affect both hardware and software?

Standardisation is the imposing, by a third party or with agreement, of a set of standards on manufacturers. There is a set of standards (rules and benchmarks) that both software and hardware must adhere to if it is to be recognised by certain bodies.

There are different standards in other types of businesses – standards for food preparation, voltage and measurements, to name a few. In ICT there are several organisations that monitor and develop standards:

- W3C – the World Wide Web Consortium develops standards for the Internet.
- ISO – the International Standards Organisation currently has over 14,000 standards.

In a perfect world everything would meet the same standard. This would mean that everything was built and worked to the same level of quality. Where the items are of a similar type, but from completely different manufacturers on different sides of the world, they would still work together using the same protocols.

Unfortunately there is a lack of standardisation in the world of ICT. This is not to say that it is altogether lacking, standards for hardware and software do exist, but there are many different standards and they are not always compatible with each other.

How does this affect the end user?

A lack of standardisation in hardware has the following disadvantages:

Cost

If you purchase a computer that is not part of a global standard, then all the subsequent upgrades and parts you purchase for that computer would have to come from specific outlets and be very expensive to purchase.

If you do not know that your computer is of a particular type and purchase a new piece of hardware, it may not work with your computer.

Availability

If there is a limited outlet for a piece of hardware then the supply itself may be limited. Limited supply has a knock-on effect on cost.

Technical support

If the hardware has limited availability and, therefore, is only used by a small number of people, technical support will be expensive and also have limited availability.

The standardisation of hardware is not just about different types of computers. It may be about computers of the same type but of different ages. Computers purchased three or four years ago will probably not be able to use new processors, RAM or graphics cards – the standard itself has moved on. This is the case with the rapid development in wireless network devices.

Software standard

Software standards are a little different. Although there is a set of standards released by the operating system manufacturers (in order to work with a particular operating system and be accredited, these standards must be met) there is limited comparability between them.

Think about word processors. In an ideal world every document written in any word processor would be able to be viewed using any other word processor.

Activity

Open up your word processor and look at the different files that can be imported. Do some research to see if there are any file types unavailable.

Software standards are not just linked to operating systems. Think about the Internet. Web pages are written for different computers, running different operating systems and different browsers. It is because of standards that these web pages can be viewed. However, there are elements of web pages that cannot be viewed correctly in different browsers – colours and alignment, for example, often vary.

A lack of standardisation among web browsers means that you may not see the page exactly as the designer intended. This may not be of relevance but it may mean the colours of a company are slightly different, or that the text does not appear where it should, or a code may not work correctly, limiting the functionality of the web site.

From a company's point of view, this lack of standardisation is not necessarily a bad thing. It means that they can continually release new hardware, which leads to obsolescence of previous versions and companies are able to make more money because of this.

Questions

1 What are standards?
2 Describe **two** effects of having different hardware standards, from a user's point of view.
3 What are the advantages of having different standards?
4 How does standardisation affect how web pages are displayed?
5 What are the advantages of a lack of standardisation to a company?

The components of a general-purpose computer

There are three main components of a general-purpose computer:

1 control unit
2 arithmetic and logic unit (ALU)
3 random-access memory (RAM).

Inside the computer is a microprocessor, also called the CPU (central processing unit). The CPU is the brains of the computer – it performs the core processing functions.

The CPU is divided into two main parts, the control unit and the ALU.

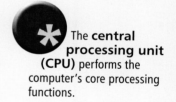

The **central processing unit (CPU)** performs the computer's core processing functions.

Figure 2.1 Central processing unit (CPU)

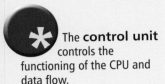

Control unit

The control unit acts as a go-between linking the ALU and the system memory. The control unit controls the functioning of the CPU and data flow. It accepts the data from the system memory, passes the data to the ALU for performing arithmetic and logical operations, and returns the processed data back to the system memory.

The control unit does not 'do', it directs – it is a conductor.

Arithmetic and logic unit

The ALU is responsible for all arithmetic and logical operations.

- Arithmetic operations include addition, subtraction, multiplication, and division.
- Logical operations compare data to determine whether they are equal and, if not, which is larger. 'Less than', 'greater than', 'equal to' and 'not equal to' are all logical operations.

Random-access memory (RAM)

This is the working memory of the computer. Anything stored in RAM is lost when the computer is switched off – it is volatile memory.

Many items can be stored in the RAM – the operating system, graphics – what is displayed on the monitor, and program data (the file that you are working on).

RAM is memory where all the memory locations can be accessed in the same amount of time as any other – there is no difference. (Compare this to disk memory where data stored in different positions on the disk takes different times to access.)

Questions

1 Describe the control unit.
2 What is the purpose of RAM?
3 Identify **three** components of a general-purpose computer.
4 Identify **two** features of the ALU.

Computer performance

When talking about computers, the term 'speed' is a little misleading. There are various parts in a computer that come together to determine the speed.

Clock speed

There are four steps that the CPU carries out for each machine language instruction:

- fetch
- decode
- execute
- store.

These four steps, taken together, are known as the machine cycle.

The instructions are controlled by a clock pulse. A clock pulse is like a metronome – an action is performed on each beat.

A machine instruction requires at least one clock cycle to execute. A clock that oscillates 1 billion times per second is a (1 GHz) clock. So it produces a clock cycle with duration of one billionth of a second (1 nanosecond). One machine instruction can be executed every nanosecond.

Increasing the speed of the clock (which is within the processor) will increase the number of machine instructions that can be processed per second, which will have the effect of speeding up the machine.

Multiple processor

A computer system in which two or more CPUs share full access to a common RAM is known as a multiple processor system. Adding a second processor will not necessarily double the processing speed. However, it will increase it.

There are various factors that need to be taken into account that can affect the speed of a computer.

Overclocking

Every processor is given a rated speed by the manufacturer. Overclocking is changing this rated speed.

The speed of a CPU is determined by two things: the FSB (Front Side Bus), and the multiplier. For example, an Intel Celeron 600MHz CPU uses an FSB of 66MHz and a multiplier of 9, 9 x 66MHz = 600MHz.

If you want to overclock the speed of this CPU you will have to change one of the parts of the equation.

Word size

A word is the amount of data that a CPU can process at a particular time.

An 8-bit processor can process 8 bits at a time. 64-bit processing systems are available and in time will be used more. The more bits that can be processed at a time the faster the computer will be. The space shuttle uses 4-bit processors!

Bus size

The bus is the pathway between components on the computer, for example, the CPU and the memory.

The **bus** is the pathway between computer components.

The bus width is the amount of data that can be transmitted at one time. An 8-bit bus moves 8 bits at a time. Think of the bus as a highway going from one place to another. The road can only have so much traffic on it. A bigger road can have more traffic flowing at the same time.

RAM

It is much quicker to retrieve data from RAM than from disk. The more data that is held in RAM the faster a computer will seem to work. Increasing the RAM is a popular way of improving a computer's performance.

The **hard disk** is
the computer's main
storage area.

Independent processing

The processing can be moved from the CPU to peripheral devices. For example, graphics cards can have their own processors. This will remove part of the processing responsibility from the main CPU, which will allow it to concentrate on other tasks.

Hard disk

The hard disk is the main storage area of a computer. Getting the data to and from the hard disk takes time. The faster the access to data, the quicker it can be retrieved.

General

You want to ensure a good match between the word size, the bus size and the clock. It wouldn't be very useful to have a bus that can deliver data 128 bits at a time if the CPU can only use 16 bits at a time and has a slow clock speed.

An important factor in the speed of the motherboard is the chipset used to control the data processing. Manufacturers place great emphasis on the processors in their advertisements but 'power' users know that the chipset is as important.

Activity

Look through a computer magazine or web site and select a computer specification. Go through each of the items on the specification in turn and see if the overall performance of the machine could be improved by upgrading them.

Software

There are also some measures regarding software that you can take to improve the performance of a computer.

Freeing up memory so that the computer has more RAM to use is always a good idea. Memory will be taken up by little programs that are running in the background.

Defragmenting the hard disk drive so that files can be read continuously without the head jumping around to find the next section of the file, and ensuring that the drive is error free, will also assist performance.

Questions

1 How does the speed of the processor affect the speed of the computer?
2 Identify **three** hardware measures that could be carried out to speed up a computer.
3 How can replacing the hard drive with a faster model improve performance?
4 Describe how the bus width, clock speed and word size can impact on performance.
5 What is overclocking and how does it improve performance?
6 Identify **three** software measures that will improve performance.

Input devices and their ergonomic design

An input device is a piece of hardware that gets data from outside the computer system into the computer system. Any input device that has a large proportion of contact with the user increases the risk of inaccurate data being entered.

There are many different input devices and it is not possible to list them all here. The key, when writing about input devices, is to be aware of their use and to know which situations they are most appropriate. This can be determined by their cost effectiveness.

Ergonomics is about designing devices that increase productivity, health and safety and comfort.

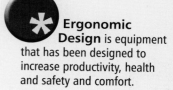

Ergonomic Design is equipment that has been designed to increase productivity, health and safety and comfort.

Keyboard

The keyboard has a typewriter-like set of keys used to input data and control commands to the computer. Most keyboards use a QWERTY layout and may also have a calculator-like numerical keypad off to one side, as well as a set of cursor-movement keys. Keyboards are good for inputting small quantities of data. There are two main keyboard layouts: QWERTY and DVORAK.

Figure 2.2 QWERTY and DVORAK keyboard layouts

Activity

Make a template (or download one) of a DVORAK keyboard and an alphabetical keyboard. What are the advantages and disadvantages of using the DVORAK layout and the alphabetical layout?

Keyboards do not necessarily just have letters in capitals. Primary school keyboards are available with lower case letters and concept keyboards are programmable.

A concept keyboard/overlay is a sheet that goes over a flat pad and allows you to create your own individual keys. These are used in bars and restaurants where the keys represent drinks and meals.

The concept keyboard is good in situations where language is a problem (perhaps in a pre-school or for the physically impaired) or where there are a set number of options (such as on tills).

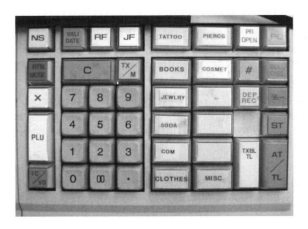

Figure 2.3 Concept keyboard used in a shop

Keyboard design has improved over the last few years with many
different ergonomic varieties. These include curved keyboards, split
keyboards and complete keyboard desks to ensure good posture.

Mouse

This is a pointing device that can be used to select items. It has buttons
on top to make the selection and a sensor underneath that allows the
pointer to move on the screen. It is a direct manipulation device.

The mouse has evolved over the last few years. The shape has changed
and it is possible to get ergonomically shaped mice that fit into the
palm of the hand. The sensor on the bottom used to be a ball but this
has been changed to an optical sensor.

The mouse needs some surface area in which to operate, a problem
with laptops. To overcome this, the mouse was turned upside down
with the ball on the top and became a trackerball.

The other pointing device that is similar to a trackerball is the joystick.
The joystick allows a device to be in one place with a stick that controls
the cursor on the screen. Joysticks have advanced ergonomically and are
now moulded to fit the hand. They are commonly used in gameplay
and flight simulators.

Scanner (OMR, bar code, flatbed, MICR)

**Optical Mark
Readers** (OMR) are
hardware devices that can
read marks made on paper.
They are used for multiple
choice tests and national
lottery tickets.

There are many different types of scanner. A scanner translates
information on paper into a form the computer can use:

- A bar code scanner reads bar codes and translates the bars into
  numbers – it is used in supermarkets.
- An OMR scanner reads the lozenges and translates them into
  numbers – it is used in lotteries, school registers and multiple-
  choice questions.
- A flatbed scanner digitises an image so that it can be processed
  later – as a picture, or using OCR to turn it into editable text.
- MICR is read and the magnetic ink turned into numbers – this is
  used on cheques.

Figure 2.4 A scanner translates information on paper into a form the computer can use

Graphics tablet

A graphics tablet consists of a flat working area, like a sheet of paper, and a stylus, that resembles a pen. They are used together to create and manipulate images on screen. A graphics tablet allows for freehand drawing.

Ergonomically, the stylus has improved and is easier to hold and the tablet has curved edges where the forearm goes. The new interactive whiteboards can be thought of as very large graphics tablets.

Graphics tablets are used by designers, and anyone involved in drawing on a computer.

Digitiser

Any device that converts analogue data to digital data is a digitiser. It is a generic description for many devices. Scanners, digital cameras, modems and graphics tablets are all types of digitisers.

Graphics tablets are input devices where the user draws with a stylus on a flat surface, and the drawing is reproduced on the monitor.

 A **digitiser** is a device that converts an analogue to a digital signal.

Activity

a) There are many other data-input devices that have not been covered above. Research the following devices, focusing on their purpose and ergonomic features:

- digital camera
- touch screen
- microphone
- switch
- sensor
- magnetic stripe reader.

b) Investigate the use of biometric devices as input devices. Describe the devices and list their advantages and disadvantages.

Specialist devices for physically disabled users, and their ergonomic design

There are a number of input and output devices for physically disabled people. There are two main groups of physically disabled users who require special devices to use the computer.

Visual impairment

The most common aid for the visually impaired is a screen reader, a program that reads out a computer display for the visually impaired or for those who do not have access to a monitor. The screen reader can read text that appears in a standard way in dialog boxes, menus, icons, and text-editing windows by attaching to the operating system components that are used to output the text. The screen reader may output information in Braille, use voice output, or use other audio signals to indicate graphics on the screen.

Other tools that can be useful in place of, or in addition to, a screen reader include:

- Text-to-speech system – takes written text and outputs it using a speech synthesizer. Text-to-speech systems are useful for the visually impaired and for situations where users are not able to view the computer screen at all times, for example when driving.
- Auditory feedback – sounds in response to user activity – noises for key presses, opening windows, menus deleting files, etc. This is useful as it confirms the action.
- Tactile interface – a user interface that uses touch (known as an embosser), such as a Braille keyboard or printer.
- Screen magnifier – a utility that can zoom in on portions of the screen to make it easier for the visually impaired to view information on computer monitors.

Motor impairment

Motor impairment is a loss or limitation of function in muscle control or movement, or a limitation in mobility. This can include hands that are too large or small for a keyboard, shakiness, arthritis, paralysis, and loss of limb. Hardware devices to assist include:

- Mouth-stick – a device for the physically disabled that enables the user to control input through a stick they control with their mouth.
- Puff-suck tube – a device that is placed in the mouth and blown through. (Also known as a blow-suck tube.)

- Tongue-activated joystick – a device that is placed in the mouth and manipulated with the tongue.
- Eye-typer – a device that fits on to the muscles around the eye and when the eye is moved a pointer on the screen moves.
- Foot-mouse – a mouse that is controlled by the foot.

Questions

1 Describe **two** input devices that can be used by a visually impaired person.
2 Describe **two** input devices that can be used by a motor-impaired person.
3 Describe how a foot-mouse works.
4 Describe how an eye-typer works.

Output devices and their uses

Output devices are used to display the result of processing to the user. They are designed to carry data from within the computer to outside the computer system. As we move towards a paperless society there is less reliance on hard copy and a lot of output is now being produced electronically, for example by email, being transferred to CD-ROMs, etc.

There are too many different output devices to list here. The key, when writing about output devices, is to be aware of their use and to know which situations are most appropriate for their use.

Monitor

A monitor is a device that takes signals from a computer and displays them on a screen. Monitors come in a variety of sizes and resolutions. The resolution is the maximum number of dots (pixels) that can be displayed on the screen at any one time. A screen resolution is given as the number of horizontal dots and then the number of vertical dots, for example, 800 x 600, or 1024 x 768.

Traditional monitors consist of a 'tube' (Cathode Ray Tube – CRT) like a television. Increasingly, monitors are also available as flat screens – these weigh a lot less than CRT and take up a lot less space on the desktop. The flat screen TFT is also better quality with no flicker and thus may cause less health problems for users.

Large monitors are used by graphic designers and newspaper editors, who need to display a lot of material on the screen at a time.

A **monitor** is a device that takes signals from a computer and displays them on screen.

Printer

Printers produce hard-copy output (output on paper). There are several different types of printer. The main ones are:

- dot matrix
- ink jet
- laser.

Dot matrix

These are impact printers – this means there is physical contact between the print head and the paper. They use an inked ribbon. Dot matrix printers can print in colour as well as black and white and their main advantage is that they will print on multi-part stationery (carbon forms).

Ink jet

These spray ink on to the paper and are relatively quiet. They are available in black and white or colour. They are relatively cheap to run, as the only replaceable component is the cartridge. They are used in homes and offices where the cost of a colour laser is prohibitive.

Laser

These are high-resolution non-impact printers that use a similar process to photocopying machines. A laser printer uses a rotating disc to reflect laser beams on to a photosensitive drum, where the image of the page is converted into an electrostatic charge that attracts and holds the toner (ink). A piece of charged paper is then rolled against the drum to transfer the image, and heat is then applied to fuse the toner and paper together to create the final image.

Laser printers are reliable and produce excellent quality in both colour and black and white. The running costs of the printer are high because not only do you have the toner to replace, you also have a drum and a fuser unit.

Laser printers are used where high-quality fast output is required – in businesses mainly, but lasers are also becoming common in homes. Schools are now using colour laser printers.

Activity

Complete the table below.

Printer	Description	Advantages	Disadvantages
Dot matrix			
Ink jet			
Laser			

There are several other types of printer. Research the following types of printer:

- daisy wheel
- line
- thermal.

When choosing a printer there are several factors to consider:

How much output?	What speed is needed?
Is heavy-duty equipment necessary?	Quality of output needed? Letter quality? Near-letter quality? Draft?
Location of printer?	How big a footprint can be handled? (The physical size of the unit.)
Is sound important?	Multiple copies needed?
Colour print needed?	

Plotter

A plotter is a mechanical device that produces printouts using vector or co-ordinate graphics. There are two types of plotter:

- **flatbed**, where the paper stays still and the pens move
- **drum**, where the paper is on a drum that moves.

Plotters are output devices that transfer drawings from the computer onto paper by moving a set of pens.

Figure 2.5 Flatbed and drum plotters

Plotters are used to draw accurate line diagrams, such as maps and building plans.

Activity

There are many other data output devices that have not been covered above. Research the following devices, focusing on their purpose:
- loud speaker
- lights
- modem.

Questions

1 Describe **three** criteria you would consider when buying a printer.
2 Identify **two** differences between a dot-matrix and a laser printer.
3 Describe a monitor.
4 Describe **two** different types of plotter.
5 Who would use the following devices and how would they be used:
   a) a 24″ monitor
   b) a flatbed plotter
   c) a colour laser printer
   d) a loud speaker.
6 Is a CD writer an output device? Give reasons for your view.

Storage devices and their use

Storage devices are used to hold data and programs. They are non-volatile (they keep their storage after the computer has been switched off).

There are many different types of storage device on the market. The main ones are included below:

Floppy disks

A floppy disk is a portable magnetic disk on which data and programs can be stored. Floppy disks are flexible plastic. They have a storage capacity of 1.44MB and are useful for transferring small files. A large number of machines, laptops in particular, are now being sold without floppy-disk drives.

Hard disks

A hard disk is a flat, circular, rigid plate with a surface that can be magnetised on one or both sides and on which data can be stored. It is a sealed unit and can be either internal (fixed in the computer) or removable.

Hard disks are the main storage device of a computer and hold the data and programs. Hard disk capacity is up to 1Tb (terabyte) at the moment and constantly improving. Hard disks can also be portable and used as external back-up units.

CD-ROMs and DVDs

CD-ROMs have a storage capacity of about 700MB and come in two varieties: a CD-R and a CD-RW. CD-Rs are WORMs (Write Once Read Many) and once the data has been written to them it is fixed and cannot be removed. CD-ROMs that you buy in shops – music, games and program CD-ROMs have already been written. You can buy blank CD-Rs and write your own CD-ROMs. CD-RW can be written to, erased and rewritten many times.

DVDs have a storage capacity of 4.7GB (or more) and, like CD-ROMs, come in two varieties – DVD R and DVD RW.

Tape drives

These are like tape cassettes and have a very high storage capacity – 2.4TB (compressed) and increasing. They are used for backing up large amounts of data.

Memory sticks

These are a series of solid-state devices. They were originally developed for digital cameras but have found a market replacing the floppy disk. They have a large storage capacity – in excess of 1GB and they come in a variety of formats.

Activity

a) Complete the table below.

Media	Description	Use	Capacity	Transfer speed	Cost per MB
Floppy disk					
Hard disk					
CD-ROM					
DVD					
Tape					
Memory stick					

b) When choosing a storage device, describe five characteristics that you would look for in order to make a comparison between devices.

Questions

1 Describe the different types of CD-ROMs and their uses.
2 Describe **three** different criteria that can be used to compare memory sticks.
3 Why is tape suitable to use for backing-up data?
4 How is a removable hard disk different from a portable hard disk?

What is the difference between magnetic storage media and optical storage media?

There are two main methods of storing data – optical and magnetic.

- Optical storage is any storage method in which data is written and read with a laser. Examples include DVD and CD-ROM.
- Magnetic storage is any storage method in which data is written and read with an electromagnet. Examples include hard disk, floppy disk and tape.

The backing-up and archiving of data – why are they necessary?

Back-up

Back-up is keeping a copy of the current data. If there is a failure of the computer system, for example power failure leading to corruption, a virus, files accidentally deleted, and so on, then the back-up can be used to restore the data.

Back-up is important so that data is not lost. Information is valuable and needs to be protected.

There are many different back-up devices:

- external memory – floppy disk, memory card
- second hard drive
- tape
- making a second copy of the same disk; possibly storing it off-site.

The back-up needs to be organised and it must be possible to locate the files that you need. If you have several copies of the file, it is important to know which one is the latest back-up. There are many different programs that will automate the back-up and restoration processes for you.

Activity

Investigate two different back-up programs. What facilities are available on them and why are they required?

Archiving

Archiving means the long-term storage of data that is not required in the short term. In fact, archived data may not be required at all. It is taken off the system and stored just in case it is required in the future. During archiving, data is written to a large-capacity storage device and this will only be done occasionally unlike back-ups, which should be written at short intervals.

Files should be archived when they are no longer needed for current use, but when you don't want to delete them permanently. Examples of these types of files would be last year's financial or sales records, completed projects, and other materials that, even though not necessary on a day-to-day basis, should be readily available if needed.

In a school, leavers' records are not required on a day-to-day basis but might be required in the future, for up to seven years after leaving, in order to write a reference for a student. The leavers' data would be archived for this purpose.

When you archive old files you:

- eliminate the waste of time and media that results from backing-up files no longer in regular use
- free up hard-drive space
- improve the performance of the system.

Questions

1 Using an example, define what is meant by the term 'back-up'.
2 Using an example, define what is meant by the term 'archive'.
3 Why is it important to back-up data?
4 What is the difference between archiving and the back-up of data?
5 What storage medium should be used for archiving?

Software types

Software is a computer program that provides the instructions that enable the computer hardware to work. There are various types of software:

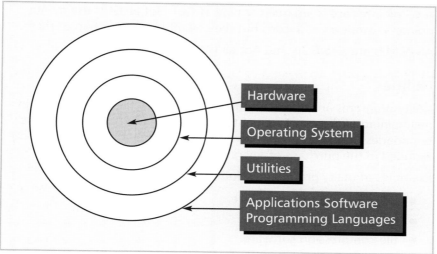

Figure 2.6 Types of software in relation to hardware

Operating system

The operating system is software that controls the allocation and usage of hardware resources such as memory, central processing unit (CPU) time, hard-disk space, and peripheral devices (for example, speakers or a mouse). It performs basic data-management tasks such as recognising input from the keyboard, sending output to the display screen and keeping track of files and directories on the disk.

The operating system is the foundation software on which programs depend. Examples of operating systems include Microsoft Windows®, BEOS®, Linux® and Unix® These are a few of the many different operating systems available.

User interface

The user interface is the means by which the user can interface with the application or operating system. User interfaces are covered in depth in the next chapter.

An **Operating System** is the software responsible for allocating system resources such as memory, processor time and disk space.

There are different types of user interface:

- menu – the on-screen list of options
- form – the on-screen space where you type
- command line – the space where you type instructions
- natural language – a voice-based interface.

User interfaces have two overriding phrases associated with them:

- GUI – Graphical User Interfaces
- WIMP – Windows, Icons, Mouse, Pulldown menu. (An alternative interpretation is Windows, Icons, Menu, Pointing device.)

A graphical user interface is the term for an interface based on graphics and pictures rather than text.

A WIMP interface is a particular type of GUI. Not all GUIs use menus, pointers, windows and icons but they might use one or two of them.

All WIMPs are also GUIs, but not all GUIs are WIMPs.

Utilities

Utility programs are small programs that assist in the monitoring and maintaining of the computer system. There is a blurring between the boundaries of operating systems and utilities with many utilities being included in the purchase of operating systems.

Examples of utility programs include:

- Printer-monitoring software
- virus checkers
- file-compression software.

Translation software

This is software that is used when programming – it converts the code written by the user into machine code that can be understood by the computer.

Application software

These are programs that allow the computer to be used to solve particular problems for the end user. Application software includes programs such as:

- word processing
- spreadsheets
- databases
- communications (email)
- graphics.

Application Software are programs that allow the computer to be used to solve particular problems for the end user.

Programming languages

These are packages that the user can use to create their own programs. There are many different programming languages available such as Visual Basic, C++ and Pascal.

Differences between types of
software and programming
language

Activity

Complete the following table and list as many pieces of software as you can. (An example has been completed for you.)

Name of software	Type	Description
Microsoft Word	Applications	Text and document processing

Questions

1 What is the role of the operating system?
2 Identify **two** different types of application software.
3 Describe **two** different user interfaces.
4 What does WIMP stand for?
5 What is a GUI?
6 Describe **two** different utility programmes.

Differences between types of software and programming language

Application software can be classified into four groups.

Generic

Generic software, also known as general-purpose software, is software that is provided for a range of tasks rather than a specific task. For example, word-processing software can be used to write letters, newsletters, web pages, memos and reports. It has a range of functions. Similarly, spreadsheets can be used to hold lists, calculate wages, work out positions in sports races, and so on.

Examples include:

- word processing
- spreadsheets
- databases
- communications (email)
- graphics.

Tailor-made

This is also known as bespoke software. It is specially written to suit a particular purpose. The software is usually produced when there is no off-the-shelf package available, or if a big company has specific requirements. It can be very expensive to create and support this kind of software.

Off-the-shelf

This is software that is created to meet a particular purpose but is available in a shop. The software is specific to a situation, for example wages software, library software, encyclopaedias, map software and route planners. These are specific pieces of software with one main function but they do not need to be created specifically for each situation. This type of software often has features that some users will not require.

Programming

This is software that can be used to create tailor-made software. It can create its own software, for example, the programmer drafts the user interface and the software creates the code to produce the user interface. There are many different programming packages available – usually each package is specific to a particular computer language.

Questions

1 Describe what is meant by the term 'generic software'.
2 What is the difference between off-the-shelf and generic software?
3 Why is there a need for programming software?
4 Describe what is meant by tailor-made software.

End of Chapter 2 tests

Test 1

A local newspaper has many computers advertised for sale within its pages.

1 The computers have hardware and software.

  Describe, with examples, the difference between hardware and software. [4]

2 One of the advertisements claims that an advantage of buying a PC from them is that they conform to industry standards.

  Explain the problems that would be brought about by a lack of standardisation in hardware. [4]

3 A general-purpose computer contains a control unit, an arithmetic and logic unit (ALU) and random-access memory (RAM).

  Describe the purpose of the control unit, ALU and RAM. [6]

4 Physically disabled users can purchase specialist input devices for computers.

  Describe a foot-mouse and a puff-suck switch. [4]

5 Give examples of optical and magnetic storage devices and describe the differences between them. [4]

6 Describe and state how a home user would make use of
   three different output devices. [6]

7 What is the difference between tailor-made and off-the-shelf
   software packages? [4]

Test 2

*An employee of an insurance company has recently been given the
opportunity to work from home.*

1 They have an old computer at home that they need to upgrade
   before they can use it for work.

   Describe how the computer performance is linked to the
   machine cycle. [4]

2 Describe **three** upgrades that could improve the
   performance of the computer. [6]

3 Identify **three** different input devices that could be used
   and, for each one, give an example of its use. [6]

4 Some data held on the computer needs to be backed-up
   and some needs to be archived.

   (i)   Describe the difference between backing-up and
         archiving data. [2]
   (ii) Why is archiving of data necessary? [2]

5 How would the employee make use of:
   (i)   DVDs [2]
   (ii) memory sticks? [2]

6 Identify **three** different types of software that might be
   found on a computer. [3]

3 | Systems and user interface software

Objectives

Your objectives for this chapter are to:

◎ know the types of operating system and the differences between them

◎ describe different styles of user interface and their characteristics

◎ know about supplementary user documentation and self-documenting systems

◎ describe a range of utilities and system software

◎ know the characteristics and purpose of translators, linkers and loaders.

Keep these objectives in mind as you work through the chapter.

Major characteristics of operating systems

The operating system (OS) is software that is responsible for allocating various system resources, for example: memory; processor time; disk space; and peripheral devices such as printers, modems, and the monitor. All application programs use the OS to gain access to these system resources.

There are different types of operating systems:

- single-user
- multi-user
- multi-tasking
- interactive
- batch processing
- real time
- distributed processing systems.

Single-user

A single-user OS provides access for one user at a time to use the computer. It is like a single machine for use at home. If someone else is using it you must wait for them to finish before you can have your turn.

Multi-user

A multi-user system lets more than one user access the system at the same time. Access is usually provided by a network. A common setup would be a network with single-user OS connected by the network to a server that has a multi-user OS.

The multi-user system must manage and run all user requests, ensuring that they do not interfere with each other. Devices that can only be used by one user at a time, like printers and disks, must be shared among all those requesting them.

Multi-tasking

This type of OS involves the processor carrying out several tasks at the same time. This could be, for example, using the Internet and writing a letter. Most multi-tasking operating systems are not actually doing two tasks at the same time – in order to achieve this it would require multiple processors. The computer is completing part of one task and then changing to do part of the second task and then back to the first and so on. It is doing this so fast that it appears that the computer is doing both tasks at the same time. The latest processors, however, can run multi-tasks, or threads, at the same time provided the OS can manage the activities.

Interactive and batch processing

Interactive is an OS that has direct user interaction while a program is running. This is the opposite of a batch-processing system where the OS is given a set of tasks to run and completes them without any intervention by the user. In batch processing the programs to be run are collected, stored and run at an appropriate time, such as when there is less demand on the processor (at night or during weekends) or just before it is required, for example, wages needed at the end of a month.

Real time

A real-time OS has been developed for real-time applications. These are typically used for embedded applications (systems within another application, for example, mobile phones within cars).

Any OS where interruptions are guaranteed to be handled within a certain specified maximum time limit is a real-time operating system.

Distributed processing systems

This is where there are a number of computers connected together. Each computer contributes by completing a part of the processing and, once it has all been completed, the results are combined to achieve the specified goal.

 **Distributed processing** is where different parts of the processing are carried out by different computers, connected together.

Questions

1 Describe **three** different types of operating system (OS).
2 What is the difference between a single-user and a multi-user OS?
3 How does a batch-processing OS differ from an interactive OS?
4 Describe real-time operating systems.

Different styles of user interface and their characteristics

The user interface is the method by which the user communicates with the computer. When deciding which user interface to implement, it is necessary to consider the situation where it is going to be used and who is going to be using it.

Command-based

This is where the user is presented with a command prompt.

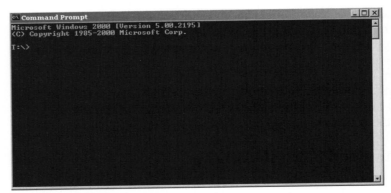

Figure 3.1 Command prompt

The commands are typed into the computer. This means that the user needs to have a good knowledge of what commands can be typed and the effect of those commands. If the prompt is not correct, it is possible that a lot of damage may be done to the computer.

Commands include:

- DIR – directory listing
- DIFF – show the difference between two files
- ENV – display environment variable.

If the interface is just command-based it takes up less memory than other user interfaces and this has the effect of running the commands faster.

Switches

A large number of commands have switches. These are parameters – additional commands, that can be added to the end of the main command and slightly change how it operates. For example:

- DIR = lists all files and directories in the directory that you are currently in.
- DIR /S = lists the files in the directory that you are in and all sub-directories belonging to that directory.
- DIR /P = if you cannot read all the files you can use this command and the computer will display all files one page at a time.
- DIR /W = this will list the files and directories horizontally.
- DIR /S /W /P = this will list all the files and directories in the current directory and the sub-directories after that in wide format one page at a time.

Switches add additional functionality to the command.

Command-based systems are for use by expert users with a good understanding of the commands. They are useful for running commands that cannot be accessed from a menu or form.

> ★ A **command-based user interface** is where the user types commands into the computer to carry out tasks.

Activity

Investigate **five** different commands from two different operating systems. Describe what the command does and its syntax, including the switches available.

Forms

A form is a limited area on-screen with boxes to fill in.

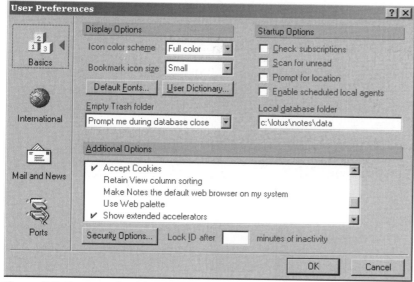

A form is a limited
on-screen area with
labels and instructions and
spaces for entering data.

Figure 3.2 Computerised form

The form has:

- labels to give assistance and instruct the user as to what to enter
  into each box
- spaces to enter data – these might be drop-down boxes, open text
  or option buttons.

Forms can guide the user through entering the relevant information in a
structured manner. They can include the default options for the user and
give context-based assistance. The data-entry boxes can also be validated.

The form on the computer can be a copy of a paper-based form, which
can make entering data easier.

Activity

Design a form to be used for entering a customer order for a new car.

Menus

Menus are a series of related items that can be selected. Menus are
either pop-up (when you press a button or a key a menu appears next
to the cursor) or pull-down (when you click on a heading the rest of the
menu appears below the heading).

Menus can be structured – the top word in a pull-down menu gives an
indication of what the menu is about. For example, in word-processing,
'File' contains all aspects to do with the file itself, 'Format' is about
changing the appearance, and so on.

Menus can be cascaded – one menu leading to another menu. Items on
menus can be greyed out and not usable. This can be done if certain
options are not available.

Menus can also be context sensitive. Depending on what you are doing
within the application, a different set of menus might appear. For

example, if you are working with tables you will get a menu relevant to tables and if you are working with pictures you will get a picture menu.

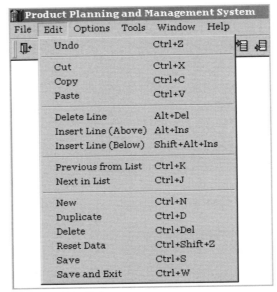

Figure 3.3 Pull-down menu

Menus can use a graphic user interface (GUI) or be text-based.

Natural language

This is currently in the realms of science fiction – *Star Trek* and HAL from *2001*. There is some progress towards a natural language interface but it requires specific key words to be included.

The idea of natural language interfaces is that they allow the users to use their own language to communicate with the computer. They do not require any specific commands.

There are two main types of natural language interface – spoken and written. Spoken interfaces are typified by voice-recognition software, which allows you to word process. Typed natural language interfaces include Microsoft Help® and Ask Jeeves®. PDAs (Personal Digital Assistants) can include software that recognises handwriting.

When natural language interfaces eventually become commonplace, they will allow all levels of user to access the computer and will revolutionise ICT.

A **Natural language** interface allows the user to use their own langauge to communicate with the computer.

Activity

Investigate and write a report on the problems of voice recognition and using voice-activated software.

Questions

1 Describe **three** advantages of using a command-based interface.
2 Where would the use of a forms interface be appropriate?
3 What are the disadvantages of a natural language voice interface?
4 Describe **three** characteristics of a menu interface.

The purpose and importance of self-documenting systems and supplementary user documentation

Self-documenting systems

One of the problems of documentation is being able to find it when you need it. If the software is installed on a network, this problem may be compounded, as there may only be one copy of the manual.

Self-documenting systems contain all the necessary documentation within the system – no external documentation is required to use it .

Methods of achieving this include:

- tool tips – quick, single-word help when you rest the cursor on an item
- internal help guides – tutorials online
- helpful error messages – messages that mean something (what you did wrong and how to correct it)
- online help – context-based help relevant to the form or menu you are using.

Supplementary user documentation

This includes all the different types of documentation that you might get when you purchase software or hardware.

It does NOT include the user documentation – it is in addition to the user documentation.

Figure 3.4 Supplementary documentation

Type	Purpose	Importance
Warranty	To let the user know their legal rights	Without it, if things go wrong, it may be difficult to find out your rights
Health and Safety guide	To set up and use the computer safely	If not followed, there may be damage to the user's health
Licence	To let the user know the limits of how they can use the software	Protects the company's intellectual property
Product key	To install the software	The user cannot install and run without this
Start-up guide	To get the software running quickly	Allows the user to get the software installed and running quickly without having to read a large manual first
Glossary	Quick reference guide to specific terms	Terms specific to the software can be looked up and understood
Troubleshooting	Guide to common errors	Allows problems to be resolved quickly and easily
Tutorial	Guide to individual tasks	If a user needs to find out how to do something specific they can use the tutorial rather than a large manual

All the documentation could be included in one document; however, this would be a large and unwieldy document. For novice users it would be very daunting. Breaking the documentation down allows each part to be stored separately. Users can have the guides but the key information – the warranty, licence and product key can be stored centrally.

Questions

1 What is a self-documenting system?
2 Describe **three** different methods of creating a self-documenting system.
3 Describe **three** items of supplementary user documentation.
4 Why is the user guide not a part of the supplementary user documentation?
5 What are the advantages of separating the documentation?

Utilities and other system software

System software is software that is used to control the basic operations of the computer. It is used to liaise with the hardware and the applications programs.

Utilities

Utilities are small programs that assist with the maintenance and monitoring of a computer system and its use.

Utilities are small programs that assist with the maintenance and monitoring of the computer system and its use. They also make the PC more convenient to use. There are many different utilities available. The following are some of the main types of utilities.

Compression software

Compression software reduces the size of a file to reduce the amount of storage space it occupies and to reduce the time it takes to transmit.

This is software that will reduce the size of the file. It is useful when sending and receiving files across the Internet. There are two different compressed files that can be made – a normal compressed file and a self-extracting compressed file. If the end user does not have the compression software installed on their machine then a self-extracting file can be created which has the uncompressing software built in to enable the file to uncompress automatically when run.

Back-up

Making back-up copies of the data is vital, so that it is retrievable if an accident should occur and the original is lost. There are many different parts of a computer that can be backed-up. You can have an entire back-up of all files and settings, back-up the working data, back-up program settings or a combination. Back-up utilities allow the different types of back-up and restore to be managed.

Anti-virus

Keeping a computer free of viruses is a time-consuming process. There are new threats all the time and it is important to keep the anti-virus software up-to-date and all machine operating systems and software patched against the virus threat. Patches are quick fixes for the software – designed to fix a specific error or hole in the code.

Activity

Investigate six different pieces of utility software and write a review on each of them, giving reasons why they are needed.

Drivers

In order for the peripheral devices to communicate with the computer and its operating system there is a need for a piece of software. This software contains the specific commands needed by the peripheral in order to work with the operating system. This piece of software is called a driver. Each peripheral will have its own driver.

Configuration files

A peripheral needs a driver in order to work. Once the driver has been loaded the computer can communicate with the peripheral and use it. To make the use of the device suitable for the particular environment that it is in, a config (configuration) file is used. The config file is used to personalise the settings, for example:

- having a particular set of icons on the toolbar
- printer settings with a certain type of paper
- connection settings, such as dial-up number and baud rate for the modem to use.

The **config file** is used to personalise settings, for example having a particular set of icons on a toolbar.

Questions

1 What is system software?
2 Why are utilities needed?
3 Describe the use of configuration files.
4 What is the purpose of drivers?
5 Describe **three** different utilities.

Translators, linkers and loaders – their use and characteristics

There are three elements within the computer that are needed to ensure that programs being created will run correctly. They are:

- translators
- linkers
- loaders.

Translator

When a program is created, it is written in a source language. Source language is a high-level language that needs to be converted to a language the computer can understand – the object code. The translator performs this task.

There are two methods of translating code:

1 Interpreting. Interpreters are like human interpreters – they cannot cope with all the code in one go but need it a bit at a time. Interpreters take one line of source code at a time and produce

Translators are programs that translate source code written in a high-level language to a language that the computer can understand – the object code.

one line of object code at a time. This takes place whenever the code is run, which means you need the source code each time. Because it takes the code a line at a time, interpreting is slower than other methods of translation. However, if the translator encounters an error it will stop, highlight the error and show variable values to help in diagnosis. This makes interpreting useful when developing code.

2 Compiling. Compiling is taking all of the source code and creating the object code in one go. The object code is then released and can be run. Depending on the size of the program, compiling can take a long time. Any errors in the code will not be found until the code has been translated and then a list of errors will be presented. It will take time to correct these and recompile. Compilation is used when releasing a program to the general public. It can optimise code so that it runs faster and it usually produces more compact code.

Linker

A **linker** puts together the modules that make up a program to create a single executable program.

A **loader** takes a program from disk and places it in memory so that it can be run.

When a program is written, it is likely that it is written in module form, in other words, lots of different parts with each coded separately and stored as separate files.

When it runs a program the computer needs one file, not lots of little ones like this. The linker puts the modules together to create a single executable program.

Loader

The user usually purchases a program on disk. In order to run, the program needs to get from the disk to the computer's memory. The loader takes the program from disk and places it in memory so that it can be run.

There are different types of loaders:

Bootstrap loader

A bootstrap loads a small piece of the program from disk at the beginning of the process and can then load the rest. This type of loader is commonly used to load the operating system.

Linking loader

A linking loader combines the features of a linker and a loader. It can link different modules and load them.

Relocating loaders

Relocating loaders can load the program anywhere in the memory.

Questions

1 What is the purpose of the translator?
2 Describe **two** different methods of translating code.
3 Describe **two** problems with giving out the source code.
4 What is the purpose of the linker?
5 What is the purpose of the loader?
6 Describe three different types of loader.

Test 1

A software developer is setting up a system for a newsagent.

1   The newsagent could have a batch processing or an interactive operating system.

   Describe the difference between these two types of operating system.   [6]

2   The developer is considering using a forms-based interface for the software.

   Describe **three** characteristics of a forms-based interface.   [6]

3   Identify **two** other types of interface.   [2]

4   The system will contain supplementary user documentation.

   Describe **three** items of supplementary user documentation and, for each, give its purpose.   [6]

5   The new system will contain drivers and configuration files.

   Describe the role of the configuration file in the system.   [2]

6   The software developer uses a translator when writing the software.

   Describe the characteristics and purpose of a translator.   [4]

7   When backing up the data on the system, the newsagent will use compression software.

   Describe the role of compression software.   [2]

Test 2

A parent has purchased a computer for himself and his family to use.

1   Although a single computer, it is advertised as having a multi-user, multi-tasking operating system.

   (i)   Describe the major characteristics of a multi-user operating system.   [4]

   (ii) Describe the major characteristics of a multi-tasking operating system.   [4]

   (iii) Are the claims made in the advert correct? Give your reasons.   [2]

2   The computer has a command line and menu interface.

Describe these two types of interface and give an
appropriate use for each.   [6]

3   The system is described as self-documenting.

Describe **three** features that would make a system self-
documenting.   [6]

4   The operating system is advertised as having 'a large range
of utilities'.

Describe **two** utilities that the computer would be supplied
with.   [4]

5   Each piece of hardware has its own drivers.

What is the role of the driver?   [2]

File and database concepts

4

Objectives

Your objectives for this chapter are to:

◎ describe the problems and benefits of storing data using fixed- or variable-length records

◎ describe the characteristics, advantages and disadvantages of serial, sequential, indexed sequential and random access to data

◎ describe how data can be organised in secondary memory

◎ know about hashing algorithms and the use of an index or set of indexes to facilitate indexed sequential access

◎ explain the advantages and disadvantages of using alternative data types

◎ describe the terms typically used in relational database terminology

◎ describe the difference between flat files, relational and hierarchical database systems, discussing the comparative benefits and drawbacks of each

◎ describe the use of access levels for online files and databases, identifying the need for the different levels of access.

Keep these objectives in mind as you work through the chapter.

Problems and benefits of storing data

A record is an organised collection of information about an object or item. For example, in an address book:

Paul Jones
302 Windsor Street
Birmingham
B7 4DW

This is a record. When storing the information on computer there are two main methods:

- fixed-length records
- variable-length records.

Fixed-length records

Each record is made up of characters – the record listed above has 44 characters. A space is included as a character. For example:

Name:	10
Address line 1:	18
Town:	10
Postcode:	6

In a fixed-length record, each record is allocated a maximum number of characters that can be stored in it. Every record, no matter how large or small the amount of information, is given exactly the same amount of space.

For example, if the amount of space given to the name was 15 characters:

Glen Millbery:	13 characters – 2 free spaces
Sonia Stuart:	12 characters – 3 free spaces

A **Fixed-length record** is a record where the number of characters that it can contain is specified.

These two names fit and have very few free spaces. However:

Robert Louis Stevenson: 22 characters – would not fit.

What happens if the name is too long? The first x number of characters is stored. In this case, the first 15 characters would be stored:

Robert Louis St

So why don't we just allocate lots of characters for each name? If you came up with the longest name you could think of – 60 characters for example, and made this the length of the name field, all names would fit. However, as most names have between 10 and 15 characters there would be a lot of wasted space. It might not seem a lot when talking about one name, but when you are talking about thousands and millions of names (for example, in a large database) it builds up, especially when you are doing the same thing for all lines of the address and any other data you might store. Historically, storage space was expensive and needed to be used with care.

When using fixed-length records, it is necessary to find a balance between allocating enough space to fit all the characters in and not allocating so much that there is lots of unused and wasted space.

Variable-length records

Variable-length records ensure that every record has just the right amount of space it requires. No information is truncated (cut off) and there are no empty characters stored. The disadvantage is that it is much more difficult to program.

Fixed-length records have a major benefit. If every record stored on the disk is of the same length, then it is possible to know where the beginning and end of every record is. This makes access to the data faster than variable-length records where the beginning and end is unknown because the length of each record is different.

Variable-length records are records where the length is automatically adjusted to fit the data being entered.

Activity

Investigate how data is stored in bits and how to convert bits to bytes, kilobytes and megabytes. Write a poster on how to achieve the conversion.

Questions

1 Describe, with examples, what is meant by a 'record'.
2 List all items you would store in a student record. Allocate maximum and minimum sizes to each piece of information and work out the overall record size for both and the difference between them.
3 What is the difference between a fixed- and a variable-length record?
4 What are the benefits of using fixed-length records?
5 What are the benefits of using variable-length records?

Accessing data

Records are stored on a storage medium – a tape or a disk. In order to be used they need to be retrieved from the storage medium, and, if necessary, replaced back.

There are four main methods of accessing data:

- serial
- sequential
- indexed sequential
- random.

Serial

Serial access is where the records are stored one after the other with no regard to the order. This is usually an unprocessed file. It might be a transaction file – in a shop where transactions are stored as they occur, or when logging the activity of a user. In such cases, records are written as they happen.

Serial files are read by starting at the beginning and reading through every record until you find the one that you want. You need to start at the beginning because, as the records are in no particular order, you do not know where the record that you want will be. You can stop when it is found but the only way to know if it is not present is to read every single record.

Tape and disk can be used to store serial files.

If you are processing a file that requires every single transaction to be read then serial access is appropriate, for example, back-up.

Sequential

Sequential access is a sorted serial file. The records have been put into some sort of order. This might be alphabetical order, date/time order or some other suitable method.

Tape and disk can be used to store sequential files.

When searching sequential files, you can begin at the beginning and read the records one by one. Once you have gone past where the record should be (and have not found it), it is safe to assume that it is not present.

The main disadvantage is that if a new record is added and needs to go in the middle of the list then the whole list will need to be rewritten.

Serial access stores records with no regard to order.

Sequential access sorts records into a particular order.

Figure 4.1 Serial and sequential access

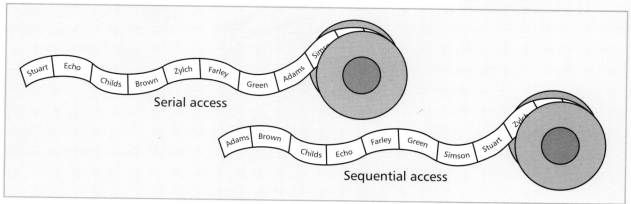

Serial access

Sequential access

Sequential access is useful for batch processing as it speeds up the job, for example, payroll, updating exam results and working out utility bills.

Indexed sequential

An indexed sequential access system organises the files sequentially but also contains an index to certain points in the file.

Imagine that you have a telephone directory. This is stored as a sequential file with every name sorted alphabetically. There is also an index that might show where every letter starts.

An **indexed sequential file** is a file that is organised sequentially (in order) but that also has an index to certain points in the file.

Figure 4.2 Index sequential filing system

As you can see, the index points to the beginning of all the entries for that particular letter. This becomes the starting point for a sequential search through the records (rather than starting at A each time).

The advantage of an indexed sequential system is that you do not have to start at the beginning of the file. You can start your search from a position closer to the target. The system then has the same advantages of sequential over serial files.

If the file you are searching is very large then it is possible that it may have more than one index.

Figure 4.3 Multi-level indexed sequential filing system

The first index gives a reference point in the second index, which in turn gives the starting position on disk.

Multi-level indexes are used because it is easier to search a small file than a very large one. If the index were located in one large file, it would not be much faster than searching the sequential file.

Indexed sequential organisation can also be used sequentially. A disk is required to allow indexed sequential file access.

As both sequential and indexed access to the records is available, this method of access is very good for sequential applications that may require individual records to be updated. For example, payroll and utility bills require sequential access when every record has to be processed. However, if someone leaves or joins the company or a person moves house and needs a final bill then indexed sequential access can be used.

Random (also known as direct access)

Using the random access method, it is possible to go directly to a record without going through any preceding records. If serial and sequential methods are like songs on a cassette tape, random access is like a CD – you do not have to go through all the previous songs to get to the one you want, you can go straight to it.

Only disks can be used for random access.

The main advantage is that when you add, remove and alter records you do not have to continually rewrite the files. The files do not have to be stored together on the disk; they can be in any location on it. The disadvantages are the requirement to have disks, and arrangements have to be made so that two records do not have the same address on the computer. We will discuss this later in this chapter.

Suitable applications include anything that requires instant access to data – for example, booking systems and bank accounts.

> * A **random-access** file is a file where an individual record can be accessed directly.

Questions

1 Describe, using an example, what serial access is.
2 What are the advantages of using sequential access?
3 Give examples of suitable applications for serial, sequential, indexed sequential and random access systems.
4 Using an example, explain how two levels of indexes can be used in indexed sequential access.
5 Explain the advantages of using direct access.
6 For each type of access, identify the type of storage medium required.

Hashing algorithms and collisions

Hashing

Direct access allows each record to be accessed without the preceding records being looked at. This is done because each record has an address and this address can be calculated. The process is known as hashing.

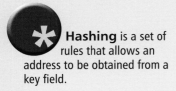
Hashing is a set of rules that allows an address to be obtained from a key field.

There are lots of different methods of hashing. Below are two examples:

1 Division method of hashing (modulo arithmetic)

This involves finding the remainder from a division. For example:

10 divided by 4 = 2 with a remainder of 2
18 divided by 7 = 2 with a remainder of 4
59 divided by 10 = 5 with a remainder of 9

When we write it out, instead of using divided by, we use the term MOD – this means find the remainder.

Hashing using modular arithmetic begins with a finite set of storage locations. This, in turn, leads to a maximum number of records that can be stored.

The address is found by dividing the key field by the number of memory spaces available. This is the formula:

Memory address = Key field MOD number of addresses

For example, a key field of 6454 and 1000 addresses available:

Memory address = 6454 MOD 1000
Memory address = 454 (6454/1000 = 6 remainder 454)

2 Mid-square hashing

In this method the key field is squared and specified digits are extracted from the middle of the result to form the address.

Key:	9876
Squared:	97535376
Middle 4 numbers:	5353

Collisions

Occasionally the hashing algorithm will give the same address from different keys.

For example, using the division method, with 1000 memory spaces, key field 4096 and 2096 will both give the key field of 96. When this happens, it is known as a collision.

There are many different methods for dealing with collisions. Two of them are given below:

1 Next free block

The record is placed in the next available free block. The hashing algorithm generates an address, if there is something in that address the addresses are searched sequentially until one is found with nothing in it and the record is placed there. To find the record, the address where it should be is searched and from there a sequential search is done to find the record.

In some systems a part of the storage area is set aside as an overflow area. This is an area where records that cannot be placed in their rightful locations are placed. If the record cannot be found in the correct storage location, the overflow area is sequentially searched.

2 Linear probing

The second method uses linear probing. This stops a sequential search by detailing exact spots where the record might be.

If the address is taken, then 1 is added to the address. If that address is taken, then 2 is added to the address and so on. Once the end memory address has been reached, it starts again from the beginning.

For example, if a record should be in position 1534 and this is taken, the 1 is added to it to get 1535, if that is taken then 2 is added to get 1536 and so on. Because it started at 1534 there may be spaces from 1 to 1533, so it then goes back to the beginning.

Questions

1 What is hashing?
2 Describe **two** different methods of hashing.
3 What is a collision?
4 Using examples, describe **two** different methods of dealing with collisions.
5 Using the division method, what would the address be for the following keys in a system with 1250 memory spaces:
   a) 76
   b) 34
   c) 874
   d) 576
6 Using the mid-square hashing method, what would the addresses be for the following keys, using the middle four numbers:
   a) 3212321
   b) 4323432
   c) 6545654

Selecting appropriate data types

More detail on data types can be found on page 7.

Data types

The main data types available are:

- text/string
- integer
- real
- Boolean
- date/time.

Text/string

Text/string data is any key on the keyboard. It can be used to store text (Mr Jones), text and numbers (TN18 7PU), or just numbers.

Numbers are only stored as text if they are not to be manipulated as numbers – if no addition, subtraction, and so on is to be performed.

Integer and real

Integer and real data are numbers – integer being numbers without decimal places and real, numbers with decimal places. When assessing

Data types are the type of data that can be located such as a field in a database.

the numerical data to be stored it is necessary to look at examples of data and decide the most appropriate numerical data type.

Currency is usually stored as a real number – £43.00 (the symbol, although text, is stored separately) but if you are talking about house prices then is it still appropriate to store currency as a real? A house price is not going to have decimal places.

Boolean

Boolean is used where only one of two values needs to be selected, for example: yes/no; male/female; true/false.

Date/time

This data type is used specifically for storing dates and times.

Advantages and disadvantages of data types

The advantages and disadvantages of using the data types are related to their use within a given scenario and what the data will be used for. For example, the data for a field, 'Does the house have a garden?' has only two possible options – yes or no. This is appropriate for a Boolean data type. Why? Because it takes up the minimal amount of memory space and can be validated to ensure the data stored is one of those two values. It also enables easier searching of the data.

Questions

1 Describe the **five** main data types.
2 When should numbers be used?
3 What are the advantages of using the Boolean data type?

Relational database terminology

A database is a collection of related data. As we saw earlier, a record is also a collection of related data so what is the difference between a record and a database? A collection of related records is called a table and a collection of tables (or just one table) is called a database.

Each of the individual lines in a record is known as a field. One of the fields is more important than the rest as it uniquely identifies the record and is known as the primary key. If you link two tables together, they are linked using a foreign key and the link is known as a relationship. Why do we link tables together? The main reason is to prevent the same data being entered into more than one table.

The above is a brief overview of database terminology. This will help you as we go through the more detailed information below, using an example.

Imagine you own a company that sells paint. You are very successful but disorganised and have decided to create a database for your business.

Entities and attributes

Having examined your business, you find that you have lists detailing:

- all the paints you have in stock – amounts, prices, etc.
- where you get the paints from
- customer information
- the products/paints each customer has bought.

These four collections of data are known as entities. An entity is a name for a 'logical or physical storage unit'. In simpler terms, an entity is the name given to anything that you store data about. A list of all the paints in stock is an entity – all the data items refer to the same thing – paints and storage.

Entities are referred to singularly and, when written, always appear in capitals. Ideally, entities should be single words. If a two-word name must be used, then the words should be joined by an underscore.

The four entities identified might be called:

PAINT   SUPPLIER   CUSTOMER   ORDER

Relational database terminology

An **entity** in database terminology, is the name given to anything you can share data about, for example, CUSTOMER SUPPLIER or ORDER.

Activity

Identify the entities contained in the scenario below and give reasons why they are entities:

A library holds details on all the books, CDs and tapes in the library. It also has details on all its borrowers and which books/tapes/CDs they have borrowed.

Entities are a theoretical aspect of databases. They are used when writing about and designing databases. Eventually, the entities will become records within tables when you actually start creating the database.

We need to add some details to the entities. We know the entities hold information – we need to decide what information.

In our paint shop, details on customers are being held. We need to identify all the different details about the customers that will need to go into the database:

- name of the customer
- their address
- their phone number.

Having come up with the details, it is good practice to reduce them to a single identifiable word:

- name
- address
- phone.

It is also good practice to reduce the contents to single pieces of data. This means that name and address need to be broken down:

- Forename
- Surname

- Address Line 1
- Address Line 2
- Town
- County
- Postcode
- Phone.

These are known as attributes. An attribute is a characteristic of an entity.

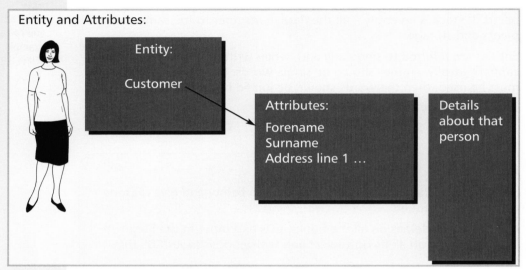

Figure 4.4 Entities and attributes

Every entity has attributes.

Activity

For the SUPPLIER, PAINT and ORDER entities, write down the information that needs to be stored for each and then break these down into single-word attributes.

So far we have entities and each entity has attributes. We have only been dealing with a theoretical database so far. When it comes to actually creating the database, the name of the entities will become table names and the attributes will become fields.

Tables and fields

The table is made up of fields. The table is the physical implementation of the entity and the field is the physical implementation of the attribute.

The field holds an individual item of information. The field is identified by the name (usually the same as the name of the attribute) and is given a data type. Validation rules can also be applied to fields. When planning the use of a table it is useful to apply validation, such as in the table below:

Figure 4.5 Fields are identified by field name, data type and validation

Table Name:	Tbl_Customer	
Field Name	**Data Type**	**Validation**
Forename	Text	Length
Surname	Text	Length
AddressLine 1	Text	Length
Town	Text	Length
County	Text	Choice
Postcode	Text	Picture
Phone	Text	Type, Length, Picture

Activity

Using the library example described in the Activity on page 75, write out the tables and field names required for a suitable database.

Records, keys and relationships

Figure 4.6 Table displaying records

Forename	Surname	Address Line 1	Town	County	Postcode	Phone
John	Green	43 The Grove	Chatham	Kent	ME1 2AB	01634 12345
Harry	Blue	18 Hilltop	Chatham	Kent	ME1 3AB	01634 22345
Susan	White	23 The Street	Chatham	Kent	ME1 4AB	01634 32345
John	Green	43 The Grove	Chatham	Kent	ME1 2AB	01634 12345

Each line is known as a record. The table above contains four records. A record is a collection of fields that all relate to the same topic.

There are rules for tables. In order for the table to conform to these rules, every row needs to be unique. In the example above, every row is not unique – the first and last contain the same details. These may refer to the same customer or they may refer to different customers – two people who live at the same address with the same name.

To make the records unique, we need to have a primary key. The primary key is a field that makes each record uniquely identifiable. Primary keys are usually numeric and, in many database systems, the data type can be

The **primary key** is a field that makes each record uniquely identifiable.

set to Autonumber. This is a number field, which the database will start at 1 and automatically increment for each new record.

Figure 4.7 Table showing primary key

Customer	Forename	Surname	Address Line 1	Town	County	Postcode	Phone
1	John	Green	43 The Grove	Chatham	Kent	ME1 2AB	01634 12345
2	Harry	Blue	18 Hilltop	Chatham	Kent	ME1 3AB	01634 22345
3	Susan	White	23 The Street	Chatham	Kent	ME1 4AB	01634 32345
4	John	Green	43 The Grove	Chatham	Kent	ME1 2AB	01634 12345

As you can see, the primary key is just a number, but it now makes every record unique – no two records will have the same primary key.

The four tables in the database, with fields, are:

CUSTOMER (<u>Customer</u>, Forename, Surname, Address Line 1, Town, County, Postcode, Phone)

PAINT (<u>Paint</u>, Colour, Name, Cost, Supplier, Type)

SUPPLIER (<u>Supplier</u>, Name, Contact Name, Phone)

ORDER (<u>Order</u>, Customer, Paint, Quantity, Date)

The primary key in each table is underlined.

One of the advantages of a relational database is that it removes duplicate data. Imagine if you had to write out the customer's name and address every time they placed an order. If they placed 50 orders that is a lot of duplicated data. Would it not be better to store their name and address once and link it to their order?

If we go back to the original paint company scenario (page 74) it will help to find the links between tables:

- Each paint has a supplier.
- Each customer orders a paint.

Look at the tables and field names in Figure 4.8 – can you see field names repeated in different tables?

- In the PAINT table there is **Supplier** (also in the SUPPLIER table)
- In the ORDER table there is **Customer** (from CUSTOMER table) and **Paint** (from PAINT table)

This can be drawn out:

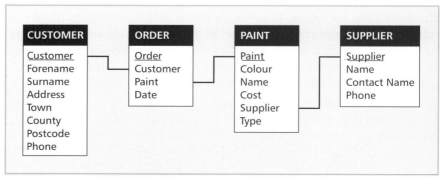

Figure 4.8 Entity with attributes and links

Notice how one of the sides of the link is always a primary key and the other is just a field. This is important. The one that is just a field but is part of the link is called a foreign key.

A foreign key is a field in one table that is also a primary key in another table and is used to create a link between the two.

Look at the tables below showing the PAINT and SUPPLIER tables. The value in the primary key of SUPPLIER matches the value of the foreign key in PAINT allowing a link between the two tables and the data to be matched between them.

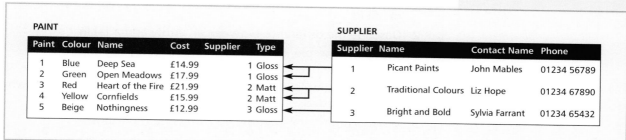

Figure 4.9 Entity with data showing link

Activity

Using the Activity on page 75, complete the tables and attributes for the library and draw out a diagram showing the links between tables.

Referential integrity

Looking at the paint company example, it is possible to have a supplier in the database that did not supply you with any paints. They may have done so in the past but you do not stock any of their paints now.

It is not possible to have paints in the database that do not have any supplier. Referential integrity makes sure that it is impossible to enter a reference to a link that does not exist:

Figure 4.10 Referential integrity working and not working

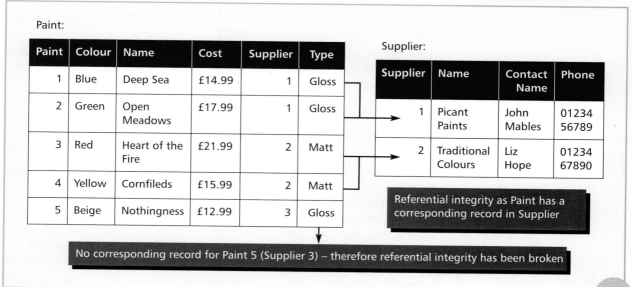

Questions

1 Describe the following database terms:
   a) database
   b) record
   c) field.
2 Describe the difference between an entity and a table.
3 Using an example, describe the term 'primary key' and explain why they are needed.
4 Using an example, describe the term 'foreign key' and explain why they are needed.
5 What is referential integrity and why is it important?

What are the differences between flat file, relational and hierarchical database systems?

There are a variety of database models. A database model is a method of structuring the data within the database. It is how the data is organised.

There are three main methods of organising a database:

● flat file
● relational
● hierarchical.

Flat file

A flat-file database is one that has a single table. The table is not connected to anything else.

Flat-file databases are used to store lists. They are very simple to set up. However, because they are like lists, they contain a lot of repeated data. In our paint company, if the data was held in a flat-file system, every time an order came in, the name and address of the person who placed the order would have to be repeated.

If the details of the person placing the order changed – they moved for example – then you would have different addresses for the same person. You would not know which one to use and problems would arise.

Customer
Customer ID
Forename
Surname
Date of Membership
Book Borrowed
Date Taken Out
Date Due Back

Figure 4.11 A flat-file database

Relational

This model of database uses lots of tables and links them together. The database that we created for the paint company was a relational database.

In a relational model, the tables are linked by foreign keys, and this means that data only needs to be stored once. This reduces data duplication. Reducing data duplication decreases the amount of storage space required and means that the data is more likely to be correct – if you are storing only one copy then you are not going to store two different versions – the data is said to be consistent and has integrity. If you are only entering the data once there is also less scope for data-entry errors.

In relational models, an update or deletion in one table can be cascaded throughout all the tables.

Searching and reporting in the relational model can utilise data from any of the tables – it is not limited to just the data held within an individual table.

The disadvantages of the relational model are the complexity of the software required to set up and maintain the database, and the expertise needed to do so.

Hierarchical

This model is where the data is held in a tree structure.

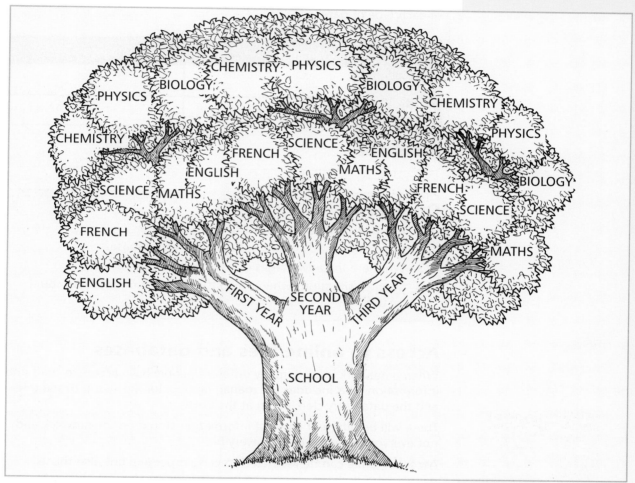

Figure 4.12
A tree hierarchical database

The main nodes are linked to subordinate nodes – often called parent and child. A main node can have many subordinates below it but all nodes link to only one node above.

It is not possible to create relationships that go across branches – they are distinct and separate.

This data model is very good for storing data that is topical. For example, all items related to a particular mobile phone could be held in one branch and those related to another mobile phone in another branch. The problems come when a particular accessory for one phone can also be used on another. This would require the data to be duplicated.

The hierarchical data model does have cascade update and delete. If you were to delete a node, all those below it would also be deleted. Likewise, if you updated a node, all related data below would also be updated.

The access to the data is very fast – for each branch you go down you automatically restrict the amount of data that needs to be searched.

Unfortunately, reorganisation of the data is very difficult and you cannot cross branches. This makes it suitable only for very specific applications, for example, transaction-orientated applications and customer-oriented applications, that have a single focus.

Activity

Complete the following summary of the advantages and disadvantages of each type of database model.

	Advantages	Disadvantages
Flat file		
Relational		
Hierarchical		

Questions

1 Using examples, describe a flat-file database.
2 What are the advantages of a relational database?
3 What are the advantages of a hierarchical database?
4 Suggest situations where the different types of database could be used.

Access to online files and databases

When a network is used, many different people have access to the same information. This includes the managing director at the top of the tree and the data-entry clerk down at the bottom.

There will be different types of information stored on the network and not everyone needs access to every file.

Access to a file can be restricted to certain people, but also those people who do have access can be restricted as to what they are permitted to do with the file. This is implemented by levels of access rights:

- Read – the user can look at (read) the information only.
- Write – the user can change the information in the file.
- Append – the user can add new information but not alter the existing information.
- Create – the user can make new files.
- Delete – the user can delete files.

Different levels of access are required to ensure that some information remains confidential. Some information can only be viewed with a high level of access. If you had a 'guest account' on a network you would not want that account to be able to view confidential information. There is also a legal requirement to keep information confidential and secure – the Data Protection Act. The same user may have different levels of access to different parts of the database.

Activity

There are three main types of user within a bank: the data-entry clerk, the network manager and the managing director. Give each user an access level for each activity listed below and give your reasons.

a) Looking at personnel records.

b) Adding a new bank account.

c) Deleting a bank account.

d) Changing a person's bank account details.

e) Looking at how much money a person has in their account.

There are different types of users. There are the users of the system and there are the managers of the system – the supervisors.

Supervisors monitor the system. They ensure that it is running and deal with the technical problems. Users deal with the actual day-to-day input and analysis of data.

Questions

1 Why are there different access rights?

2 Describe, with examples, **five** access rights.

3 What is the difference between a user and a supervisor?

4 Why do supervisors need more access rights than users?

End of Chapter 4 tests

Test 1

A scout group has decided to computerise the information it holds on its members. It has decided to use a database.

1 The database will have tables, fields and records.

Describe, using examples, the terms 'tables'; 'fields'; and 'records'. [6]

2 The scout group could use a flat-file or a relational database system.

Describe **two** differences between the two types of database system. [4]

3 The information that is held on members includes:

forename; surname; mobile phone number; age; address and postcode.

For each piece of information, give an appropriate data type and a reason why that data type is appropriate. [6]

4 When storing the data, fixed- or variable-length records could be used.

Describe **two** benefits of using fixed-length records. [4]

5 Random access to the data will be used.

Describe the characteristics of random access to data. [4]

6 The database uses usernames and passwords.

i) Describe the purpose of the username.
ii) Describe the purpose of the password. [4]

Test 2

A computer company is rewriting the database of its suppliers. The old database was a flat-file database.

1 The company cannot decide between a relational and a hierarchical database.

Describe the difference between the two types of database system. [4]

2 The database will contain relationships and foreign keys to ensure referential integrity is maintained.

Using an example, describe the terms: 'relationship'; 'foreign key'; and 'referential integrity'. [6]

3 Describe how a set of indexes could be used to find a supplier called Robert Smith Ltd. [4]

4 When data is stored using random access a hashing algorithm is used.

Explain hashing algorithms and give an example of what happens if there are collisions. [6]

5 The data could be stored using fixed- or variable-length records.

Describe **two** advantages of using variable-length records. [4]

6 Different levels of access can be given to different staff using the database.

i) Identify **three** different access rights that can be set on the database. [3]
ii) Why are different levels of access required? [2]

The role of communications and networking

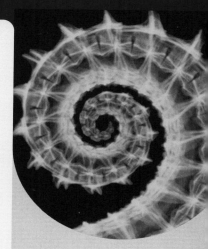

5

Objectives

Your objectives for this chapter are to:

◎ explain why protocols are needed

◎ describe the characteristics of a local area network (LAN) and a wide area network (WAN)

◎ describe the star, ring and bus network topologies

◎ describe how analogue signals are converted to digital signals

◎ explain the importance of bandwidth when transmitting data

◎ know about different items of hardware and software required to create a network

◎ describe the advantages and disadvantages of networking

◎ explain why IDs and passwords are required and how to make them effective

◎ compare different communication methods.

Keep these objectives in mind as you work through the chapter.

Why do computers need to communicate?

A network consists of two or more computers connected together so that they can communicate. Without communication between the computers and the peripherals information cannot be exchanged.

In order for computers to communicate they need to be talking the same language. This means that they need to be running the same protocol. TCP/IP is one example of a protocol.

A protocol is a set of communication rules. It governs:

- the format of the message
- the type of error-checking to be used
- any compression
- how the sending device indicates that it has finished sending
- how the receiving device indicates that it has received the message.

There are many different types of protocols available.

Protocol is a set of rules that allows communication between computers.

Activity

Investigate and compare three different types of protocols, looking at where they are used and their advantages and disadvantages.

Questions

1 What is a network?

2 Why do computers have to communicate?

Cont...

3 Identify **three** items that need to be communicated.
4 What is a protocol?
5 Why must the computers have the same protocol running?

The characteristics of a local area network and a wide area network

Local area network (LAN)

This is a set of computers that are:

- within a locally defined area – the computers are in close proximity to each other
- connected by high-speed connections
- able to have direct connections between them
- only connected by cables that are owned by the company/user
- able to share local peripherals.

An LAN is a small network – usually within a school, library, doctor's surgery or small business.

Wide area network (WAN)

This is a set of computers that are:

- geographically remote – with large distances between them
- connected by equipment that is owned by a third party – telecommunications lines, satellites, etc.

The most common example of a WAN is the Internet.

Questions

1 Describe a local area network (LAN).
2 Describe a wide area network (WAN).
3 What is the main difference between a LAN and a WAN?
4 Give examples of an LAN and a WAN, explaining why they are LANs and WANs.

The star, ring and bus network topologies

Definition: A topology is a description of how the physical devices within a network are connected together. It is a layout – a plan of the network.

There are three main topologies:

- star
- bus
- ring.

Star

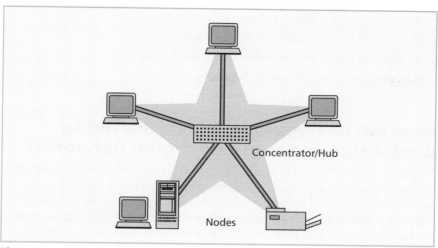

Figure 5.1 Star network topology

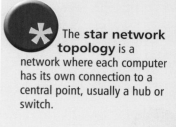

The **star network topology** is a network where each computer has its own connection to a central point, usually a hub or switch.

This is where there is a central point of the network. This central point could be a server or, more likely, a hub or a switch. All computers have their own connection into the central point.

The data flows both to and from the computers and the central point – it is two-way.

Bus

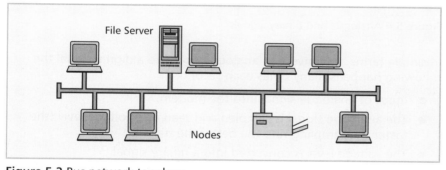

Figure 5.2 Bus network topology

The **bus network topology** is a network where there is a single cable with the computers connected directly to it.

The **ring network topology** is a network where the computers are connected together to form a circle or ring.

The bus is a single cable with the computers connected directly to it. The data is sent both ways down the cable.

Ring

The computers are connected together to form a circle, or ring. The data travels one way only.

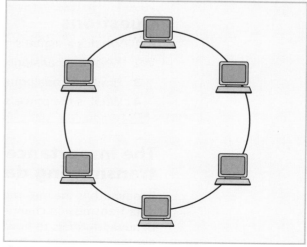

Figure 5.3 Ring network topology

87

An **analogue
signal** consists of a
continuously varying voltage.

Digital signals
consist of only two
states, on and off (0 and 1).

Questions

1 Identify **three** characteristics of a bus topology.
2 Identify **three** characteristics of a ring topology.
3 Identify **three** characteristics of a star topology.
4 Draw and label the **three** topologies.

How are analogue signals converted to digital signals for use by digital networks?

The computer system is a digital system. This means that it works on the binary system of 0 and 1. The telephone system is an analogue system and operates on a continuously varying electronic signal. For the two to work together the analogue signals need to be converted to digital signals (and vice versa). This process is known as digitising or demodulation.

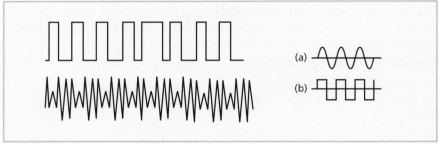

Figure 5.4 Analogue and binary signals

In simple terms, to convert an analogue signal to a digital signal the following happens many times each second:

● Input of analogue signal into the modem.
● The analogue signal is sampled and read as a voltage level (the faster the sampling rate the better the transfer).
● The voltage level is converted into a binary signal.
● The binary signal is passed on to the computer.

Questions

1 What is a digital signal?
2 What is an analogue signal?
3 How is an analogue signal converted to a digital signal?
4 What is the process of conversion known as?

The importance of bandwidth when transmitting data

Bandwidth is the maximum amount of data that can travel over a given data transmission channel in a given amount of time. Put simply, bandwidth refers to how much data can be sent from one computer to another at a point in time.

It is not to do with the speed of the data, but how much data. A large bandwidth is like a three-lane motorway, a small bandwidth is like a single-track road.

The more bandwidth you have the more data you can move. Video, for example, needs a large bandwidth because of the amount of data being transmitted per second.

Questions

1 What is bandwidth?
2 What happens when there is limited bandwidth?
3 When is it important to have a large bandwidth?

Bandwidth is important when sending time-sensitive data, for example downloading a video file to view off line can use a low bandwidth, but downloading a video for streaming requires a high bandwidth.

Hardware and software needed for a LAN and a WAN

To create a network, additional hardware and software is required to that needed for a standalone computer.

Hardware

Network interface card (NIC)

This allows the device to be physically connected to the network and allows communication to pass to and from the computer.

A wireless network interface card would perform the same function but eliminate the need for a direct physical connection. These are being used more in schools

Wireless access point (WAP)

If you have any wireless NICs then you need a device that will send and receive the wireless signals. The WAP will be connected into the physical network by a cable and be positioned so that it can send and receive the wireless signals.

Modem (modulator/demodulator)

This is a piece of hardware that converts digital to analogue signals and back again. Modems allow computer data (digital) to be transmitted over voice-grade telephone lines (analogue).

Router

This is a device that routes information between networks that use the same topology. It can select the best path to route a message, as well as translate information from one network to another. It can connect a LAN to the WAN – a 'digital modem'.

Hub

This is a concentrator that joins lots of computers to the network through a single link. Signals received on any port are broadcast to all other ports. Hubs can be active (where they repeat signals sent through them) or passive (where they do not repeat but merely split signals sent through them).

Switch

A switch has a number of ports and it stores the addresses of all devices that are directly or indirectly connected to it on each port. As data comes into the switch it is examined to see the final destination and then directed to the port where the device it is seeking is connected.

Gateway

A gateway connects and passes packets between two network segments that use different communications protocols.

Bridge

A bridge connects and passes packets between two network segments that use the same communications protocol.

Repeater

This is used in a network to strengthen a signal as it is passed along the network cable. A signal degrades over distance so a repeater can boost the signal to extend the maximum cable length.

Server

There are several different kinds of server. Some of the most common are computers that can:

- verify and route requests (proxy server) and ban those that are not permitted
- route email (email server)
- control printing, including quotas (print server)
- run an intranet (intranet server)
- be used to host a web site (web server), if a permanent connection to the Internet is available.

Communications media

This is the means used to transmit the signals – for example, analogue telephone line, ISDN, ADSL, fibre, Broadband.

Activity

Investigate the advantages and disadvantages of UTP (unshielded twisted pair) cable, coaxial, fibre optic and wireless as means of transmitting data signals.

Software

The network will require additional software as well as hardware in order for it to function correctly.

Network operating system

This will provide network services – file sharing, printer sharing and security.

Protocol

This allows a device to communicate with other devices on the network.

Internet browser

This allows web sites to be browsed, information to be found, goods ordered and tracked, and so on.

Email client

This sends and receives emails, including attachments.

File transfer protocol (FTP)

This uploads and downloads files from the Internet.

Chat software

This engages in interactive, real-time chat on the Internet.

Compression software

This reduces the size of files prior to transmission across the Internet, thus speeding up the download/upload time.

Application software

This includes word processing, spreadsheets, and so on – allows work to be done by a number of different people.

Questions

1 Identify **three** items of hardware needed to create a network.
2 What is the difference between a switch and a hub?
3 What is the role of a router?
4 If a client wanted to set up a wireless network, what items of hardware would they require?
5 Compare the use of fibre optic and UTP.
6 Identify **one** essential item of software required to create a network.
7 Why is an Internet browser required?
8 Describe **four** features of an email package.

Networking – the advantages and disadvantages

There are many different types of network, the two main ones are:

- peer-to-peer
- client-server.

Peer-to-peer

A peer-to-peer network is a computer network where all of the connected computers are of equal status. An example would be the linking of two home computers together. Any of the computers connected can provide printer or file-sharing resources.

Advantages of peer-to-peer

- Only normal computers are required – there is no need to purchase an expensive server.
- Each user manages their own computer. This means that a network manager is not required.

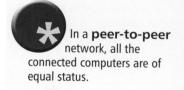
In a **peer-to-peer** network, all the connected computers are of equal status.

- The set up is done via wizards within the software. No technical knowledge is required.
- There is no reliance on a central computer, which means there is less chance of things going wrong.

Disadvantages of peer-to-peer

- Each computer is fulfilling more than one role – it may be printing or file sharing. This increases the load.
- The data can be stored on any computer – there is no organisation to the data storage.
- The security, anti-virus and back-up is the responsibility of the individual user.

Client-server

A client-server network has a powerful controlling computer – the server. This computer controls the peripherals, for example printers and back-up, and the security of the network.

Advantages of client-server

- Back-up, security and anti-virus are centralised.
- The shared data is centralised and organised.
- The user is not involved with any of the management of the computers.
- Network processing is done centrally, not at individual computers, freeing them to do what the user wants.

Disadvantages of client-server

- The server has additional costs, as does the network operating system.
- A network manager is required.
- There is a reliance on the central server – if it fails, no work can be done.

Standalone

If the computers are not networked then they are standalone. This is where a single computer is not connected to any other computer. There are general advantages and disadvantages of networking over standalone computers.

Advantages of networking

The advantages of networking include the following:

- The sharing of peripherals. Colour printers and scanners can be shared among several workstations, reducing the cost (as you do not have to buy one for each computer) and the quality of the device purchased can be better than the quality you would buy for individual devices – if you are buying one printer instead of 10, you can spend more money making sure it is of a high quality.
- Data can be shared. This allows standard files, such as templates, to be available from a central source. Data can also be shared amongst several people in a team allowing them to work on the same document.

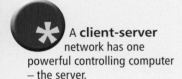

A **client-server** network has one powerful controlling computer – the server.

A computer is **standalone** if it is not connected to any other computer.

- The network can control access to data through user IDs and access rights. The network manager can also log information on who has used which files and ensure that security is not breached.
- Access to applications can be controlled from a central area. This can ensure that licensing is correct and no laws are broken.
- The resources used by individuals can be monitored and logged, allowing for access to the resources to be charged to the appropriate department.
- Back-up and virus checking can be controlled from a central location.
- On a network the users can communicate with email systems and an intranet can disseminate useful information.

Disadvantages of networking

The disadvantages of networks include the following:

- Relying on a network being in place and the components of the network to be working. The devices that are required to build the network depend on the different topologies.
- If a virus is introduced into a single workstation it can use the network connection to infect all computers on the system.
- If the network is particularly busy, it may have a detrimental effect on the work that a user can do.

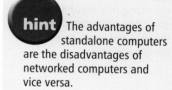

hint The advantages of standalone computers are the disadvantages of networked computers and vice versa.

Questions

1 Describe **two** different types of networks.
2 What are the disadvantages of standalone computers?
3 What are the disadvantages of networks?

User IDs and passwords – why do we need them?

When you logon to a computer system you are asked for two pieces of information:

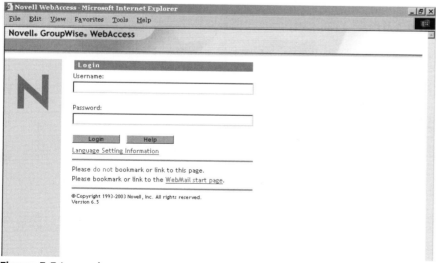

Figure 5.5 Logon box

The User_ID

The User_ID:

- is a unique identifier for a user. It identifies who the user is to the system.
- can be allocated to groups and those groups can have access rights and programs allocated to them. According to which user group they belong to, they might just be allowed to read a file, while other groups might have edit or delete access.
- can also restrict the user to logon to only certain machines or at certain times of the day.
- can also be used to log what the user is doing.

Passwords

A password is one method of restricting access. Unless you know the password for a particular level of access, you will not be permitted to perform tasks. When used in conjunction with a User_ID, the password authenticates who the user is – in other words, that they are who the User_ID says they are. This assumes that only the user knows the password.

Passwords are the weak link in any system. User_IDs tend not be kept secret, passwords need to be.

The network manager can apply controls to the password to make them more difficult for people other than the user to find out. Such controls might include:

- using a minimum number of characters
- using a combination of numbers and letters
- not using any word in the dictionary
- changing passwords regularly: monthly, for example.
- Keeping a record of passwords so you cannot reuse one you have already had
- restricting the number of attempts, for example, three wrong passwords and the account is locked.
- insisting that the password is impersonal.

> **Passwords** are security devices consisting of a set of letters and numbers known only to the user that allow access to a computer system.

Activity

Create a poster for the ICT room explaining password security. Give examples of good and bad passwords.

Questions

1 Why are User_IDs required?
2 What is a password?
3 What is authentication?
4 Why are User_IDs not kept secret?
5 Describe **three** measures the network manager can undertake to ensure that passwords remain secure.

Communication media and its merits

Once a network has been established, one of the uses it can be put to is communication. There are many different ways a network (WAN and LAN) can assist in communication.

Comparing communication methods

When comparing the different methods available, a set of criteria is required:

Access to the resource

This is how accessible the end product is – from within the office or even worldwide.

Download speed

This is the speed of access to the resource. It is usually related to the bandwidth available.

Hardware and software requirements

In order for the communication method to be made available, are there any additional hardware and software requirements? These will cost money.

Security

How secure is the information contained within a message?

Quality

This relates to both the size of the item and how good the quality of the end product is.

Having established some criteria for comparison, it is necessary to keep these in mind when looking at different communication methods.

Communication methods

Fax

This is a method of transmitting text and graphic documents over telecommunication lines.

* If the sending and receiving equipment is compatible then faxes can be sent and received in colour, otherwise they are received in black and white.
* The received document cannot be directly edited.
* Fax is not secure – it can be encrypted but this is not practical.
* There is no guarantee of where you are sending the fax to – it could be the wrong fax number, or the fax machine could be in the middle of an office where lots of people can read it.
* The fax machine does give a receipt of delivery to the number you entered.
* The quality is variable – it depends on the quality of the sending and receiving machines and on the quality of the original.
* Sending a fax is dependent on the line being clear and there being paper and ink in the receiving machine.
* Modern fax machines have the ability to hold address books and to send faxes to groups of people.

Fax is a means of transmitting text and graphic documents over the telephone network.

95

Email

This is the sending of an electronic message from one computer to another.

- Email allows you to send messages to many people at the same time and you can send the electronic equivalent of carbon copies (cc).
- It is possible to add a digital signature to the message and encrypt it to increase security.
- The email client can send back a confirmation of delivery and of opening, but as this is not always required, with some software it is possible to cancel this and stop these confirmation emails from being sent.
- Pictures and text can be sent and, providing there is the correct software on the receiving computer, they can be edited.
- There is a 24-hour service to anywhere in the world. A single point of contact (email address) can be picked up anywhere in the world, so the location is not an issue.
- The email can sit on a server until the recipient is ready to read it, improving security. Providing the password is secure, no one else will be able to read it.

Bulletin boards

These are part of a web site where users can post and read messages from other users.

- A bulletin board accessed through the Internet can be used to give information or contain links to downloadable documents. These documents can be edited.
- The bulletin board is accessible anywhere in the world and can have many recipients.

A **bulletin board** is part of a web site where messages can be posted and read.

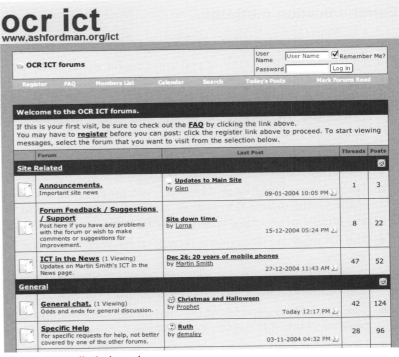

Figure 5.6 Bulletin board

- Parts of the board can be password protected as can the documents that are downloaded.
- A bulletin board can set up threads of conversations and ensure that all elements are kept together. Users can be notified of new postings by email.
- Bulletin boards can have the postings moderated before they are made accessible to the users.
- Parts of bulletin board can be set aside for selected groups of users.
- Multiple people can access the site as long as they know the URL (web address).

Video conferencing and teleconferencing

This is conducting a meeting with people who are geographically remote through the use of video/sound equipment.

- Video conferencing can be achieved via a direct line or across the Internet. If it is via a direct line it will be secure, whereas across the Internet it will not be.
- The equipment required can range from simple (a web camera) to complex and, therefore, very expensive.
- The individuals involved in the conference need to be present at the same time and there can be a slight delay, which can make conversation difficult.
- The image size is not likely to be large and the quality may be poor, especially when simple equipment is used.
- The conference can be recorded for playback at a later date.

Teleconferencing is where there is real-time interaction between people without video. This could be chat rooms or interactive discussion boards.

Video conferencing is conducting a meeting with people who are geographically remote through the use of video/sound equipment.

Teleconferencing is where there is real-time interaction between people without video, for example chat rooms.

Activity

Investigate three other methods of communicating – courier, world wide web (WWW) and file transfer protocol (FTP).

Questions

1 Describe **four** different methods of communicating on a network.
2 Compare fax and email as methods for sending a legal document.
3 What is the difference between video conferencing and teleconferencing?
4 Describe **four** features of a bulletin board.
5 Describe **four** criteria for comparing methods of communication.

End of Chapter 5 tests

Test 1

A local computer store is offering a 'home networking package' to its customers that will allow several computers to be connected together and an Internet connection shared between them.

1   Installing the home networking package will allow customers to create a local area network (LAN).

    Describe **two** characteristics of an LAN.   [4]

2   The package allows its customers to set up a star network topology.

    Describe a star network topology.   [3]

3   Identify **two** items that would be in the home networking package and, for each, give its purpose.   [4]

4   Describe **three** advantages of networking computers within a home.   [6]

5   A customer who has purchased the package has two children under the age of 11.

    Explain how User_IDs and passwords can prevent them from accessing unsuitable materials on the Internet.   [4]

6   Identify **two** facilities offered by video conferencing.   [2]

7   A customer who has purchased the package wants to start using email instead of fax for sending and receiving documents to their offices in the USA.

    Discuss the use of fax and email as media for sending and receiving documents.   [7]

Test 2

A primary school currently has one computer and a dial-up connection to the Internet. It is looking to expand and purchase several new computers and upgrade its Internet connection to Broadband.

1   The existing connection to the Internet uses a modem, which converts digital signals to analogue and back again.

   Describe how the modem coverts the digital signals to analogue signals.   [2]

2   Several new pieces of hardware and software, in addition to the computers, are required to create the network.

   Describe **one** piece of hardware and **two** pieces of software that will be required to create the network and to connect and use the computers on the Internet.   [6]

3   A bus or a star topology could be used for the new network.

   Describe a bus network topology.   [3]

4   Describe **two** disadvantages of networking the school.   [4]

5   The school wants to use live video links between the classrooms.

   Explain the importance of bandwidth when using live video links.   [3]

6   The school is concerned that children are sharing work and has implemented passwords on all accounts.

   Describe **three** methods for ensuring that the passwords remain effective.   [6]

7   With the new computers, and a faster connection to the Internet, the school wants to increase its use of pen pals.

   Compare the use and facilities available with video conferencing and bulletin boards for communicating with schools in other countries.   [6]

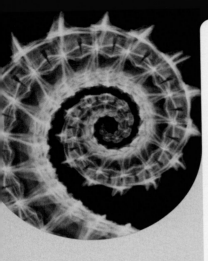

Objectives

Your objectives for this chapter are to:

◎ describe the main aspects of the Data Protection Act and discuss its purpose and implications

◎ discuss the purpose of the Computer Misuse Act, Copyright, Designs and Patents Act, Regulation of Investigatory Powers Act and Electronic Communications Act

◎ describe methods for combating a range of ICT crimes

◎ discuss ethics and ICT with reference to codes of conduct

◎ describe the purpose and activities of professional bodies

◎ describe a range of health and safety problems related to working with ICT and measures for avoiding them

◎ discuss the capabilities and limitations of ICT and how communications systems have changed our use of ICT

◎ discuss the social impact of ICT upon individuals

◎ discuss the impact of ICT on organisations

◎ discuss the impact of ICT on society.

Keep these objectives in mind as you work through the chapter.

The **Data Protection Act** is designed to regulate and safeguard data held by organisations about private individuals.

The Data Protection Act (1998)

The Data Protection Act (DPA) was set up to protect individuals from the misuse of information stored about them by organisations. There is a lot of information available on individuals and this is collected by lots of different organisations and government agencies.

Activity

List three organisations and three government agencies. For each, list all the information you can think of that would be stored by them on individuals.

The DPA was introduced to limit the information held by individual organisations to only what they needed. It was meant to stop organisations holding excessive quantities of data on individuals for no immediate purpose.

Technical terms

There are a number of technical terms related to the DPA:

Personal data

Personal data means data that relates to a living, identifiable individual.

Data

Data is any information that is held which can be said to be part of a record. This covers both manual and computer data. If you store data about people, such as their health or education records, whether it is on paper or on computer, it is classed as data. Data is also anything stored which is processed by a computer.

Processing

This means obtaining, recording or holding the information or data. It also covers any operation performed on the information or data.

Operations on the data may include organising it (sorting, indexing), changing it, retrieving it (searching) and using it in some way. Operations on the data also include disclosing it (telling someone else or passing it on) and destroying it.

There are several people who are specifically mentioned by the Act and have different rights and responsibilities.

Data subject

The data subject is the living identifiable human being about whom the data is being held.

Data controller

This is the individual within the company who is responsible for making sure that all the provisions of the DPA are being complied with. This is also the person who you would contact if you had any queries with a company about the DPA.

Data processor

This is any person (other than an employee of the data controller) who processes the data on behalf of the data controller. For example, some companies hire third parties to process their data for them.

Even if the processing is done by a third party, the data controller retains responsibility for making sure that the DPA is not broken.

Recipient

This is the individual who is given the data in order to do some form of processing upon it. They are usually employees of the data controller or are data processors.

Third party

This is the person who receives the data after it has been processed. A company may need to pass on its data to certain people in order to do its job – schools will give references and information to the government.

Information commissioner

This is the individual who is responsible for ensuring that the DPA is being adhered to. An information commissioner will give advice, run training sessions and investigate complaints.

Rights under the DPA

As an individual, you have certain rights under the DPA. There are six main rights that you possess as follows:

1 Right to subject access

You are allowed to see what information a company is holding about you. You need to write to the data controller and request a copy. You will need to pay an administrative charge. The company must provide the information within a reasonable time of receiving the request (credit agencies – 7 days, schools – 15 days, other organisations – 40 days).

2 Right to prevent processing likely to cause damage or distress

If the processing of the data is going to cause you damage and distress you can ask the company to stop. The level of damage and distress needs to be very high and, if the company does not agree that it is causing damage and distress, then the matter would need to go to court.

3 Right to prevent processing for the purposes of direct marketing

Direct marketing is mail that is sent to you advertising goods and services. You can request that it be stopped.

4 Rights in relation to automated decision-making

Some decisions are taken by computers. Credit checks are an example – points are awarded for things such as time in work, owning your own home, and so on and, based on the number of points you get, a decision is made as to whether you can have a credit card or not. You can request that a person takes the decision, not a computer.

5 Right to compensation if damage and distress is suffered by the Act being contravened

If you can prove that the data controller did not follow the requirements of the DPA, and by not doing so you suffered both damage and distress, then you are entitled to compensation. Damage is physical or financial loss. You cannot be compensated for distress on its own.

6 Right to rectify, block or erase incorrect data

If the data that is held is wrong then you can get it changed.

The DPA is very long and complicated. The points above are a very simplified version of the main points.

There are some exemptions from the Act. A few of them are listed below:

- national security
- crime and taxation – you cannot see your records
- health, education and social work – if giving the subject access will cause them harm
- domestic purposes – data held on your own computer for your own use, such as mailing lists for Christmas cards.

Activity

Investigate and summarise the main exemptions from the Data Protection Act.

Questions

1 Describe what is meant by a data controller.
2 What is the difference between a recipient and a third party?
3 What are the implications for a company under the Data Protection Act (DPA)?
4 What does the DPA mean by data?
5 Who does the DPA apply to?
6 Describe the rights of the individual under the DPA.
7 Describe **four** exemptions under the DPA.

The main aspects of the DPA (1998)

The DPA has eight principles that must be followed:

1 'Personal data shall be processed fairly and lawfully.'

This means that there should be consent for the processing to occur.

2 'Personal data shall be obtained only for one or more specified and lawful purposes, and shall not be further processed in any manner incompatible with that purpose or those purposes.'

When a company wants to collect and hold personal data, it must let the information commissioner know what it is going to hold and what it is going to do with the data. The companies can only collect and process data that meets these requirements.

3 'Personal data shall be adequate, relevant and not excessive in relation to the purpose or purposes for which they are processed.'

Holding more information than is necessary is not allowed. For example, there is no need for a school to hold information on the pets that pupils' parents had as children. It would not be relevant.

4 'Personal data shall be accurate and, where necessary, kept up to date.'

The company must endeavour to ensure that it only has accurate information on you. This may entail them sending out the information they hold for you to check. If they find any inaccurate information, they must correct it.

5 'Personal data processed for any purpose or purposes shall not be kept for longer than is necessary for that purpose or those purposes.'

You cannot hold data indefinitely. Eventually it will no longer meet the purpose. For example, schools keeping records on student detentions from five years ago are not needed or consistent with the current purpose. But schools are required to hold student records for seven years in case of requests for a reference.

6 'Personal data shall be processed in accordance with the rights of data subjects under this Act.'

The data subject has certain rights. These include access to the data, the right to correct data if it is wrong, the right to compensation if the processing has caused damage and distress and the right to prevent processing from causing damage and distress.

7 'Appropriate technical and organisational measures shall be taken against unauthorised or unlawful processing of personal data and against accidental loss or destruction of, or damage to, personal data.'

The company must ensure that there is sufficient security in place and back-ups to prevent the data being deleted or being stolen.

8 'Personal data shall not be transferred to a country or territory outside the European Economic Area, unless that country or territory ensures an adequate level of protection for the rights and freedoms of data subjects in relation to the processing of personal data.'

This is to ensure that data is only given to companies in other countries where there is a similar law to the DPA. This protects the rights of the data subject. However, if the data subject gives their consent for a transfer then the data can be transferred anywhere.

Questions

1 Describe the implications for companies of the 7th principle.

2 What do companies need to do to ensure they comply with principles 2 and 3?

3 Why is a DPA necessary?

4 Is the DPA a workable Act? Describe the problems with the DPA.

What are the purposes of Acts relating to ICT?

There are many Acts of Parliament that relate to ICT, concerning everything from copyright, to data privacy and theft. The four Acts below are the main ones that you need to know in detail.

Computer Misuse Act (1990)

Main provision

The **Computer Misuse Act** makes unauthorised access to, and modification of, computer material, i.e. hacking illegal.

The Computer Misuse Act (CMA) was introduced to protect data held by companies from hackers. It has three main provisions:

1 Unauthorised access to computer material. This covers entering a computer system without permission having guessed or discovered an individual's password. This is 'hacking' into a computer. The maximum sentence is six months in prison and/or a fine of up to £2000.

2 Unauthorised access with intent to commit or facilitate the commission of further offences. This is in addition to entering the computer system. This could be to gain access to a user account and use it to transmit illegal material. The maximum sentence is a five-year jail term and/or an unlimited fine.

3 Unauthorised modification of computer material. This is making changes to the contents of a computer. It includes deletion and corruption of programs and data. The maximum sentence is a five-year jail term and/or an unlimited fine.

Benefits

Until the introduction of the CMA, theft of electricity was the only crime a hacker could be charged with. The Act allows companies a legal recourse if their security has been compromised.

Problems

Intent has to be proven. Accidental intrusion is not a crime. There is also the problem of finding out who is responsible. Just because you can track a computer that is being used for hacking to a property, does not mean that you know who was responsible. You then need to prove who within the house was using the computer at the point in time that the crime was committed. As with all laws, the CMA is only enforced once the crime has been committed. If a hacker does gain access and obtains confidential information, they could have disseminated it before they are caught. Another problem is that the organisation is the body that determines what is authorised and what is not. If a code of practice for a school indicates that only you are allowed to use your account, if you give your password to your friend and they use your account, technically they have broken the law.

Activity

a) Discuss the problem of users sharing their passwords in the context of 1) a school and 2) a company.

b) Investigate the number of cases that have been brought against people, using the CMA? Why do you think this number is so low?

Copyright, Designs and Patents Act (1988)

Main provision

Among many items, the Act makes it illegal to steal or create unauthorised copies of software. It also covers manuals, books, CD-ROMs and music.

Benefits

A lot of time and effort goes into the production of software, books and music. The people who put in that effort deserve to be rewarded – the reward is in royalties. If the items are copied and distributed then they will not receive any money. By having the Act in place, it allows the individuals and corporations who invest time and money in a product, a certain amount of protection from their work being pirated for profit.

Problems

There are many different types of software license. Some do not allow the software to be run on more than one machine. Some allow it to be run on a desktop and portable as long as they are not used at the same time. Then there are site and network licenses for multiple use. Understanding the license can be difficult. The absence of a visible victim makes it hard for many people to see what they are doing as a crime. Copying a CD-ROM or downloading copyright music from the Internet is a crime, however, and there are people who it is damaging at the end of the chain. 'Microsoft already has too much money, they won't miss me not paying' is a common defense for copying software but it is still illegal. 'If I had to pay for it I would not buy it' is not an excuse, nor is arguing that 'everyone does it'.

The **Copyright, Designs and Patents Act** makes it illegal to steal or create unauthorised copies of software and to reproduce manuals, books, CD-ROMs and music.

The **Regulation of Investigatory Powers Act** relates to the monitoring of communications (telephone calls, emails, post, and so on).

Regulation of Investigatory Powers Act (2000)

Main provision

Nicknamed the 'snooper's charter', the Regulation of Investigatory Powers Act (RIPA) was introduced to address concerns about the use and misuse of communication interception techniques by public and private organisations.

The Act makes it a criminal offence to monitor communications without lawful authority. Communications being telephone calls, emails, post, etc.

To be lawful, 'the interception has to be by or with the consent of a person carrying on a business, for purposes relevant to that person's business, and using that business's own telecommunications system'.

Organisations may monitor and record communications:

- to establish the existence of facts to ascertain compliance with regulatory or self-regulatory practices or procedures or to ascertain or demonstrate standards which are, or ought to be, achieved
- in the interests of national security
- to prevent or detect crime
- to investigate or detect unauthorised use of telecommunications systems
- to secure, or as an inherent part of, effective system operation.

There are some circumstances where the organisation may monitor but not record:

- received communications to determine whether they are business or personal communications
- communications made to anonymous telephone helplines.

Public interceptions can also be made with 'lawful authority'.

Benefits

The benefits to the company are that it can monitor what its employees are doing. This, in turn, can ensure that the facilities are only being used for legitimate work and that company secrets are not being revealed.

Problems

Any form of monitoring may be seen as a breach of trust. Some people take the view that, if we have nothing to hide, we should not be afraid of being monitored. Others, however, see it as an intrusion into their privacy. The RIPA could be seen as being part of that intrusion. Some people may also be concerned about what controls there may be on the organisations that monitor communications.

Activity

Carry out some research into the RIPA – discuss the benefits to companies and what they need to have done before they can 'snoop'. What is your attitude to someone looking at all your post and emails?

Electronic Communications Act (2000)

Main provision

The Government wanted 'to make the UK the best place in the world for e-commerce' and to 'create a legal framework so that people can be sure about the origin and integrity of communications'. In order to achieve this, the Electronic Communications Act (ECA) was made law.

The legislation is in two main parts:

- Cryptography Service Providers: This allows the Government to set up a register of 'approved cryptography suppliers'.
- Facilitation of Electronic Commerce, Data Storage: This recognises digital signatures. They are now admissible in law.

There is a lot of legislation that is in conflict with digital signatures being acceptable. The ECA gives ministers the power to make delegated legislation to remove any restrictions in other legislation which prevent use of electronic communications in place of paper.

Benefits

Contracts that are signed over the Internet have the same legality as those signed by hand. This increases the security with which individuals can engage in e-commerce and the contracts entered into have legal backing.

Problems

Although there is legislation in place to remove many of the laws that prevent digital signatures being accepted, this will take time in many instances. Conveyancing (buying and selling a house) and wills are two areas where digital signatures will take a long time to be introduced.

There is always a security risk. The first digital signature made by a cabinet minister was effectively hijacked within 24 hours of its creation. In this instance, a document, digitally signed by the Trade and Industry Minister had an additional statement opposing the Government's cryptographic policy inserted into it.

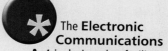

The **Electronic Communications Act** is designed to facilitate e-commerce and recognise digital signatures as well as setting up a register of cryptography service providers.

Questions

1 What are the main provisions of the Computer Misuse Act (CMA)?
2 Explain the disadvantages of implementing the CMA.
3 Explain the problems of enforcing the Copyright, Designs and Patents Act.
4 Describe the main provisions of the Regulation of Investigatory Powers Act (RIPA).
5 Why do you think there is so much opposition to the RIPA? Explain your reasons.
6 What are the benefits of having a RIPA?
7 Who benefits the most from the Electronic Communications Act (ECA)? Why?
8 Explain the problems associated with the ECA.

Combating ICT crime

ICT crime is crime involving a computer. It could be the physical theft of the computer or its components, or using one computer to attempt to gain access to another computer system and commit a crime.

The computer crimes that are seen in films are not usually possible in the real world – stopping time, stealing money. Collecting all the fractions of money and getting them paid to you or hacking into a bank and transferring money to your account all sound easy enough, but are extremely rare if not impossible to achieve.

However, computer crime does exist. It can be industrial espionage – finding out what a business competitor is doing, breaking into a computer system or trying to find personal data.

There are two main groups of methods for combating computer crime:

- physical methods
- logical methods.

Physical methods

Physical methods prevent a person from gaining access to a computer in person. Instead of gaining access across the Internet or dialing in, physical access means actually walking in and sitting at a computer yourself.

Ways to protect against physical access include having security guards on the door and giving each employee a pass that the guard checks. The computers could be kept in locked rooms with only specific people given access to them. Security cameras could monitor corridors and rooms.

Physical methods also include the positioning of the screen and keyboard. If the machine is in an open access area, like a reception, positioning the screen so it cannot be seen by the public and hiding the keyboard so they cannot see a password being typed is only sensible.

The use of wireless networks has increased the difficulty of physical security.

Increasingly biometric measures, such as scanning a person's iris, are being used to provide physical security.

Activity

For each of the physical methods described above, give their disadvantages. How might someone determined to get into a building overcome the physical methods intended to stop them?

Logical methods

These are computer-based methods that can be applied to the computer by a system administrator. They include usernames and passwords, access rights and user groups. Other logical methods include: screensaver passwords, so if you leave your desk for any length of time no one else can use the machine; firewalls and anti-virus software; logging actions and analysing these logs.

Password security is important as is education of the users – in not giving out passwords, correct selection of passwords (not using dictionary words, for example) and educating users about computer use – logging off and so on.

Questions

1 Describe **three** physical methods of preventing computer crime.
2 How can using access rights combat computer crime?
3 Describe **three** laws that would be broken by hacking.
4 Describe **five** different ICT crimes.

Ethics and ICT

Ethics and ICT is about the sensible – legal and moral – use of ICT. It is about developing and implementing policies that do not take advantage of any individual and utilise the technology to the best of its capabilities. The ethics of a company are usually found documented within a code of conduct.

Code of conduct

A code of conduct is a non-legislative (not part of the law) set of principles that an organisation draws up that lays down standards in the workplace. These are expectations of mutually agreed behaviour.

A code of conduct is not a one-way agreement – it sets out what both the company and the employee should do.

Codes of conduct:

- set boundaries for what is expected. These are not likely to be written into the employees' contracts explicitly so are put into a code
- establish what can and cannot be done on the computers
- give expectations of behaviour
- set out the rights, roles and responsibilities of employees and employers in their actions with each other and with customers.

ICT and ethics are continually changing. A code of conduct, because it is not a specific part of the contract of employment, can be updated to take into consideration the shifting environment and technical nature of ICT. This can be a disadvantage – with the goalposts and the boundaries ever changing there is no stability. What might have been acceptable one week, may not now be allowed.

Other disadvantages may include a perceived lack of trust in the workforce – employers having to spell out exactly what is and is not allowed may make employees feel like they are back at school!

The Association for Computing Machinery (ACM) and the British Computing Society (BCS) both have codes of conduct available on the Internet.

Activity

Find the ACM and the BCS codes of conduct and compare them. Discuss the points contained within them with specific reference to how they should be implemented in an organisation, how flexible they are and how likely they are to change.

Questions

1 How do ethics affect ICT?
2 What is the relationship between ethics and a code of conduct?
3 Describe **four** items that should appear in a code of conduct.
4 Why should a company have a code of conduct?
5 What are the disadvantages of having a code of conduct?

What do professional bodies do and how important are they?

The **BCS** and the **IEEE** are the main professional bodies that oversee the ICT industry in the UK.

A professional body is a formal group that is set up to oversee a particular area of industry. The two main professional bodies that oversee the ICT industry in the UK are the British Computing Society (BCS) and the Institute of Electrical and Electronics Engineers (IEEE).

Professional bodies perform a variety of roles and offer their members many benefits:

- The BCS promotes education and training – they liaise with universities to ensure that the skills required in the industry are being provided by the universities.
- They set standards for employees within the industry. This involves creating a code of conduct that its members must uphold.
- Examinations are provided by the BCS. They set a standard and maintain it. A qualification from the BCS is valued worldwide and recognised by similar bodies in other countries.
- They provide publications and discussion papers on a variety of topics. These enable the members to keep up-to-date.
- They hold conferences where members can meet like-minded individuals and ensure that they are aware of any new developments in the industry. They can also have an input into legislation concerning the industry.

Professional bodies are not the same as trade unions, which are more directly involved with pay and conditions of service negotiations. Professional bodies are not likely to offer specific technical advice to individuals outside of their publications and conferences.

Activity

The BCS has different categories of membership. Investigate the BCS web site and describe the benefits of becoming a member and what advantages there are in the different categories.

Questions

1 What is the purpose of a professional body?

2 What are the advantages to an ICT professional of joining a professional body?

3 Describe **four** activities of a professional body.

Health and safety

Working with ICT can be a dangerous activity. There are several problems that can be caused by using computers for long periods of time.

These problems can be divided into two groups – those relating to health and those that cover safety.

Health

Health risks are those based on activities that can cause physical damage to the body due to the prolonged use of computers. Some examples are given below. The causes given are not the only causes.

Figure 6.1 Health problems associated with prolonged computer use

Heath risk	Description	Cause	Prevention
Deep-vein thrombosis (DVT)	Blood clot, usually in the leg	Sitting in a chair that puts pressure on the back of the knees	Stand up and move around. Ensure that the posture when sitting in a chair is correct.
Repetitive strain injury (RSI)	Chronic pain experienced in the arms, hands, shoulders or back.	Repetitive actions, poor posture while working, maintaining a fixed, forced position.	Ensure workstation is correctly adjusted, and use keyboard rests, foot stools, adjustable chairs. Take frequent breaks from repetitive activity.
Carpal tunnel syndrome	Pressure on the median nerve in the wrist.	Repeated wrist movements, such as typing.	Avoid the repetitive actions as much as possible. Take frequent breaks between the actions.
Ulnar neuritis (Cubital tunnel syndrome)	Compression of the ulnar nerve in the elbow.	Leaning on the elbow for prolonged periods of time.	Use wrist rests, adjust height of chair and correct desk height.
Eyesight	Hazy vision, tired eyes.	Looking at a monitor for long periods of time, dehydration of the eyes. Drink plenty of fluids.	Take frequent breaks. Ensure monitor is correctly adjusted, and flicker-free.
Back pain	Muscle spasms, aching back.	Poor posture, sitting in the same position, forced position.	Ensure correct posture. Use adjustable chair.

A lot of the health problems are caused by incorrect posture and not taking enough breaks from the activity.

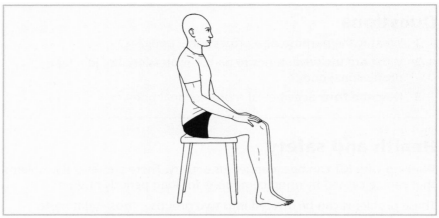

Figure 6.2 Correct sitting posture

Activity

Investigate the health and safety regulations for the use of computers. Make a list of the equipment that could be provided by a company to prevent health problems and, for each item, explain the problem that it prevents.

Safety

Safety risks are external items that can cause injury or damage. They are likely to be immediate rather than built up over time. Some examples are given below.

Figure 6.3 Safety issues associated with computer use

Safety risk	Description	Prevention
Trailing wires	Wires from computers trailing on to the floor	Cable management systems to cover wires
Fire	Overheating of computers can cause them to catch fire. Overloading of plug sockets can cause fire.	Ventilation of computers – space on all sides. Do not overload plug sockets. Correct number of sockets on a breaker. Correct (CO_2) fire extinguisher.
Electrocution	Water and electricity can cause electrocution. Bare wires, when touched, can cause electrocution.	No drinking near computers. No water near by. All wires to be frequently checked and repaired.
Unstable surfaces and chairs	Desks and surfaces that wobble can cause computer equipment to fall off.	All surfaces to be stable before computer equipment is placed on them.

Activity

Investigate the room you are sitting in. Make a list of the possible health and safety problems that exist and, for each, explain how they could be alleviated.

Questions

1 What is the difference between a health risk and a safety risk?

2 Describe **three** health risks affecting a computer operator.

3 For each health risk you have described in Question 2 above, describe an appropriate solution.

4 Describe **three** safety risks that could be taken into account when installing a new computer room.

5 For each safety risk you have described in Question 4 above, describe an appropriate solution.

What impact does ICT have on people, organisations and society?

Capabilities and limitations of ICT systems

ICT is often put forward as the solution to many problems. It is certainly true that ICT has assisted in many areas but it should always be seen as a tool – a tool that we control and decide when to use. The use of ICT is not always appropriate and there are occasions where its use should be discouraged.

Advantages

The main advantage of ICT systems is that they can perform the same actions over and over again, and they can do this very quickly. For example, calculating interest on bank accounts or working out electricity bills – the same processing is performed on every single account and because of the number of accounts is vast. It is a great advantage if a system can perform the action very quickly.

Computers can search large volumes of data and they can do it very quickly. At an ATM (automatic teller machine) the computer needs to search through vast numbers of customer accounts to find yours. You do not want to be standing waiting so it needs to do it quickly.

Think about the amount of data being stored by a company like a bank – every single transaction on every single account – and not just for this year, for previous years as well. It is no good storing the data if you cannot find your way around it and access it when you require it. The bank's storage needs to be structured and accessible.

Disadvantages

There are limitations on the use of ICT – it is not always the answer and there are some disadvantages.

One of the main limitations is hardware. The speed of hardware development is phenomenal. In 1965 Gordon Moore made a prediction for processing power – the number of components on semiconductor

hint Discussion questions will appear at the end of every 2512 paper. It is important that you read the section on examination technique and practise answering discussion questions. You must look at what you have given as an answer and see if you have given an implication – positive or negative. Have you stopped too soon? If you were giving the same answer to your teacher orally in class, would they be waiting for you to add something more to the answer? If so, add some more to the written answer.

chips with the lowest per-component cost, doubles roughly every 12 months. This has also been applied to storage. Put simply, the same amount of money will purchase twice the speed or twice the storage it did 12 months ago. For the most part, this has proved, until recently, to be true.

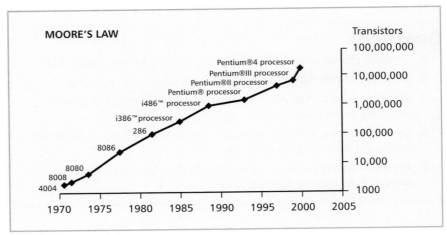

Figure 6.4 Moore's Law

However, hardware limitations are beginning to have an impact on future developments. People want things done now, not in a few seconds' time. The interface to the computer, such as the keyboard, is archaic and not useful for entering vast quantities of data quickly.

The software that is used limits what can be done. It can still be cumbersome to use and require training. The design and development of software itself can limit what can be done with it.

As we utilise the communications available within computers more and more, so we demand more and more bandwidth. We want video on demand; faster downloads of software, music and movies; interactive conversations with people on the other side of the world. At the moment this is not possible because of limitations in bandwidth.

Activity

Describe the ICT and technology that you have seen in films and television programmes recently, for example the ability to manipulate images on a computer screen by hand in 'Minority Report'.

a) How realistic is the technology that was used?

b) Do you think that it will eventually be introduced?

c) What are the advantages and disadvantages of such technology?

Communication systems

One of the biggest improvements brought about by technology is in the arena of communications. Communications have shrunk the planet – we can now send messages in seconds to countries anywhere in the world.

One effect of this is to increase the globalisation of companies – they can retain control over offices and employees from anywhere in the world.

The terms 'communications' and 'ICT' cover a variety of areas: Internet, intranet, mobile phones, telephone systems and interactive television, to name a few.

Telephone

The telephone is, relatively, an old method of communication, but it has had an upgrade over the last few years. The telephone allows you to contact another individual quickly and have an element of personal contact (even if it is only by voice) with the other person. It is now possible to have conference calls, answer phones, remote access, alternative ring-tones, call forwarding, SMS messaging and many other features.

The telephone has its disadvantages though – you cannot send documents (only voice), you cannot be absolutely sure who you are talking to and it is not always possible to get in contact with the person (they may be out or may be in a different time zone).

On the positive side, it is a relatively easy system to set up and use and with future advancements – with videophones for example – some of the disadvantages are being overcome.

Activity

The use of mobile phones has increased over the last few years.

a) What are the features available on a mobile phone and what new features would you want?

b) Describe the advantages and disadvantages of mobile phones.

Internet

The Internet is a vast collection of interconnected computers for the purpose of sharing data. One of the biggest benefits and problems of the Internet is that it is outside of any government's control. (Governments can attempt to filter or restrict access but they cannot control the content – attempts to do so have resulted in the content being relocated to countries with laws that allow that content.) The fact that it cannot be turned on or off or controlled can be an advantage. However, the disadvantage is that it causes security issues, for example, material can contain pornography or violence, and criminals and terrorists can use the Internet along with everyone else.

The **Internet** is a network of computers spanning the whole world.

Activity

What are the costs related to the Internet for a) a user and b) for someone wishing to set up a web site?

What can be done on the Internet? Primarily, you can find information. This can be by using web sites (which, when taken together, contain the largest encyclopaedia available) or downloading files. The Internet contains a large repository of information. It is useful for technical support – almost every topic has a help page. Drivers for computers can be located, as can updates to software. You can use the Internet to chat with friends and relatives and take part in discussions.

However, with all the unregulated information on the Internet, it is sometimes not possible to tell what is true and what is false. Anyone can create a web site and put their views and opinions on it. It is necessary to consider carefully all information posted on the Internet and not believe everything read without checking its validity.

The Internet is also a repository for viruses – downloading files and opening them could cause a virus on your machine. It is important that when using the Internet you have an appropriate firewall and virus checker.

Identification of individuals is difficult on the Internet. When chatting, how do you know who you are talking to? The person may say they are 16 and a student at a local school, but how can you verify this?

Copyright is a problem on the Internet. The ease of posting and availability of files – movies, music and software – makes it difficult to apprehend people who break the copyright laws. The location of the server being used to disseminate the data can also cause problems. As there is no government control, laws that govern one country are different from those that govern another. Crimes in one country may not be crimes in another. The location of the web server may be in a country where it is not illegal to post certain content that would be illegal elsewhere.

Laws regarding tax and purchases on the Internet are difficult to enforce. If you purchase items from the Internet and you are getting them from another country then they are subject to taxation and import regulations when they come into the country. Enforcing this is difficult.

Email

Email is the reading and receiving of messages through computer communications.

Email is electronic mail – messages, including documents, sent from one person to another. Email allows communication within offices as well as worldwide. You can send text and attachments. Recently, (see Electronic Communications Act on page 107) emails that have been digitally signed can be accepted as a legal contract.

Activity

We now have many more methods of communicating at our disposal. Have they shrunk the world or increased our physical isolation?

Copy and complete the table below. Give examples of advantages and disadvantages for each method of communication and give reasons why they are advantages and disadvantages. Add other methods of communication that have not been covered above.

Method	Advantages	Disadvantages
Telephone		
Mobile phone		
Email		
Internet		

Effect of ICT on organisations

Organisations as well as individuals are affected by ICT. There was a fear that introducing ICT into offices would mean unemployment. In many organisations computers would be able to do the same jobs as people, which would mean that fewer people were required. The actual effect has been to increase employment. ICT has an industry that surrounds it – network managers, technicians, web site designers, ICT trainers, etc. Organisations have had to employ more people to install and maintain the ICT equipment. There has been a redistribution of employment.

For example, if a shop closes to become an Internet-only shop it will need web site designers, packers and delivery people. These are different to the jobs required when it needed shop assistants and shelf stackers.

Those employees who use ICT in their work have benefited from the advantages of electronic filing systems, the ability to edit a document rather than retype it, and from being able to use email.

The effect on organisations has been to increase communication – email, fax, video conferencing and shared diaries have meant that it is easier to track down and get in touch with people. So the workload of an organisation has not decreased with the introduction of ICT – instead, more work is being done in the same amount of time.

Structure of the organisation

The structure of organisations has altered. With electronic communications there is no longer the need for the headquarters to be in a major city – they can be anywhere – they do not even have to have all departments in the same location. Decentralisation of the organisation is therefore partly a result of ICT.

New departments and directors have been created with the advent of ICT. ICT directors, network managers and training departments have all had to be incorporated in the organisational structure.

Teleworking

One major change in recent years is teleworking. This is working from home. Employees spend the majority of their time at home instead of in an office.

Teleworking is where employees work from home and communicate with their company by computer.

The advantages of this for the organisation are that a central location for employees to travel to is not required. They can move out of town to places where the rent is cheaper. The size of building required is smaller as there are fewer permanent employees.

But how does the organisation keep control of its workforce? How can it make sure they are meeting targets and doing the work? Not every person has the right temperament for working from home. They have to be self-disciplined and able to work on their own. To some extent, the organisation can keep track of them through email and through target setting.

Advantages

The advantages to the employee are that they do not have to commute to work – they can get up later as there is no travel and be back 'at home' earlier. There are no travel costs and less pollution because of the reduction in traffic. More time can be spent with the family – and perhaps less childcare will be required (although this will have a knock-on effect on the economy).

Disadvantages

The disadvantages include a possible lack of motivation – if there is no boss it may be very easy to put some work off until tomorrow. There may be a lack of social contact. For many people, an important part of the working day is the social interaction with colleagues. Additional equipment may be required, for example, a high-speed Internet connection, fax, and so on. If this is provided by the company, can it be used for personal use? With the equipment and important files around, there is a privacy implication and a data protection implication to keep data secure.

Activity

Would you be suited for teleworking? How would you cope with only having deadlines and no imposed structure? As a boss, what would you do to try and make sure your employees were working while they are at home?

How has ICT changed society?

The introduction of ICT into society has brought about some major changes, particularly in the areas of shopping, medicine and health care, education and facilities for disabled people.

Shopping

Most of the high street stores have a web presence. Some shops do not have a physical presence. You cannot walk into their shops; you can only buy things from them online. Amazon is perhaps the most well known of this new generation of shops.

The advantages of Internet shopping for the customer include availability – the web site is open 24 hours a day, 365 days a year. It does not matter where the 'shop' is – it could be in this country or on the other side of the world. Currency is not an issue. If you possess a credit or debit card then the conversion is done automatically. There are sites that will compare prices for you to enable you to get the best deal – all without leaving your home. This is particularly useful for those people who are housebound such as the elderly and disabled.

This is not all good news, however. How do you know that the web site is genuine? How do you know that the site has not been set up purely to get credit card details? If it is on the other side of the world, it may look genuine. If it has the goods that you want, you hand over your credit card details but you may never see the goods. At least when you go to a shop, you come out with the goods at the end of the transaction. You also need to be at home when the item is delivered or arrange to collect it from the delivery company.

The equipment that is required to shop on the Internet includes a computer and Internet connection. This can be expensive.

There may be a tendency for people to become lazy and unhealthy. If you can shop without leaving your home this may reduce the amount of exercise you take and this, in turn, could lead to an unhealthy lifestyle.

Food shopping on the Internet has increased in popularity. The web site allows you to maintain a weekly shopping list – the staples that you need every week can always appear on your list and you can add and remove items. However, you are reliant on someone else selecting your food – fruit, vegetables and meat.

For the companies, Internet shopping means fewer shops and outlets, which can mean fewer employees. However, there will need to be web site designers, technical support, food packers and an increase in delivery firms required.

There will be fewer journeys made – one delivery vehicle can take the place of several car journeys. This could decrease congestion and pollution.

Activity

Summarise the advantages and disadvantages of Internet shopping for both the customer and the company.

Medicine

Medical improvements are occurring all the time. The impact of ICT in medicine has been in two main areas:

- administration
- treatment.

Administration

The use of computers in administration has enabled medical staff to have access to patients' notes, treatment records and information on treatments as well as latest research. The medical staff can create care plans, drug administration records and monitor the patient more effectively than they could without the use of ICT.

Treatment

ICT has been used in the treatment of people with hearing and visual problems, for example, signal processing for digital hearing aids, and laser eye treatment. It has improved the manufacture of artificial components such as limbs and allowed 3D images to be created of the body for surgeons to examine.

Not everywhere has access to medical ICT facilities. It is important not to become over-reliant on the technology to the extent that medicine cannot be practised without it.

ICT and the Internet have also assisted in the sharing of research into medical conditions. Universities are enabled to share their findings and collaborate on research.

With the large amount of information on medical conditions available on the Internet, many people may use this as their first port of call when they have a health problem. Unfortunately a little knowledge can be a dangerous thing and information, whether from a book or online cannot replace a fully trained medical practitioner.

There are medical expert systems that you can consult. They will ask you questions and, based on your answers, recommend treatment or a further consultation with a doctor.

Activity

Research and produce a report on all the different parts of the body
that can be replaced by an artificial component.

Education

There are three aspects where ICT has affected education:

- administration
- students
- teachers.

Administration

Electronic registration is common in many schools with parents able to
be contacted at the beginning of the day if their child is absent. Details
on students – for example, exam results, detentions and medical
conditions can be stored and accessed. This allows students to be given
appropriate help and support. Their performance can be monitored and
any problems picked up before they become serious.

Students

Students benefit from access to a wide range of information on the
Internet, the use of computers to write up their work, electronic
documents placed in a single location that all students can have access
to, the use of presentation software and handouts to liven up the
lessons. Virtual learning environments (VLEs) allow for topics to be
structured and all materials and testing made available.

Many schools have the facility for the student to access work stored on
the school's computer system from home. This eliminates the need to use
portable devices to transfer the work or the problem of forgotten work!

Teachers

Teachers benefit from ICT in lessons by being able to pre-prepare their
lessons on presentation software with handouts. They can also make use
of the electronic administration aids for registering and recording marks.

Activity

Only a few aspects of education have been touched on above. Think
about your school.

    a) How is ICT used by yourselves as students, your teachers (in ICT
    and other subjects) and in the administration of the school?

    b) What are the advantages and disadvantages of using ICT?

Dependence on ICT

As individuals we rely on ICT a lot more than might first be apparent.
Banks, ATMs, electronic management systems in vehicles, alarm clocks,
heating systems all rely on ICT to some degree.

We have become deskilled as a population – this means losing the skills
that we did have but not replacing them with skills that are equally
useful. We may have acquired skills in software use and word

processing but we have lost some basic survival skills. The majority of us could not survive without ICT – remove all phones, television, radio, computers and we would be limited to living within a radius of about 10 miles. We take ICT for granted – we place our trust in it and then get annoyed and angry when it fails. Supermarkets in a power cut are interesting places to be – freezers not working, no lights and no tills, no one knows the prices of anything and even if the staff did they cannot accept your credit or debit card.

With mobile phones and texting, a new language is being developed – is this good or bad? Communication is happening, but are traditional languages and people skills being lost?

ICT has its advantages – there are places where it has made a large difference. But it is not the solution to all our problems. There are areas where it has caused problems and our reliance on ICT is an issue that will come to the fore over the next few decades.

Activity

Describe a typical day from the moment you get up. List all the ways that ICT directly, or indirectly, affects your life. If ICT was not available what impact would it have on the way you do things?

Questions

1 Think about the use of ICT in hospitals. Discuss the effect that ICT has had on patients and medical staff.

2 Explain the advantages to students of teachers using ICT in their lessons.

3 Describe the advantages and disadvantages of teleworking.

4 How can the introduction of ICT affect organisation change?

5 Discuss the impact of ICT on the elderly and the disabled.

6 Explain the advantages for a shop becoming an Internet-only shop.

7 Discuss the implications for customers of shopping online.

8 'Our reliance on ICT will eventually lead to a decline in our standard of living and a return to an existence similar to that of nineteenth-century Britain.' Discuss this statement.

End of Chapter 6 tests

Test 1

A cinema has created a membership scheme for its regular customers.

1 The cinema needs to register with the Data Protection Act (DPA, 1998). One of the principles of the DPA is that the data be kept safe from unauthorised access.

  Identify **four** other principles of the DPA. [4]

2 The cinema must make sure that the data is secure.

  Describe **two** methods the cinema can implement to ensure that the data is not accessible by unauthorised users. [4]

3 The cinema is introducing a code of conduct.

  Identify **three** statements that should go into a code of conduct and, for each, give a reason for its inclusion. [6]

4 The British Computer Society (BCS) is a professional body.

  Describe **two** activities of the BCS that would be useful to the cinema. [4]

5 Identify **two** safety risks associated with working with computers. [2]

6 There are many health risks associated with working with computers. Two of these are ulnar neuritis and deep-vein thrombosis.

  Describe ulnar neuritis and deep-vein thrombosis. [4]

7 Discuss how ICT has affected the cinematic experience. [7]

Test 2

Mr Jones works for a large insurance company. He is nervous about the amount of information stored on him by the company.

1   Describe **three** of the legal rights Mr Jones has under the Data Protection Act 1998. [6]

2   Describe the impact of the Regulation of Investigatory Powers Act 2000 on Mr Jones. [4]

3   The insurance company is concerned that employees copy software illegally.

    Describe **two** measures they could introduce to prevent employees copying software. [4]

4   The insurance company has a code of conduct.

    Explain what is meant by a code of conduct and why the company needs one. [4]

5   Mr Jones is a member of the British Computer Society (BCS).

    Describe the purpose of the BCS. [2]

6   Explain, with examples, why ICT is not always the answer to every problem. [5]

7   Mr Jones is currently looking at increasing the amount of work he does from home.

    Discuss the effect that ICT has had on teleworking. [7]

Objectives

Your objectives for this chapter are to:

◎ discuss the drawbacks and advantages of features found in word processing and desktop publishing packages

◎ identify the basic tasks which may be performed using word processing and desktop publishing packages

◎ explain how word processing and desktop publishing packages may be used for mail merge purposes

◎ describe the attributes of documents

◎ evaluate how text can be reformatted to meet the needs of a task or user.

Keep these objectives in mind as you work through the chapter.

✳ Word Processor is the term for a generic application package that allows the entry, editing and formatting of text to create a range of documents.

Word processing

Word processing packages are among the most commonly used computer software. We use the term 'word processing' to mean the activity of writing with the aid of a computer. Writing, when used in association with word processing, is generally used to mean the production of business or personal documents. These documents may include:

- letters
- memos
- theses
- reports.

The use of word processing packages has replaced the use of pen and paper and typewriters in many businesses. These packages enable the user to enter data using a keyboard so that the data appears on the monitor as though on a piece of paper. The data may also be input through the use of speech via a microphone. The text on the screen can then be formatted to meet the needs of the user, edited, saved and printed.

Most word processing packages have WYSIWYG features. This means:

[What-You-See-Is-What-You-Get]

Through the use of the WYSIWYG feature the user can be sure that the screen layout will match the printed layout.

Many word processing packages have the facility to view the document in more than one view-option. For example:

Normal view

The user can see and edit text but is not able to see the text laid out in columns or any imported graphics.

Outline view

The structure of the document will be shown using symbols and indentations. The indentations and symbols in outline view do not affect the way your document looks in normal view and do not print.

Print/page layout view

The document will be shown exactly as it will be printed, including all graphics.

Word processing packages have many other features that can help users format their documents in whatever way they wish. Users can format the attributes of documents including:

- page size, settings and orientation
- text position, size and style
- headers and footers
- paragraph styles
- style sheets
- sections
- footnotes.

Page size, settings and orientation

The size of the page, and the size of the paper to be printed on, can be selected by the user to meet their needs. Figure 7.1 below shows the A5 page-size selected.

Page margins are the blank space around the edges of the page. In general, text and graphics are positioned in the printable area inside the margins. However, some items can be positioned in the margins, for example headers, footers, and page numbers.

The user can also select the orientation of the page – either portrait or landscape. The screenshot below shows the landscape orientation selected.

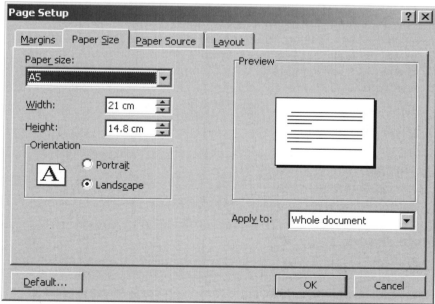

Figure 7.1 Page Setup menu

Text position, size and style

Text position is also known as alignment. The user can select the most appropriate alignment to meet their needs. Headings are often centred, but the user may also choose left, right or justified alignment.

The user may also select the font they wish to use; there are many different fonts to choose from. Some fonts are easy to read, such as

Verdana (this font), Arial or Times New Roman. Other fonts are very difficult to read such as *Palace Script MT* or *Mistral*. The user may also choose to highlight some words or phrases through the use of **bold**, *italic* or <u>underline</u> features. The style of font selected must be appropriate to the document being produced and the needs of the end users.

The size of the font may also be selected. The size of the font also needs to be appropriate to the document being produced and the needs of the end user. It would be very difficult to read a business report in 'size 8 font' as the end user would have to strain their eyes.

Headers and footers

A header is text that appears on a document in the top margin of a page. A header may include the writer's name, title and date. A footer is text that appears on a document in the bottom margin of a page. The general rule is that the footer contains the page numbering, date or file name.

You can use the same header and footer throughout a document or change the header and footer for part of the document. For example, you can use a unique header or footer on the first page, or leave the header or footer off the first page. You can also use different headers and footers on odd and even pages or for part of a document.

Paragraph styles

Paragraph styles are generally used when a long document is being created. The paragraph styles may be pre-defined (for example, the use of a corporate or house style), or they may be defined by the user. A paragraph style defines the features of the text. These features may include the paragraph alignment (left, right, centred or justified), indentations, line spacing, font size and style and bullets or numbering. Styles are generally applied to paragraphs and headings but may also be applied to frames and tables. An example paragraph style definition is given below:

> Style: Heading 3
> Font: Verdana, 20 pt
> Format: Bold
> Paragraph Alignment: Centred
> Spacing Before: 12 pt
> Spacing After: 6 pt

Style sheets

Style sheets are similar to templates and are used to set out the layout of documents. Style sheets can also be referred to as master documents. Style sheets can relate to word-processed documents or those produced using a desktop publishing (DTP) package. Style sheets are very similar to paragraph styles except that they refer to complete documents. The use of a style sheet ensures that all documents produced conform to a pre-determined layout, yet still give the producer of the documents some scope for creativity. For example, a company may decide that the company newsletter should be formatted with:

- Headings in Arial, font size 32 pt, bold and centred
- Body text in two columns, Arial, font size 13 pt and justified.

Advantages and disadvantages of using paragraph styles and style sheets

The advantages include:

- All company documents are produced to a consistent house style making them recognisable.
- Style sheets mean that different people can work on parts of the same documents but the use of a style sheet will ensure that the end results will be consistent and conform to house style.

The disadvantages include:

- All documents can end up looking exactly the same.
- There is no facility for documents to be tailored to meet the needs of the targeted audience.
- Someone must be paid to develop the style and this will be money wasted if the style is not appropriate to the needs of the company.

Activity

Collect a range of business documents. Describe the styles that have been used and whether they make the document 'fit for purpose'.

Sections

A section is a portion of a document in which page-formatting options can be set. A new section can be created when properties such as line numbering, number of columns, or headers and footers need to be changed. Until section breaks are inserted the word processing package will treat a document as a single section. Sections can be used to vary the layout of a document within a page or between pages. Section breaks are inserted to divide the document into sections, and then each section can be formatted to meet the needs of the user.

A **section** is a portion of a document in which page formatting options can be set.

Footnotes

Footnotes are used to briefly explain a word or phrase without including the explanation in the body of the text. A reference number is placed next to the word or phrase within the text and the explanation is placed at the 'foot' of the page, identified by the same reference number. Here is an example to explain the word 'footnote'.[1]

A **footnote** is a note commenting on a point in a document, printed at the bottom of the page.

Questions

1. Describe, giving an example of its use, what is meant by a footer.
2. How can style sheets be used to aid the production of documents between a team of people?
3. What are the disadvantages of style sheets?
4. Describe, giving an example of its use, what is meant by a footnote.

---

[1] A footnote is found at the foot of the page.

Other word processing features

There are many other features of a word processing package that can
help the user in creating documents. These include word wrap,
templates/standard formats and wizards.

Word wrap

When the user has typed text to the end of one line, the word
processing package automatically moves to the beginning of the next
line. The Enter key is only used when a new paragraph is needed or a
blank line is to be inserted.

Templates/standard formats

A template is a standard document with pre-set layouts and formats. A
template determines the basic structure and settings of a document
and includes:

- formatting – font size, colour, style
- page formatting – margins, size, layout
- inserting text – standard words, date, time, etc.
- graphics – standard logo, position.

Every word-processed document is based on a template. When a new
blank document is created, the package's pre-set 'normal' option is
selected by default. Many word processing packages also have a range
of templates that can be selected by the user. The templates cover a
range of different documents including memos, reports, letters and
faxes. These templates have pre-set formats and the user simply inserts
the text required. Figure 7.2 below shows the pre-set templates
available for the production of a letter or fax.

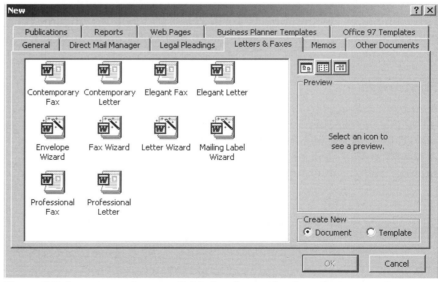

Figure 7.2 Pre-set templates available for the production of a letter or fax

Wizards

The wizard facility also assists the user in the production of a document.
Figure 7.3 below shows the options that can be selected and completed by
the user to produce a letter. The wizard offers the user a range of screens
into which the information is inserted. Once all the information has been

> **Word wrap** is the
> facility within a word
> processor to automatically
> move a word onto the next
> line when it will not fit on the
> current line.

completed the wizard is closed and the user is presented with the completed document containing the information in the pre-set format. However, there are a limited number of options available in wizards and documents produced in this way may not exactly meet the needs of the user.

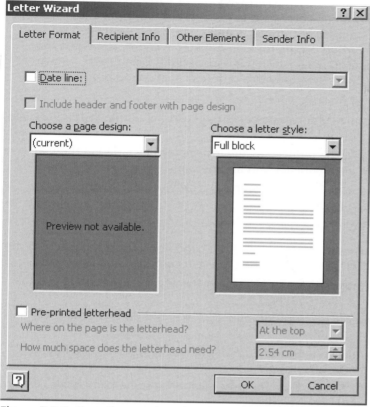

Figure 7.3 Options that can be selected by the user to produce a letter

A **wizard** is a facility that assists the user in the production of a document. It offers a series of screens into which the information is inserted.

There are advantages and disadvantages to using the pre-set templates and wizards that are included with a word processing package.

Advantages of wizards:

- They save time for the inexperienced user.
- They ensure that no important information is forgotten.
- Standard formats can be used.
- There is an element of user friendliness.

Disadvantages of wizards:

- There is no individuality to the documents produced.
- The document produced may not fully meet the needs of the user.

Activity

Investigate the pre-defined templates that are available on the Word processing package you use. Using the table headings below, identify the advantages and disadvantages of using templates for each different type of document.

Type of document	Advantages	Disadvantages

Macros

A macro enables the user to automate tasks that are performed on a regular basis. This is achieved by recording a series of commands, which can then be run whenever the task needs to be performed. For example, a macro may be recorded to add a name as a header to documents. Once the macro has been recorded, it can be run by pressing the keys assigned to it during recording. Macros can also be activated through the use of a button on the toolbar. A macro will only run when the application program to which it is associated is being used. A macro will not run on its own or with a different application program.

Advantages of macros:

- A repetitive task can be performed using a simple instruction (key press, button click).
- Errors may be reduced as the instructions included in the macro are run automatically and are the same every time.
- Inexperienced users can perform complex tasks by using a pre-recorded macro.

Disadvantages of macros:

- Error messages may occur if the conditions when the macro is run are different to those when it was recorded.
- Users must know and remember the key combination to run the macro.
- As a macro is pre-programmed, it may not do what the user wants.
- If the macro is run from a different starting point than intended, then it may go wrong.
- To correct any errors, the user must have some knowledge of how the macro was recorded.

Advantages and disadvantages of using word processing packages

While there are many advantages to using Word processing packages to produce documents, there are also some disadvantages.

Advantages of using a Word processing package:

- The user can keep going back to the document and amending it without the need for retyping/rewriting the whole document.
- Documents can be saved.
- If correct security and back-up procedures are followed, data held in a document will be securely stored.
- The quality of the final document can be very high, especially if graphics are used to enhance the appearance.

Disadvantages of using a word processing package:

- There are generic concerns about security and loss of data.
- The use of wizards and templates may appear to have led to a decline in the personalised letter.

Questions

1 Identify **three** features of a word-processed document that can be set in a template.

2 What is the purpose of wizards?

3 What are the advantages of using macros?

4 How can a 'house style' improve the efficiency of a secretary in producing word-processed documents

Desktop publishing

Desktop publishing (DTP) packages allow users to combine images and text to create publications. Among the publications that can be produced using a DTP package are:

- flyers
- brochures
- posters
- magazines/newsletters.

There are many similarities between word processing and DTP packages. Many of the features discussed in the previous section, such as style sheets, wizards, templates and macros, can be found in a DTP package but with the options presented to the user applying to DTP rather than to word processing.

The main difference between a Word processing package and a DTP package is that of emphasis. A Word processing package focuses on the creation of text-based documents while a DTP package focuses on the manipulation and accurate positioning of graphical objects on the page, including text, to create a composite publication.

A DTP package incorporates specific features to enable the end user to design, create and produce very professional-looking publications.

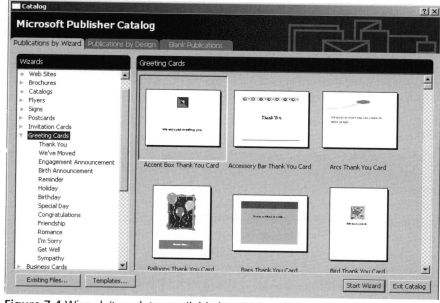

Figure 7.4 Wizards/templates available in a DTP package

* A **frame** in an area
of the screen that can
contain text or graphics and
that can be positioned and
resized independently.

Frames

A frame is an area of a page that can contain text or graphics. The frames can be positioned anywhere on the page. Changes to the content of one frame will not affect the content of another. A DTP package usually makes use of frames.

Word processing packages can use frames but are not exclusively frame-based. Therefore, in word processing the position of each object on the page depends on the position of everything else. For example, if a paragraph or sentence is deleted, everything else moves to take its place.

> Word processing packages are not frame-based.
>
> The position of each object on the page depends on the position of everything else.
>
> For example, if a paragraph or sentence is deleted then everything else moves to take its place.

> Word processing packages are not frame-based.
>
> For example, if a paragraph or sentence is deleted then everything else moves to take its place.

If this paragraph is deleted then everything else moves up to take its place.

This paragraph has now moved up to fill the space.

In a DTP package, each individual frame can be easily moved or resized. This means that a page in a DTP publication can be edited by changing the size or position of the frames. A frame can also be moved from one page to another. (See Figure 7.5 on next page).

Text, as well as graphics can be positioned in a frame. A text frame is created, positioned and resized. Text is typed or imported into the frame. If all the text will not fit in the frame, the excess text can be flowed into another frame. The DTP package may do this automatically. Alternatively, the text may need to be edited to fit the original frame.

Grouping

Frames can be grouped. Grouping makes several objects/frames behave as if they are one. This means that they can be moved, resized, or rotated all at the same time. Grouping objects preserves the arrangement of the objects. Both text and graphics frames can be grouped together. The contents of the frame do not change the principle of grouping. Frames containing either text or graphics can be grouped together. A DTP package works like a notice board, through the use of frames. The frames act as different sections, which can be moved around on the page until the layout is fit for purpose and meets the needs of the user.

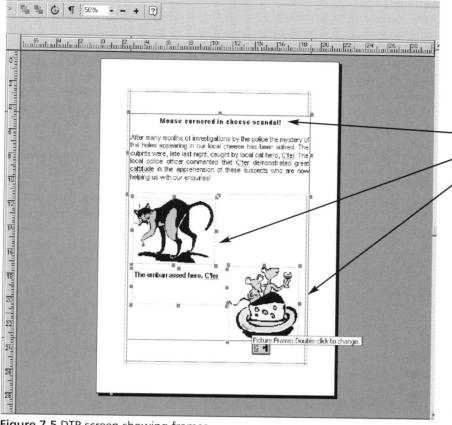

Figure 7.5 DTP screen showing frames

Each block of text or graphic is in its own frame so it can be moved on its own. A frame tends to be empty; once text or graphics are inserted into the frame then it can be called an object.

Layering

Frames and objects can also be layered. Objects can be stacked in layers, with the first object you create at the bottom of the stack and the last object at the top. If two or more objects overlap, the object closest to the top of the stack covers the ones beneath it. Sometimes it is possible to see the relative position of layered objects within a stack by the way they overlap.

Shifting one object to a different layer in the stack can also change the way objects overlap. It is possible to move an object to another layer, by selecting it and then selecting one of the layering commands on the Arrange menu. An object can also be made transparent so that the object in the layer beneath it can be seen through it.

Grids

When a publication is being created, it is important to line-up all the objects within the publication accurately. The design elements must be properly aligned vertically, horizontally, and in relation to each other.

A grid, composed of horizontal and vertical layout guides, usually defines the basic layout of a page. The layout guides define page sections and help the user to align elements on the page with precision. Layout guides are present on the background of every page.

The layout guides are usually visible on the screen, but they don't appear on the printed page. However, text frames and other design elements that are placed on the page can obscure them, and they can also be turned off if not required.

Layering is where frames or objects appear in different layers in a document.

A **grid** is composed of horizontal and vertical layout guides and defines the basic layout of the page.

Different types of publications use different grids. A booklet might use only four basic layout guides to define its margins; a three-panel brochure might use horizontal layout guides to define the areas to be folded; a newsletter might use vertical layout guides to define a multi-column format. When a grid is created, it can be the same for every page or a mirrored grid for a two-page spread (facing pages). In this case there will be one set of layout guides for the odd-numbered, right-hand pages and another set for the even-numbered, left-hand pages.

It is also possible to manipulate graphics in a DTP package. (See Chapter 10 Graphics.)

To word process or DTP?

There are very many similarities between Word processing and DTP packages. But, as explained earlier in this chapter, the focus of each type of package is different. Both word processing and DTP can be used to create a range of documents including leaflets, newsletters and brochures. However, the layout can be changed more easily using a DTP package than a word processing package. This means that a DTP package should be used when there are a lot of text and graphics that need to be layered or grouped. A Word processing package is more suitable when the document consists mostly of text with very few graphics, for example, letters, reports and memos. It is also possible to create the text for a publication in a word processing package and import this text into a DTP package.

Questions

1 Describe, giving an example of its use, what is meant by a frame.

2 In DTP, what is 'layering' and how should it be used?

3 Describe **three** features found in a DTP package.

4 Describe the differences between a DTP package and a word processing package.

5 Giving reasons, describe when it is more appropriate to use a DTP package than a word processing package.

Mail merge

A standard document created in a Word processing or DTP package can be combined with information from a spreadsheet or database. Mail merging allows the user to create and send a personalised version of the same document to many different people or organisations (recipients).

A data source is created containing all the information to be included in the document. The data source may be created specifically for the mail merge process or it may be an existing data source, for example customer records or student records.

The standard document/template is then produced including merge fields. These are based on the fields in the spreadsheet or database being used as the data source. An example would be, **Dear <title> <lastname>** where 'title' and 'lastname' are fields in the data source. The standard document can be a letter, address label or envelope.

Mail merge is combining information from a spreadsheet or database with a standard document to allow the user to create and send a personalised version of the same document to many different recipients.

The data source and the standard document/template are then linked and merged. The software merges the data by inserting the appropriate fields from the data source into the standard document/template to produce the personalised letter.

The personalised documents can be sent to a printer or used to create a new file.

If there were 100 customer records held in the data source then the mail merge process would produce 100 letters.

Advantages of using mail merge:

- Documents can be produced very quickly.
- Only one copy of the document needs to be proofread to ensure that all the others are correct.
- The data source can be used for many different mail merge processes.
- The standard letter/template can be saved and reused.

Word fields

By using word fields it is possible to run a customised mail merge process. Word fields can be used to add additional information to a mail merge document or to select specified recipients for the document. For example, it is possible, using a word field, to send the document only to those people who live in London. There are many different word fields all of which have different purposes. The five word fields shown in Figure 7.5 below are the ones you need to be able to explain:

Figure 7.6 Five word fields

Word field	Explanation of usage
ASK	Is used to prompt a user for information during the mail merge process. This is useful for variable information not available from the data source. ASK has the same result as using the FILL-IN word field.
FILL-IN	Is used to prompt a user for information during the mail merge process. This is useful for variable information not available from the data source. FILL-IN has the same result as using the ASK word field.
IF… THEN… ELSE	Is used to set conditions to limit which records are printed. For example, this word field could be used to select documents to be sent only to those recipients who live in Lancashire.
NEXT RECORD	Is used to merge the next data record into the current merged document rather than creating a new document. This is useful if a number of record details are to be included on one document, for example names and addresses.
SKIP RECORD IF	Is used to miss (or skip) a record if a given condition is met. Two conditions are compared, if the comparison is true, SKIP RECORD IF cancels the current merge document, moves to the next data record in the data source, and starts a new merge document. If the comparison is false the current merge document is continued. This could be used to skip all records of recipients living in Kent.

Questions

1 What is mail merge?
2 What are the disadvantages of mail merge?
3 What is the difference between a merge field and a word field?

End of Chapter 7 tests

Test 1

*A company is producing a flyer to be sent with a mail-merged
letter to all its customers.*

1 Using an example, describe the use of each of the following word
   fields when implementing the mail merge facility:

   i)   FILL-IN
   ii) SKIP RECORD IF
   iii) IF… THEN… ELSE.   [6]

2 Explain the process of mail merging.   [4]

3 Explain an example of using grouped text frames in a Word
   processing template for the mail-merged letter.   [2]

4 The company uses a DTP package to produce the flyer. Describe
   the benefits of using the following features to create the flyers:

   i)   wizards
   ii) templates
   iii) macros.   [6]

5 The flyer is to be created without using wizards and templates.
   Describe how the use of the following features could assist in the
   design of the flyer:

   i)   layering
   ii) grids
   iii) frames.   [6]

Test 2

A one-page, word-processed document is to be faxed to the customers of a company. The draft document produced covers more than one page.

1 Describe the following features of word processing software that could be used to create the draft document:

   i)   frame

   ii) footer

   iii) paragraph style. [6]

2 Describe **four** ways that could be used to make a document fit on to a single page without removing any of the content. [8]

3 Explain **two** advantages and **one** disadvantage of fitting the draft document on to a single page. [6]

4 Describe how style sheets could assist in the production of this document. [4]

Objectives

Your objectives for this chapter are to:

◎ describe the characteristics of modelling software and give reasons why a model might be used

◎ explain how variables, formulae, rules and functions are used in modelling software

◎ describe how a data model may be used for answering 'what if?' questions and explain the benefit of being able to answer such questions using a data model

◎ explain the purpose and use of cells, ranges, rows, columns, worksheets and workbooks in spreadsheet software

◎ describe relative and absolute cell referencing, and give examples of typical uses of each method

◎ describe the ways in which numerical data can be presented graphically and match the appropriate types of chart to a given task

◎ describe ways in which worksheets in spreadsheet software can be customised using form controls and macros, giving examples of use.

Keep these objectives in mind as you work through the chapter.

✳ Modelling is creating a computer model of a real world situation so that variables can be changed to answer 'what if' questions.

Characteristics of modelling software and its use

There are two main types of modelling used in ICT:

● Modelling of objects (rooms, buildings, cars, etc.).
● Mathematical modelling (financial calculations, spreadsheets, etc.).

Modelling of objects

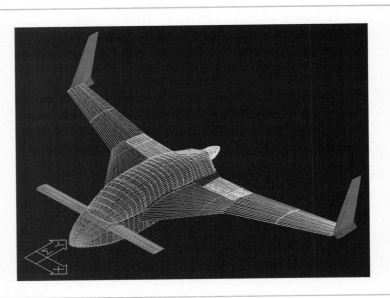

Figure 8.1 Modelling of an object

This allows you to create a virtual representation of the item within the computer. You can model large items such as buildings and look at the effect on them from different external influences, for example earthquakes, fire and explosions.

It is possible to see different layers – external view, electrical wiring view, basic frame and so on. The model can be rotated so that different aspects can be viewed. It is possible to zoom in on a particular part (for example, in a model of a vehicle individual nuts and bolts can be viewed). How individual components will react can also be seen.

An important characteristic of software used to model objects is the ability to ask questions of the model – to change the components and see how it reacts, to move an item and try out a different design. The effects can be gauged at the touch of a button.

Mathematical modelling

Forename	Surname	ICT Project 1	ICT Project 2	Exam 1	Exam 2	Total / 240
Paul	Cassidy	45	34	41	36	156
Mike	Turpin	54	54	35	41	184
Alan	Oakley	34	31	21	45	131
Joe	Masterton	41	56	45	34	176
Nigel	James	46	43	56	41	186
Sue	Younger	57	17	43	23	140
Michelle	Parker	43	32	23	43	141
Laura	Kelly	60	58	43	50	211

Figure 8.2 Mathematical modelling

Models that represent mathematical elements, such as finances, are commonly produced through the use of spreadsheets.

Spreadsheets have many characteristics that assist with the modelling process. They can be based on functions and formulas. These allow numbers to be input into the spreadsheet and for any changes to be automatically recalculated. This means that many different scenarios can be tried out using a single model.

The answering of questions is a powerful characteristic. 'What if?' questions allow the user to change values and see what the effect would be. An alternative method of asking questions is to start with the result and to see what would need to happen for that result to occur – this is known as goal seeking.

There are various features of spreadsheets that are used to allow modelling to occur. Spreadsheets can use variables and constants. Variables are values entered into a cell that are then used in a formula. The variable can be changed by the end user as required, which will lead to a recalculation of the figures. Constants are values that are used in formulas but cannot be changed by the end user.

In spreadsheets, individual cells or ranges of cells can be given easy-to-remember names. For example, instead of referring to C10, you can give the cell a name relating to its contents, for example, VAT_RATE, which can then be used to refer to the cell. This makes formulas easier to understand.

Spreadsheets are based on a layout of rows and columns. This layout assists financial modelling. It allows items to be laid out in a logical and easy-to-follow format. The use of rows and columns leads to the use of sequencing. Replication is the copying of a cell either horizontally or vertically. The value of the cell can be incremented. If the value is an item in a list, the next item in the list can be given in the next cell, for example, days of the week or months of the year. Formulas can also be copied and cell references automatically adjusted.

Other features include the use of multiple worksheets and graphical representation of data.

Why is computer modelling used?

There are many reasons why computer modelling is used. It is safer to test how an on-screen object reacts than to create it in reality and test it. For example, to build an aircraft, test it and to have it go wrong can cost human lives.

Only one model needs to be created in a computer. The model can be altered and changed. If a real model or the real thing was created, a new one would need to be created for each different alteration. This would cost time and money.

A computer model can be backed-up and shared. Since it is stored electronically, it can be backed-up on a disk. It can be emailed or sent to a third party who can also work on the model.

Computer models can be accelerated or slowed down to see effects that could not be viewed in reality. For example, a nuclear explosion in reality happens very quickly. A computer model can slow the process down so that it can be viewed in slow motion.

The creation of the universe happened over a long period of time. A computer model can simulate the process and speed it up and this simulation can be used effectively for research purposes.

hint It should be remembered that ultimately, all modelling is mathematically based. The creation and manipulation of objects is mathematical as are financial models.

Questions

1 Describe **three** characteristics of software used to model objects.

2 Why is software used to model objects?

3 What are the disadvantages of using software to model objects?

4 Describe **three** characteristics of software used to model financial data.

5 What are the advantages of using a software modelling package to model next year's accounts?

6 Describe the similarities between software used to model objects and software used to model financial data.

Variables, formulae, functions and rules

A model contains four main features that allow it to manipulate numbers and text. These features allow the model to recalculate values when a number changes. They also allow for questions to be asked and answered with the minimum amount of effort and for different scenarios to be tested. These features are:

- variables
- formulae
- functions
- rules.

Variables

A variable is an identifier associated with a particular cell and within the cell there will be a value. The variable could be a cell reference (D4) or the cell could have a name (VAT_RATE). When the variable is used in a spreadsheet, it is the value contained within the variable that is used.

Formulae

A formula is the way that a calculation is represented in a spreadsheet. Formulae use numbers, addresses of cells (either references such as A12 or names) and mathematical operators (such as + / * −).

An example of a formula is:

A12+(A12*VAT_RATE)

A formula is a mathematical expression in a spreadsheet cell that is automatically calculated.

Functions

A function is used to represent a formula that is too complex or too long to expect an ordinary user to enter. A formula uses reserved words that are built into the spreadsheet.

Examples include:

SUM: calculates the total of a range of cells.

MAX: returns the maximum value from a list.

LOOKUP: returns a value from an array, based on a given value.

A function is a pre-defined formula in a spreadsheet that can be entered in a cell to carry out a specific calculation.

Rules

These are a set of procedures that must be followed. For example, if a calculation requires two values, then these values must be supplied. A validation rule can be applied to make sure that the value is given.

A rule can also be the sequence of events required for the calculation to work.

This set of rules in Figure 8.3 will enable the procedure to be followed by different people and a comparable result obtained.

		Max Mark	UMS Mark			
Candidate A					A	240
	2512	90	56		B	210
	2513	120	99		C	180
	2514	90	67		D	150
					E	120
		Total Mark	222			

Rule: For each candidate

      For each module

            Enter a UMS mark

Add all the marks together

Look up the mark in the grade table

Return a grade

Figure 8.3 Rules to work out an AS grade

Questions

1 Define the term 'variable'.
2 What is the advantage of naming a cell?
3 Describe the differences between functions and formulae.
4 Give an example of a function and a rule that perform the same action.
5 In modelling, what is a rule?
6 Describe the rule required to work out the age of a person on a given day.

Using a data model to answer 'what if?' questions

A 'what if?' question is an attempt to find out what is going to happen in the future. It requires a value to be changed and other values to be recalculated.

Examples include:

- How much do I need to increase the price of X brand of trainers for my profit to increase by 3%?
- What would happen to the number of accidents on X road if we cut the speed of cars by 10 miles per hour?
- If I was to add a second staircase to the building how many extra people could get out within five minutes of an alarm going off?

Models contain calculations, formulae, functions and rules. They contain cell references and named cells. They can recalculate automatically and present data in a variety of formats – textually, numerically or graphically. Models can have interfaces built to increase their usability. These features assist in answering 'what if?' questions.

The benefits of using the model include recalculation – the model can be changed many times and lots of different values and figures observed. The only cost involved is time. Once the model has been created it will answer as many 'what if?' questions as you want it to.

The cost and time involved in using a model are both likely to be less than when creating physical models. To answer 'what if?' questions using physical models will require a new model to be created for each question. If testing the structure of a building in wind, physical buildings would have to be created and then tested (ending in their destruction). Virtual models of buildings can be tested in many different scenarios without being destroyed.

If there is an error in the model, it is simpler and faster to alter it on a computer than in a physical model. It may require the rewriting of a rule or function, but this can be done quickly.

Questions

1 Describe what is meant by a 'what if?' question.
2 Give **three** examples of 'what if?' questions that could be asked of a model of an aircraft.
3 Describe **two** advantages of using a computer model to answer 'what if?' questions instead of a physical model.
4 Describe **three** features of models that make them suitable for answering 'what if?' questions.

Cells, ranges, rows, columns, worksheets and workbooks

A spreadsheet is made up of different parts. Each part has a different function and purpose.

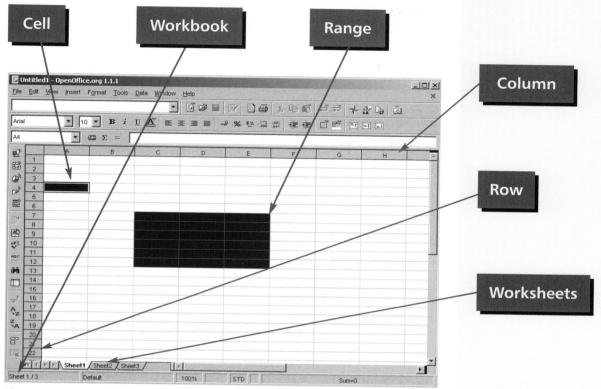

Figure 8.4 Different elements of a spreadsheet

Cell

A cell is an individual data store identified by a row and a column indicator. The highlighted cell in Figure 8.4 is in Column A and Row 4, so it is identified as A4. Every cell in the spreadsheet can be uniquely identified. Cells can also be given names as unique identifiers.

Formatting can be applied to cells. Each individual cell can be formatted independently of the others. This includes background colour, font, font size, validation, alignment and conditional formatting.

Cells can also be protected – you can stop the data within them being altered without a password having been entered.

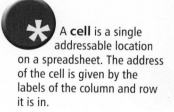

A **cell** is a single addressable location on a spreadsheet. The address of the cell is given by the labels of the column and row it is in.

Range

A range is a group of cells. The group can be given a name or just known by their cell references. A range is usually given top left to bottom right and separated by a colon:

A4:B6

C7:G12

A range is used when the cells within it contain similar data. They may contain grades, marks for an exam or names of stock items. Ranges are often used in formulae and functions. They make it easier to understand the spreadsheet and how it is working and allow the same formatting to be applied at the same time (instead of individually to a cell).

Rows and columns

A row is a range of cells that goes across the spreadsheet. A column is a range of cells that goes down the spreadsheet. In most packages, rows are given numbers and columns are given letters.

Rows and columns are used to organise the data. They can hold headings to show where the data is stored and be used to hold the data within a tabular structure.

	A	B	C	D	E
1	No of sales by groups of item each quarter				
2					
3		1st Quarter	2nd Quarter	3rd Quarter	4th Quarter
4	Pens	576	454	876	343
5	Pencils	345	232	545	323
6	Pads of Paper	54	45	76	43

Figure 8.5 Rows and columns within a spreadsheet

The width and height of rows and columns can be altered. For example, columns can be widened to fit the text.

If necessary, rows and columns can be hidden. If a set of columns contained some calculations that you did not wish to be visible, you could hide them from the user.

Worksheet

A worksheet (called sheet, or spreadsheet in some applications) is a large range of cells – all of the cells on a sheet. A worksheet can be used to hold data on a single area of the business. For example, it can hold the sales data, the expenditure or the stock. Worksheets can be given names.

Workbook

More than one worksheet, in the same spreadsheet, is known as a workbook. A workbook is a collection of worksheets. If each worksheet contains a separate area of the business, workbooks contain data about the whole business.

For example, a workbook might contain worksheets on income, expenditure, stock and a summary (four worksheets within the worksheet).

Workbooks can be used to divide data up and to organise it – if an individual owns a chain of shops, they could have a workbook on each shop, or a worksheet on each shop and a single workbook for all of them.

One advantage of using workbooks is that data changed in one worksheet will automatically change in all worksheets across the whole workbook. Another advantage is that different access rights can be given to different worksheets. For example, if a workbook contained several worksheets and each worksheet contained data relating to a single shop, you could allow the manager of each shop access to the data for their own shop only.

A **worksheet** is a single sheet of rows and columns in a spreadsheet package.

A **workbook** is a set of linked worksheets in a spreadsheet package.

As a workbook is saved as a single entity, it is easy to back-up, copy and send it to other people. All the data required is in a single location.

Questions

1 Describe how a cell would be used in a financial spreadsheet.
2 What is a range? Give an example of how a range would be used in a sports-league spreadsheet.
3 Describe the benefits for a sweet shop of using a worksheet.
4 Describe how a furniture shop might use a workbook.

Relative and absolute cell referencing

Referencing in spreadsheets is the use of cell identifiers to include the value contained within the cell in a formula or function. For example, C2+D2 uses two cell references.

When you copy formulae or functions in a spreadsheet there are two ways the cell reference can be affected. It can move in relation to the direction of the copy or it can stay the same.

Relative referencing

Relative referencing is when you copy a formula or function and the cell reference within the formula or function will move.

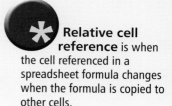

Relative cell reference is when the cell referenced in a spreadsheet formula changes when the formula is copied to other cells.

	A	B	C	D	E	F
1						
2						
3						
4		23	43	54	23	
5		34	54	2	12	
6						
7		B4+B5	C4+C5	D4+D5	E4+E5	
8						
9						

Figure 8.6 Copying formulae across columns

If the formulae are copied from one column to another, then the column identifier will change. In Figure 8.5, when copying from column B to column C the cell references have changed.

If formulae are copied from one row to another, then the row identifier will change. In Figure 8.6, when copying from row 3 to row 4 the cell reference has changed.

	A	B	C	D	E
1					
2					
3		23	34	B3+C3	
4		43	54	B4+C4	
5		54	2	B5+C5	
6		23	12	B6+C6	
7					

Figure 8.7 Copying formulae down rows

Relative referencing is used when you want the cell reference to change when you copy the cell.

Absolute referencing

This is when you copy a formula or function and the cell reference within the formula or function will not change.

This is used when you have a value entered into a single cell that the formula or function refers to, for example:

- VAT – all individual figures need to be multiplied by VAT.
- Postage – all individual sales totals have the same postage added on.

	A	B	C	D	E
1		P&P		£1.99		
2					
3					
4		Order Number	Order Total	Total with P&P	
5		A123B1	£45.33	C5+$C$1	
6		B432H7	£27.54	C6+$C$1	
7		J345U9	£19.99	C7+$C$1	
8		F342K8	£56.87	C8+$C$1	
9					

Figure 8.8 Absolute referencing

In Figure 8.7, P&P (postage & packing) is in cell C1. All the Order Totals need the same P&P adding.

By using an absolute reference (a cell reference that does not move when copied) you can refer to P&P in D5, copy the cell down and those references that are relative – C5, C6, C7 and so on move when the formula is copied while the absolute one does not.

The spreadsheet knows that it is absolute because of the $ signs. Instead of using $ signs, you could use the name of the cell instead:

	A	B	C	D	E
1		P&P		£1.99		
2					
3					
4		Order Number	Order Total	Total with P&P	
5		A123B1	£45.33	C5+Post	
6		B432H7	£27.54	C6+Post	
7		J345U9	£19.99	C7+Post	
8		F342K8	£56.87	C8+Post	
9					

Figure 8.9 Using the name of the cell in absolute referencing

In Figure 8.8, C1 has been given the name of Post. When Post is used in the formula it refers to cell C1 and because it is not incremented when copied, the name makes it an absolute reference.

The main advantage here is that if you wanted to change the cost of P&P, you only need to change the value in C1 and all associated formulae will recalculate.

Absolute referencing is used when a value is used in the same formula or function many times.

Presenting numerical data

Spreadsheets can present information in numeric or graphical form. Within each spreadsheet there are many different types of graphs and charts that can be used to display information. Not all the possible chart types are given below, only the most common. Note though, that although the charts are described here as being commonly used in spreadsheet software, British mathematicians may use slightly different definitions.

Bar chart

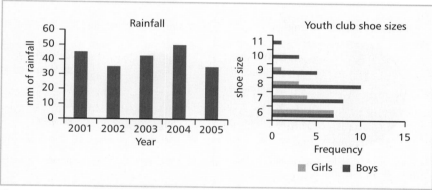

Figure 8.10 Bar charts

The bar charts in Figure 8.9 show data changes over a period of time, and illustrate comparisons between items. The length of the bars represents frequency or quantity and each column is labelled. Some software refers to vertical bar charts as column charts.

Bar charts are useful when comparing different sets of data.

Bar charts could be used to show:

- rainfall in different years
- marks in different subjects
- sales in different areas.

Line chart

Line charts are often used to show changes in a variable over time. (See Figure 8.10 overleaf).

Line charts could be used to show:

- temperature readings for a hospital patient
- a company's monthly sales
- population changes over several years.

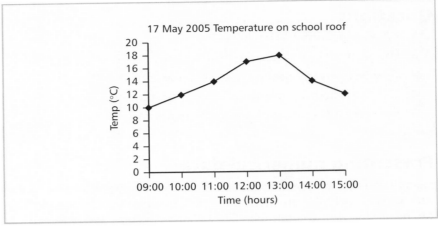

Figure 8.11 A line chart

Pie chart

A pie chart shows groups or classes of data in a proportional size to the sum of all items that make up the data series.

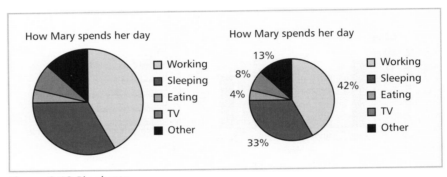

Figure 8.12 Pie charts

They are useful when you want to show how something is shared or divided.

Pie charts could be used to show:

- how much of the population voted for each political party
- how the manufacturing cost of an item is divided between different raw materials
- the most common hair colour in a group
- the proportion of A, B, C, D and E grades achieved by a group of students.

Scatter chart

A scatter chart shows the relationship between two variables. The two values are used to plot coordinates on the graph.

Scatter graphs are useful when you want to see the correlation between two sets of results.

Scatter charts could be used to show:

- the relationship between marks in two different subjects
- the correlation between height and weight
- the association between a town's population and its football team's league position.

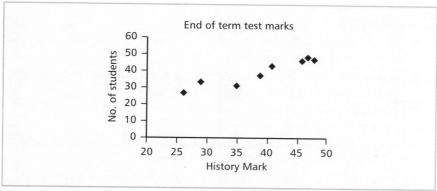

Figure 8.13 A scatter chart

Radar chart

Radar charts are sometimes called spider charts or star diagrams. They are used to plot several different factors that all affect the same item. They show different facets of the same item. The chart will have several axes radiating from a central point. It is like a bar chart wrapped into a circle.

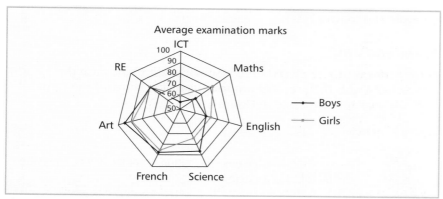

Figure 8.14 A radar chart

Radar charts are useful to compare areas of relative strength and weakness.

Radar charts could be used to:

- compare the amount of different vitamins in a variety of food items
- show economic indicators such as average earnings and unemployment in different towns
- compare performance in different subjects for different groups of students.

Activity

Investigate the following graph types below. For each one, draw an example of the graph and give examples of its use.

   a) histogram

   b) pictogram

   c) stem and leaf diagram

   d) population pyramid.

Customising worksheets

The interface for a worksheet is simple – rows and columns. The cells can be coloured and borders can be added. Gridlines can be removed, as can row and column headings. Fundamentally, all the user can do on a standard worksheet is enter data in cells.

It is possible to customise the worksheet. This is done using form controls and macros.

Form controls

Form controls can be placed on the spreadsheet to increase the interactivity with the user and improve usability. Some of the form controls available are listed in Figure 8.14.

Figure 8.15 Form controls

	Button – the user can push the button to start an event. The button can be linked to a macro.
	Check box – options can be ticked (when an invoice is paid, for example).
	Group/Frame – form controls can be grouped together. For example, if you have two option buttons, by grouping them you can make them into choice buttons so only one can be selected at a time.
	Option button – options can be selected and given values.
	Text box – this allows text to be written and picked up and used in the spreadsheet.
	Combo box – items can be selected from a drop-down box.
	List box – this gives a list of items. Either single or multiple items can be selected.
	Image – a picture can be inserted.
	Label – instruction labels or titles can be added.

The spreadsheet can also be customised through validation. This can restrict the entry of data into the spreadsheet and, where appropriate, given an error message.

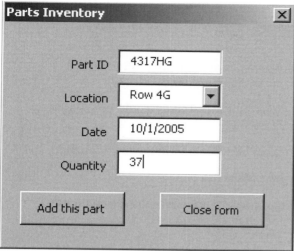

Figure 8.16 A completed form

Macros

Macros can be used to give additional functionality to the spreadsheet and increase the customisation of the interface. A macro is a sequence of instructions that are defined as a single event. The macro can be attached to a button, opening a worksheet or initiating an event (such as a cell becoming a particular value). The macro can do anything that can be programmed. Some examples include:

- moving to a different part of the spreadsheet or a different worksheet
- running a calculation
- closing the application
- printing the application
- adding a header and footer to the spreadsheet.

The complexity of the macro is only limited by the task requirements and the ability of the programmer.

A **Macro** is a set of stored commands that can be replayed.

Questions

1 A school uses a spreadsheet to enter exam results. Describe **three** ways the interface can be customised.
2 Describe **two** advantages to the user of using a customised interface.
3 Define the term 'macro'.
4 Give **three** examples of how a macro could be used in a spreadsheet.

End of Chapter 8 tests

Test 1

Mrs Adams has four shops. At present the accounts for the shops are done on paper.

1 Describe **three** characteristics of modelling software that could help Mrs Adams with her accounts. [6]

2 Use an example to show how Mrs Adams would use relative and absolute cell referencing. [4]

3 Describe **two** differences between a formula and a function. [4]

4 How would Mrs Adams make use of a workbook? [4]

5 Identify the most appropriate types of graphs she could use to show:

   i) comparison of the profit for each shop each month over a year
   ii) prediction of the profit for the four shops over the next five years. [2]

6 Describe **two** form controls that could be used to customise the user interface. [4]

7 Describe **three** ways the user interface could be customised and, for each, give an example of how it might benefit Mrs Adams. [6]

Test 2

An estate agent is moving to bigger premises.

1 Describe **two** characteristics of modelling software that could assist the estate agent in creating a virtual model of the new premises. [4]

2 Describe **three** benefits to the estate agent of using a virtual model instead of a physical model. [6]

3 The estate agent is going to use a spreadsheet to work out the cost of the move.

   i) Describe how 'what if?' questions could be used. [2]
   ii) Describe **three** features of spreadsheet modelling software that allow it to be used to answer 'what if?' questions. [6]

4 Describe how the estate agent could use a range in the spreadsheet. [2]

5 Describe **two** advantages of being able to give a cell a name instead of using the column and row identifier. [4]

6 Explain, using an example, the difference between absolute and relative cell referencing. [4]

7 Bar and pie chart are two types of graph.

   Identify **two** other types of graph and give an example of how the estate agent could make use of them. [2]

9 | Presentations

Objectives

Your objectives for this chapter are to describe:

◎ the use and purpose of presentation software and multimedia presentations

◎ the main features of presentation software

◎ how a team of people can develop a presentation

◎ different modes of navigation used in presentation software

◎ the differences between the use of overhead projector transparencies and presentation software.

Keep these objectives in mind as you work through the chapter.

Presentation software and its features

Presentation software enables the user to create, link and run slideshows on a screen either automatically or through user control. The slides created can contain text, graphics and sound/video clips. Presentations that include sound and/or video clips as well as text and graphics are called multimedia presentations.

Buttons and hotspots can be used to move between slides. If buttons and hotspots are used then the presentation is interactive as it allows the user to interact with the presentation and to choose how they move through it.

Presentations can be displayed on a large monitor or screen. In addition, speaker's notes can be prepared, outlines can be viewed, and audience handouts can be printed in a range of formats.

Frames

Frames can be used to position the different elements contained within a slide. These frames can include text, graphics, movies, sounds, graphs, charts and tables. The elements contained within the frames can be created in the presentation software or imported from other software packages. Text is generally typed directly into the frames as the amount of text on each slide is limited and normally in bullet-point form.

Slide transition effects

Transition effects can be applied to a slide to make the presentation more interesting. Transition effects govern how the presentation software moves from slide to slide. The transition effect does not have to be the same throughout the presentation. It can be changed to indicate a new section of a presentation or to emphasise a particular slide.

Presentation software offers a range of different transition effects that can be used. Some of the effects that may be available are:

● cut

● dissolve

● wipe left.

It is also possible to set the speed at which the transition occurs.

A transition effect can be applied to one particular slide or to the whole presentation. Transition effects can also include the use of sound. The sound effects connected to each slide transition can be set to occur with one specific transition or with the whole presentation. Sound effects, however, should be used sparingly as they can detract from the presentation and its contents.

Activity

Investigate the different transition effects available on the presentation software you have access to. Identify the advantages and disadvantages of using transition effects.

Animation effects

Animation effects are special sound or visual effects that can be added to text or other objects, such as a chart or picture. Through the use of animation effects, it is possible to control the way that objects appear on each slide. For example, the presenter may want to introduce a bulleted list on a particular slide, one bullet at a time. Each bullet point can be made to appear when the presenter performs an action, for example a mouse click.

To give another example, as English is read from left to right, the animation effect on the bullet points is set up so that they appear from the left. If a bullet point needs emphasising, it could be animated to appear from the right instead. The change will grab the audience's attention and reinforce that bullet point.

All the elements of a presentation including text, graphics, movies, charts, and other objects, can be animated. This is done in order to emphasise important points, control the flow of information within the presentation and to add interest. As we saw above, it is possible to control the way text or an object appears on the slide, for example, you may wish it to fly in from the left. Text can also be animated to appear by the paragraph, word or even one letter at a time.

Other effects can also be employed. For example text or objects can be dimmed or change colour when a new element appears on the slide during the presentation.

The order and timing of animations can also be changed. If the presentation is to be shown without a presenter then it is possible to set the animations to occur automatically without any human intervention.

When the animations for a presentation have been set up it is possible to preview the presentation to ensure that all the effects are appropriate and that they do not detract from the content of the presentation.

Sound

Sound in a presentation can be used in many different ways. Sound effects are available when animation effects are being set. These sound effects can be used to signify the 'arrival' of a piece of text on the screen. Sound effects available include:

- clapping
- drum roll
- chime.

155

If used appropriately these sounds can be used to emphasise an important piece of information and add impact to the slide. Sound effects should be used sparingly as they can detract from the contents of the information contained within the slide.

Sound can also be used in a presentation in other forms, such as speech and music. Sound files can be a pre-existing file, such as a company advertising jingle, or downloaded from the Internet. It is also possible to record sound files to meet the specific needs of a particular presentation.

Video

It is also possible to insert video clips into a presentation, for example, part of a company's advertising commercial. The video clip can be set up to play automatically when the slide is shown or can be started by the presenter taking some action, usually a mouse-click. Do not use too many video clips in a presentation. Frequent use of special effects can draw attention away from the content of the presentation.

Handouts

It is useful to provide handouts for the audience when a presentation is being delivered. These handouts will enable the audience to make additional notes as they are listening to the presenter. The slides can be printed with two, three, four, six, or nine slides to a page. If handouts are produced with three slides to an A4 page, lines are automatically provided for the audience to use to make their notes. Handouts show only the slides; they don't include any corresponding notes.

However, each slide can be printed with additional notes if required. These notes can be created for the presenter to be used as an aide-memoire during the presentation, or they can be used to provide extra information and clarification for the audience.

The layout of a handout with three slides per A4 page. This option has lines on which the audience can make additional notes.

The layout of a handout with six slides per A4 page. This option has no lines for additional notes.

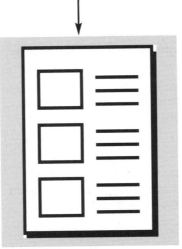

Figure 9.1 Handout layout options

Hyperlinks

A hyperlink is coloured, underlined text or a graphic that, when clicked, takes the user to a file, a location in a file, an HTML page on the world wide web, or an HTML page on an intranet. Hyperlinks can also link to newsgroups and to Gopher, Telnet, and FTP sites.

A hyperlink can be added to a presentation and used to move to a variety of locations, for example, a custom show, a specific slide within the presentation, a different presentation, a document or spreadsheet, or an Internet, intranet, or email address. A hyperlink can be created from any object including text, shapes, tables, graphs, and pictures.

Hyperlinks are coloured, underlined text or a graphic that, when clicked, takes the user to another location/file.

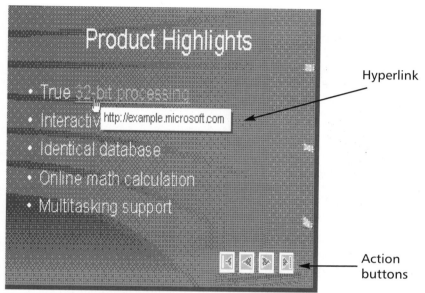

Figure 9.2 Slide with hyperlinks and action buttons

Questions

1 What is meant by slide transition?
2 Explain the disadvantages of using sound in a presentation.
3 Explain the advantages of using video in a presentation.
4 How could hyperlinks be used in a presentation?

Design templates

A design template specifies the colour scheme as well as the master slide and master title-slide layouts with custom formatting and fonts. These are all designed to create a particular look. When a design template is applied to a presentation the master slide, master title-slide and colour scheme of the new template replace the existing design of the presentation. When a design template is applied, each new slide will follow the same customised look.

Most presentation software comes with a wide variety of professionally designed templates. However, the user can also create a design template from scratch. If an original design template is created then it can be saved as an additional template to be used again.

A variety of pre-designed colour schemes are also available in most presentation software packages. These are sets of balanced colours designed for use as the main colours of a slide presentation. They detail the colours to be used for text, background, fill and accents (highlighting). Each colour in the pre-designed scheme will be used automatically for the appropriate element on the slide. A colour scheme can be selected for an individual slide or for an entire presentation. When a pre-set design template is applied to a presentation then the presentation software will offer a set of pre-designed colour schemes made to go with that design template.

Auto layouts

When a new presentation is being created the presentation software will offer a choice of pre-designed slide layouts. Each auto layout has placeholders where different elements of the slide can be placed. Placeholders are boxes with dotted outlines that appear when a new slide is created. These boxes position the objects contained within the slide such as the slide title, text, charts, tables, organisation charts, and clip art.

Master slides

A master slide enables a team of people to work on the same presentation separately. When the presentation is collated, all the elements of the presentation follow exactly the same format. The master slide will show:

- the theme to be used for the presentation
- the position of any graphics to be shown on each slide in the presentation (for example, a company logo)
- the positioning of any information which must appear on each slide such as the date, slide number and any footer/header text.

The master slide also controls certain text characteristics – such as font type, size, and colour – called 'master text', as well as the background colour and certain special effects, such as shadowing and bullet style. Objects appear on slides in the same location as they do on the master slide.

The master slide contains text placeholders and placeholders for footers, such as the date, time, and slide number. When a global change is needed (that is, a change to all the slides in the presentation), each slide does not have to be changed individually. The change is made on the master slide and the presentation software automatically updates the existing slides and applies the changes to any new slides added to the presentation. The formatting of the text can also be changed on the master slide by selecting the text in the placeholders and making the changes required. For example, if the colour of the placeholder text is changed to blue, the corresponding text on the existing and any new slides will be changed to blue automatically.

The master slide can be used to:

- add a graphic
- change the background theme
- adjust the size of the placeholders
- change the font style, size, and colour.

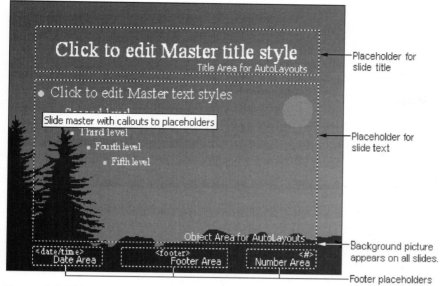

Figure 9.3 Slide master with callouts to placeholders

It is possible for a team to work on the development of a presentation. Through the use of the templates and master slides a team can work individually on different parts of the presentation and then collate their work once it is finished.

Modes of navigation

Navigation through a slideshow may be by the use of a manual or automatic transition method, or through the use of an on-screen button that is then clicked to advance the presentation. Hotspots may also be used to move between slides in the presentation.

Manual

Manual transition involves some form of action from the presenter to move on to the next slide. If the slide contains a number of items then each item can be displayed manually. For example, if the slide contains a bulleted list, then using the manual method, the presenter can perform an action to display each bullet point in turn. Manual navigation is best suited to a presentation given by a speaker to an audience – a verbal presentation. The presenter is able to control when each slide, or item, is displayed, and can tailor the navigation to meet the needs of the audience.

Automatic

A presentation can be set up to run automatically with no intervention required to move on to the next slide. The software can be set up so that the next slide is displayed automatically after a pre-specified time period. The timings must be set to give the audience sufficient time to read the information contained on a slide before the presentation moves on to the next one. The presentation can also be set to restart as soon as it has finished. This navigation method is suitable for presentations where no presenter is involved, such as at an exhibition. Automatic navigation is not suitable for verbal presentations as the presenter may struggle to keep pace with the presentation.

On-screen buttons

A button can be used to move the presentation from one slide to the next. When this method of navigation is used the presentation is interactive. This means that the user of the presentation is interacting with the presentation and is using it to meet their needs. By using this method the user can select the slides viewed and sometimes even select the order of viewing. This method is useful where the user needs to jump to another part of the presentation to view the information they need.

Hotspots

A hotspot is an area on a screen display that responds to a mouse click. This may be a piece of text or a graphic; either will take the user to another page or screen when clicked. A hotspot is normally used in a multimedia presentation.

 A **hotspot** is an area on a screen display that responds to a mouse click.

Questions

1 Describe the disadvantages of using design templates in the production of a presentation.
2 What is a master slide?
3 Identify an appropriate situation where manual slide transition would be used.
4 Identify an appropriate situation where automatic slide transition would be used.
5 Describe **three** different methods of navigating around a slideshow.

Structure

A presentation is made up of a number of slides. When designing a presentation, the structure of the presentation should be developed carefully. There are three main structures a presentation can take. These are:

● linear
● hierarchical
● mesh.

The structure of the presentation should be selected to meet the needs of the content of the presentation and the target audience. The structure of the presentation will provide the routes that can be taken through the presentation. (See Figure 9.4 overleaf).

Activity

Investigate the third structure that can be used for a presentation (the mesh structure). Draw a mesh structure diagram for a presentation.

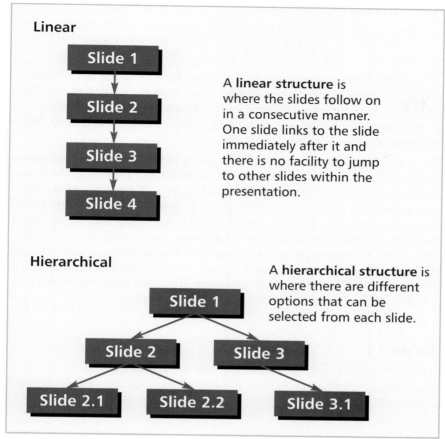

Linear

A **linear structure** is where the slides follow on in a consecutive manner. One slide links to the slide immediately after it and there is no facility to jump to other slides within the presentation.

Hierarchical

A **hierarchical structure** is where there are different options that can be selected from each slide.

Figure 9.4 Linear and hierarchical structures of presentations

Overhead projector transparencies versus presentation software

Presentations can be given with presentation software, using a computer and screen, or by using an overhead projector (OHP) and transparencies (OHTs). Presentation software can be used to create and print OHTs.

There are many benefits to giving the presentation using a screen and computer. The full range of software facilities available can be used when creating the presentation. The presentation can be shown using animation effects and include multimedia elements such as sound and video files. These effects are not possible using OHTs.

The presenter may have a bulleted list of information on a slide which they need to reveal one bullet at a time. As we have seen, using a computer-based presentation it is possible to animate each of the bullets and reveal them one at a time. If OHTs are being used, the presenter will have to cover the slide and slowly reveal the bulleted list one at a time! This does not look very professional and it is possible for the presenter to forget to uncover a bullet.

If the presentation has been created using a hierarchical structure on a computer, then the presenter can use hotspots and hyperlinks to automatically move through the presentation. With OHTs, it is difficult to select the required transparency if a different route through the presentation is required.

Once a presentation has been developed and saved using presentation software then it is relatively easy to edit the presentation. If OHTs are used, then any edits to the presentation will normally mean the presentation having to be reproduced, for all the affected pages.

If a presentation is produced on OHTs then each time the presentation is given the OHTs have to be handled. Over time the quality of the OHTs will begin to diminish until some of them may become unreadable. With presentation software, the quality does not diminish and so the presentation can be used a great many more times.

There are, however, some benefits to using OHTs to give a presentation. The only equipment that is required is an overhead projector. These are relatively inexpensive compared to computers and screens and there is very little that can go wrong with them. Computer-based presentations may also cause a problem if the presenter is travelling and has to show the presentation at many different locations. Each computer, projector and screen may have different instructions and facilities, which may be difficult to understand and learn quickly. In addition, it is possible to write on an OHT in response to audience questions and responses. This is not possible with a computer-based presentation.

Activity

Using the table headings below, identify the advantages and disadvantages of giving a computer-based presentation, and of giving a presentation using OHTs.

	Advantages	Disadvantages
Computer-based		
OHTs		

Questions

1. What are the advantages of using OHTs instead of presentation software?
2. Identify **two** situations where the use of a slideshow on a computer would be more appropriate than using OHTs.

Rules!

If a presentation is carefully designed then it can be an effective tool to communicate information. There are some rules that must be considered when designing a presentation to ensure that the presentation is effective and meets the needs of the presenter and the audience.

1. The font styles and size of the text should meet the needs of the presentation and the audience. There should be no more than three different font styles on each slide in the presentation. More than this and the slides will be difficult to read.
2. The size of the text should be large enough for an audience to be able to read from a distance.

3 When an on-screen presentation is being developed the slide background should contrast with the text colour. Consideration should be given to avoid clashing, garish colour schemes, for example bright green and bright pink, as these can cause eyestrain for the audience and the presenter.

4 The text on the slides should be kept to a minimum. The text contained within the slides should be a summary with the presenter expanding these points in their talk.

5 Graphics should be very carefully selected. A graphic can add impact to the points being made but if too many graphics are used then they will distract the audience.

6 Animation, sound and transition effects should also be carefully considered. As with graphics, these features can add to the impact of the presentation, but if too many are used then they can detract from the content of the presentation.

hint In your exam you will be asked to provide examples. The examples you give **must** be relevant to the context of the question being asked in the examination. If the question is about a car showroom, give an example to do with car showrooms.

End of Chapter 9 tests

Test 1

A teacher is to give a presentation to a group of new students.

1 Describe why the teacher might prefer to use an overhead projector and OHTs for the presentation. [4]

2 Identify and explain **three** advantages of using a computer-based presentation rather than OHTs. [6]

3 Describe **two** methods of moving to the next slide in a computer-based presentation. Identify a situation when each method would be suitable. [6]

4 Describe how templates and wizards could be used to produce the presentation. [6]

5 Describe how sound could be used in the presentation. [2]

Test 2

A manager is to give a presentation to a group of new employees.

1 Describe, giving reasons, **four** features of multimedia software that could be used to produce the presentation. [8]

2 Describe **two** advantages of using multimedia software to create OHTs for the presentation. [4]

3 Describe **two** reasons why the manager would prefer to use a computer to deliver the presentation. [4]

4 Describe how master slides could be used in the production of this presentation. [4]

5 Describe how video clips could be used to enhance the presentation. [2]

10 | Graphics

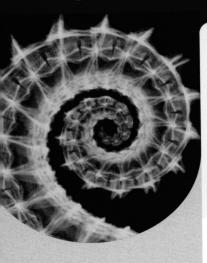

Objectives

Your objectives for this chapter are to:

◎ describe specified features found in graphics software

◎ analyse graphic images and explain how they are created

◎ describe the differences between bitmap and vector-based graphics and evaluate their suitability for given applications

◎ explain how graphics libraries are used in applications

◎ discuss the advantages and disadvantages of using clip art and image libraries

Keep these objectives in mind as you work through the chapter.

What are graphics?

The term 'graphics' is defined as:

'Pictures on a computer display, or the process of creating pictures on a computer display.'

(*The New Penguin Dictionary of Computing*, Dick Pountain, Penguin Books Ltd, 2001)

Specified features found in graphics software

Software packages used to create, edit and manipulate images have a range of built-in features. The OCR AS specification covers ten of the most commonly used features that may be available. There are many more features available for the manipulation of graphics in a variety of software packages.

Fill

This is filling an object with colour. The colour can be constant or it can have a gradient or an effect. The fill tool can also be used to replace colour. All pixels of one colour can be replaced with those of another, using fill.

Shade

This is the difference between light and dark. With 3D modelling packages, the light source can be moved around and the shading is automatically calculated by the package, based on the intensity of the light (distance of object from source) and the size of the object.

Layering

This is when one image is placed over the top of another. This creates an overlap. If the top image is made transparent then what is underneath can show through. It is possible to send layers to the back, to the front or to move one layer backwards or forwards. Layering allows you to build up images in the same way as an artist does on paper.

Fill is a command in graphics software that allows an enclosed area to be filled with a particular colour or pattern.

Shade is a tool in graphics software that allows the application of shading to an object.

Layering is when one image is placed over the top of another.

Brightness

Brightness is the total amount of light in a colour. Zero brightness is black and 100% is white, intermediate values are 'light' or 'dark' colours.

Contrast

The contrast is the difference between light and shade in an image. Changing the contrast changes the amount of shading between areas. It can be used to sharpen or blur an image, and to make colours appear more saturated, and make specific areas stand out.

Size

The image can be enlarged or shrunk. This can be done proportionally or disproportionally. The size of the canvas can be increased – this places the background colour around the image and can be used as a frame.

Orientation

This is the direction of the canvas – portrait (longer length than width) or landscape (longer width than length).

Negative

Creating a negative image replaces each pixel colour with its opposite on the colour wheel. The brightness value of the pixel changes to 255 minus the original value. Zero becomes 255, and 50 becomes 205 and so on. The new image is like a photographic negative. This function can be used to create a positive image from a scanned negative.

Specified features found in graphics software

Brightness is the total amount of light in a colour.

Contrast is the difference between light and shade in an image.

Orientation is the direction of the canvas – either 'portrait' or 'landscape'.

a

b

c

d

Figure 10.1 a) Original image, **b)** Effects of contrast, **c)** Effects of brightness, **d)** Effects of negative

Soften

Soften smoothes transitions and decreases contrast by averaging the pixels next to the hard edges of defined lines and areas where there are significant colour transitions. It is used for photo retouching.

Sharpen

Sharpen produces the opposite effect of soften, by increasing the contrast between adjacent pixels where there are significant colour contrasts, usually at the edges of objects. It lightens the light pixels and darkens the dark pixels.

Components of graphic images

There are many different ways in which graphics can be created.

The entire image could be created from scratch – the artist could set up the canvas, create backgrounds, and use lines, shapes, and so on to produce a picture or import a pre-existing graphic such as clip art as part of the image.

A template could be used as a starting point and then edited to make it individual.

An existing picture, for example, a scanned image, an image from a digital camera or clip art, could be edited to create a new picture.

To create and edit graphic images an editing package is needed. To edit an existing image, a method of capturing the original image is also required.

Graphical images may be made up of many different components. Each component is manipulated to ensure that the final image meets the needs of the creator and the target audience.

Figure 10.2 Graphical images may be made up of many different components

The graphic shown in Figure 10.2 is a very simple combination of components. A rectangle has been used as the outer shape of the logo; this was created using the AutoShape facility. The text 'The Pie Shop' has been created using a WordArt facility with the basket being taken from a clip art file. The logo has then been filled with a colour with the text being edited to be in a different colour.

By analysing the components that make a graphic it may be possible to identify the way in which the graphic was created. The graphic shown in Figure 10.2 was created from scratch.

Bitmap and vector-based graphics

There are two main ways in which graphics are stored; these are as a bitmapped graphic or as a vector-based graphic.

Bitmap graphics

These are also known as raster graphics. A bitmap graphic is made up of pixels. Each bit in a stored, true black-and-white graphic tells the computer whether a pixel is to be switched on or off (1 or 0). The number of bits representing each pixel dictates how many colours are available to the user. If a pixel is represented by 4 bits in a black and

Bitmap graphics are made up of a number of dots or pixels.

white graphic, then 16 different shades of grey are available, while 8 bits per pixel means that 256 different shades of grey can be used.

Most graphics are stored in colour. These graphics combine the primary colours of red, green and blue to produce a palette of different shades. Each primary colour, if represented by 8 bits, can have a value between 0 and 256, depending on the shade of the colour. When combined this gives 256 x 256 x 256 = 16,777,216, i.e. more than 16 million possible shades.

Figure 10.3 The values of red, green and blue can be allocated to a specific pixel

Primary colour	Value
Red	190
Green	55
Blue	137

Each pixel has two key properties associated with it: a position on the grid that makes up the image and a colour value. These properties are stored as data in the computer's memory. When the graphic needs to be displayed the data held in the bit-mapped file is used to reconstruct the graphic.

A bitmap graphic will be produced when an image is taken from a scanner or a digital camera.

Bit-mapped files appear in a number of different formats. Some of these are shown in Figure 10.4.

Figure 10.4 The different file formats of bit-mapped graphics

Format	Description
BMP	Bit Mapped Picture. The standard file format used with Windows applications.
GIF	Graphics Interchange Format. These files are often used on web sites especially in their animated format (animated GIFs). They have a 256 colour limit (8 bits per pixel) and use a lossless compression algorithm to save on the amount of memory used.
JPEG	Joint Photographic Experts Group. These are also frequently used on the Internet. JPEGs are often used when good-quality photographic images need to be stored, as they can store 24 bits per pixel and have the capability to store 16 million colours. There are different JPEG formats, which relate to the level of compression used.
TIF / TIFF	Tagged Image File Format. The file structure here is more complex than some of the other formats but this format can be used on several different platforms.

Vector-based graphics

Vector-based graphics are also known as object-orientated graphics and work in a different way to bitmap graphics. Rather than being stored as data relating to a grid of pixels, this type of graphic is stored as geometric-based data. The file for a vector-based graphic contains

Vector graphics are represented by objects or geometric shapes that can be moved around the screen and positioned.

mathematical data that defines the key properties of every element in the graphic. Instead of individual pixels storing the required data, vector-based graphics work on the basis of lines, where drawing starts from a certain point central to the image.

If, for example, there is a straight line in the graphic then the data in the file will define its starting point, length, thickness, location within the graphic, and so on. The file data, also known as the display list, will also specify the order in which each component will be displayed. This is also known as the hierarchy of the objects.

Although a vector-based graphic is stored according to its mathematical properties, it is still displayed as a temporary bit-mapped graphic.

Vector-based graphics are mainly used for design purposes and are usually used in computer-aided design (CAD) programs. Vector-based graphics are used by architects and designers who need to adjust the size, perspective and proportions of their diagrams. A vector-based graphic can be resized with no distortion occurring. Vector-based graphics are essential when CAD/CAM systems are being used. This is when the whole or part of the graphic is being used as the basis for instructions to automated machines.

Bitmap or vector?

Figure 10.5 shows the main differences between bitmap and vector-based graphics.

Figure 10.5 The differences between bitmap and vector-based graphics

Bitmap	Vector
When resized there is a lowering of image quality. The image will become blurry and can appear 'pixellated'.	Can be re-sized or re-scaled with no loss of definition.
As each pixel in the image has to be saved individually a bitmap graphic file can be very large.	The size of a vector-based graphic file is relatively smaller than a bitmap graphic file for the same size of image.
The components of the graphic are only stored as pixels with their attributes.	Every component of the graphic is described by its features (length, colour, thickness, etc).
Bitmap graphics are more consistent with the general computing environment, i.e. display and printing devices tend to use a series of dots to define images and text.	Vector-based graphics can be grouped; this keeps the components in the same position relative to each other.
Bitmap graphics are popular as they deal well with complex, highly detailed images such as photographs. As each pixel is an addressable unit, it is possible to make subtle changes to the properties of a graphic.	The facility for producing simple vector-based graphics is often included as part of a word processing program. These allow the user to create simple graphics such as squares and lines that can enhance the presentation of a document.
Bitmap files can be compressed.	Vector-based graphic files cannot be compressed.
The screen resolution of the display equipment can affect the display of the colours used in a bitmap graphic.	The processing power required to display a vector-based graphic on display equipment is high.
Editing of bitmap graphics relates to changing the properties of the pixels in the graphic as a whole or an area of it.	Individual elements that make up a vector-based graphic can be edited independently, e.g. moved, resized, copied.

Graphics libraries

Graphics software for specialist applications, such as kitchen design and map making (cartography) provide libraries of graphical images and symbols that are commonly used in the application. For example, a kitchen-design software package will have standard symbols for cupboards and kitchen appliances (cookers, dishwashers, and so on), which are used when planning and designing a kitchen layout.

These specialist software applications are developed with the involvement of manufacturers and professional bodies. For example, specialist cartography software would, most likely, have been developed in consultation with the Ordnance Survey and Land Registry to ensure that industry-standard symbols are available. This approach also means that all software relating to the production of maps uses the same symbols with the same meaning.

Clip art and image libraries

Clip art libraries contain images that are either supplied 'free' with other software packages or at a cost from a software manufacturer. The clip art images can be edited or used as they are.

Clip art libraries contain pre-drawn pictures that can be copied and edited.

Figure 10.6 Advantages and disadvantages of clip art

Advantages	Disadvantages
Images are readily available.	Choice of images is limited to what is available.
Images are available immediately.	The quality of the images ranges from very poor to good.
The use of clip art can reduce the cost of the design process, e.g. when designing a logo a designer may not have to be employed.	Clip art is neither original nor unique.
Extra equipment, such as scanners and digital cameras, does not have to be purchased.	Clip art images, especially if taken from the Internet, may be subject to copyright.

Image libraries are collections of small images (thumbnails) based around a topic showing a preview or a representation of the actual image. When the image is clicked then the actual image is shown.

Using image libraries and thumbnails enables many images to be shown together, although the quality of the images may be poor. Images that are alike can be grouped together. It is also possible to add descriptions to the images so that they can then be searched. It is not always possible to tell whether the actual image is of a better quality or a larger size than the preview or thumbnail image. If the image library holds a large number of images then it can also take a long time to load.

hint In your exam you will be asked to provide examples. The examples you give **must** be relevant to the context of the question being asked in the examination. If the question is about the use of graphics by an architect then give an example to do with architects.

Questions

1 What is a graphic library?
2 How is a graphic library used in cartography?
3 What is an image library?
4 What is clip art?

End of Chapter 10 tests

Test 1

A school needs a logo for their new 'Eat Healthy' snack bar.

1 State **two** advantages and **two** disadvantages of using an image library to select the logo. [4]

2 The image library is displayed as a set of thumbnail images. Describe the benefits of using thumbnails. [6]

3 The selected logo could be modified by using brightness and contrast. Describe what is meant by these terms. [4]

Test 2

A poster is to be created for advertising the local pre-school group.

1 State **two** advantages and **two** disadvantages of using clip art in this poster. [4]

2 The clip art can be either a vector-based graphic or a bitmap graphic. Describe vector-based graphics and bitmap graphics. [6]

3 The clip art graphic could be modified using fill and shade. Describe what is meant by these terms. [4]

Internet

Objectives

Your objectives for this chapter are to:

◎ compare web-authoring software with standard applications software for creating web pages

◎ evaluate the use of static information sources compared to dynamic sources, including the use of indexes and keyword searches

◎ explain the purpose of filtering access to information that can be obtained over the Internet.

Keep these objectives in mind as you work through the chapter.

The Internet

The Internet is, basically, a very large network of computers that provide the facility to link computers worldwide using telecommunications systems, for example, telephone lines. The Internet allows fast communication between people, the transfer of data between computers and the distribution of information.

There are two main approaches to creating web pages, and these are covered by the OCR ICT AS specification. They are:

● using web-authoring software
● using standard applications packages and converting to HTML.

Web-authoring software

Web-authoring software enables the creation of web pages. The software has built-in functions to enable well-designed web pages to be created with a variety of features to meet the needs of the user.

The user interface of web-authoring software is similar to that of a standard applications package but there are some functions that are different, for example, changing the font style. Some technical ability is, therefore, needed and training may be required to use the software.

Web pages are visual representations of code, generally HTML (Hypertext Markup Language). Most web-authoring software packages do not require the user to write any code. Pages are created using a graphical interface, where objects are dragged and dropped on to a page template. It is then possible to access and amend the code if the user has sufficient knowledge to do so.

The majority of web-authoring software packages are aimed at the general user. Templates are available in the packages (usually an outline web site structure that just require details to be added) and wizards are also included (a series of questions/dialogue boxes that take the user through a procedure one step at a time).

The user can determine the final look and structure of a web page through formatting. Most web-authoring software packages offer formatting facilities such as:

 **Web authoring software** provides tools to enable the creation of web pages without the need for detailed knowledge of a web programming language.

- colour options for background, text, lines and boxes
- font and point size options for text
- the positioning of objects on the web page and layout items such as columns, tables and forms.

As well as text and layout items, web pages contain graphical objects. A web-authoring software package will allow the user to access these objects, for example by providing a clip art library. The user can then import these graphics into a web page and manipulate them, so they meet the needs of the web page and its users. Other objects, such as animation, video and sound clips, can also be used in the creation of web pages.

Web pages normally contain links to other pages within the site or to other related and linked sites. These are hyperlinks. When the user activates these hyperlinks, a request is sent for the linked page to be downloaded. The web-authoring software package will allow the user to create and add new links to their page(s). The hyperlinks may show the URL (Uniform Resource Locator) directly, or they may be activated by clicking on a graphic.

Many web pages allow user interaction. The web page may contain an interactive form. This form may allow the user of the web page to, for example, register their details or place an order. This facility requires the use of CGI (Common Gateway Interface) script. Most web-authoring software packages will enable the creator of the web page to produce forms without having to write any code.

Standard applications package

Another approach to creating web pages is to use a standard applications package and use the inbuilt facility to convert the document to a web page. This is a quick and simple method of distributing a document on a web site, which requires very little knowledge of web-authoring and HTML. Also, as very little technical ability is needed no training should be necessary.

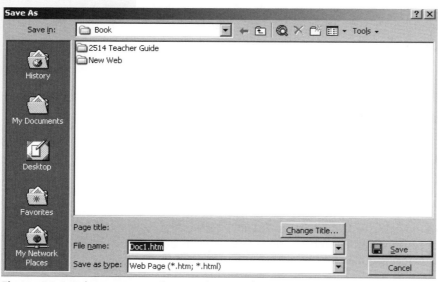

The pages are created in the standard applications package, saved using the web-page option and then viewed using a browser. The screenshot in Figure 11.1 shows the option of saving a document as a web page.

Figure 11.1 A document can be saved as a web page

Comparison between web-authoring software and standard applications software to develop web pages

Advantages of using web-authoring software

- The exact effects required can be developed directly.
- Wizards for specific tasks are built in – creating HTML tables, for example.
- It has WYSIWYG (What You See Is What You Get) – the layout on the screen is what will appear. Some packages allow the representation of different screen sizes and different browsers.
- Some packages include web site management tools, for example to assist the user to check versions of their pages as they progress.
- A site manager can be used; with this facility, if the name of a page is changed then all links to that page within the site are automatically updated.
- With specialist software, code samples/scripting language can be integrated and tested. These can then be integrated into other packages within the authoring software – you can integrate Flash® and Fireworks® into Dreamweaver®, for example.
- Editing of the code can be done by either using the WYSIWYG feature or editing the HTML directly.

Disadvantages of using web-authoring software

- Some degree of knowledge and technical ability is required as not all concepts from word processing will apply, for example, changing the size of the font is performed differently.
- Web-authoring software packages can be more expensive to purchase than a standard applications package.

Advantages of using standard applications software

- Very little technical knowledge is required. If a standard word processor can be used then a web page can be easily created and saved using the automatic conversion facility.
- It is likely that a standard applications package will already be installed, so there will not be any additional cost.

Disadvantages of using standard applications software

- It is very difficult to get the page to look exactly how it is wanted, as this method of creating web pages is not truly WYSIWYG.
- The code that is created is 'messy' – it is bloated and often not very good or compatible with all browsers.
- Limited tools are available – there is likely to be no site management or uploading tool, very few wizards and no tools to assist in script generation.

Static and dynamic information sources

An information source is a repository of information that can be accessed when required. There are two main types of information source – static and dynamic.

A static information source is one that once created does not change. A dynamic information source is regularly updated.

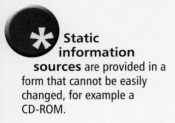

Static information sources are provided in a form that cannot be easily changed, for example a CD-ROM.

Dynamic information sources can be constantly updated, and include the World Wide Web.

Static information sources include books and CD-ROMs. Dynamic sources include the World Wide Web.

With static information sources, the information contained does not change. This means that it can be found when needed. If a teacher creates a worksheet based on a static source they know that the student will be able to find the information. Web sites can be static. A web site that is static can only supply information that is written into the code and this information will not change unless the change is written into the code. When a web browser requests a specific static web page, a server returns the page to the browser and the user only gets whatever information is contained in the HTML code.

The information stored on a CD-ROM is also static. Once the information is burned to the CD-ROM it cannot be changed. A common use of static information and CD-ROMs is an encyclopaedia. Companies may also use CD-ROMs to promote their products by producing a catalogue or brochure on a CD-ROM and sending it to all their customers or clients.

It is likely that static information sources have gone through some editing process – if it is a book or a CD-ROM there is a rigorous system for checking the data. The end result is content that can be relied upon to be accurate.

A dynamic source can frequently change. A web site that once existed can vanish and even if the web site is still present, the content may have changed. Dynamic information is information that changes or can be changed. A dynamic web page contains content that a user can interact with, such as information that is tied to a database. The user can request that the information, such as ticket availability or product information, be retrieved from a database.

Anyone with a computer and a telephone line can create a web site. They can put whatever they want on the web site and it can be viewed worldwide. Therefore, material posted on the web may not always be correct, and there may not have been a rigorous editing process (or indeed, any editing at all). Any information found on the web needs to be treated with caution until it is verified by a separate source.

A book or a CD-ROM (static) has limited accessibility. Only one person can see a single copy of a book and possession of the CD-ROM is required to view its contents. Information on web sites, on the other hand, is accessible by thousands of people simultaneously.

Comparison of CD-ROMs and the Internet

There are advantages and disadvantages to information being held in a static form, on a CD-ROM, and in a dynamic form on the Internet.

Figure 11.2 lists the differences between holding information on a CD-ROM or on the Internet.

Figure 11.2 The differences between holding data on a CD-ROM and on the Internet

CD-ROM	The Internet
There is a limited amount of information available.	The WWW has a large volume of information.
Users do not require access to the Internet.	Only people with Internet access can access the data.
The information should be reliable.	The information is not always reliable.
A suitable computer with a CD-ROM drive is required.	The user does not need a CD-ROM drive.
Data cannot be upgraded very quickly.	Data can be upgraded very quickly. The data is up-to-date.
The CD-ROM can be scratched/broken or lost/stolen.	
Software to search the data on the CD-ROM can be included with the CD-ROM along with any necessary additional software.	The user may not have the correct version of the software, or all the required software installed.
If there are errors, erratum notices would have to be sent round to purchasers.	The WWW has many different opinions, and material may not be accurate or corrected.
There is a cost involved in producing, selling and dispatching the CD-ROMs.	Can reach a large variety of people with minimal cost.
CD-ROMs can take time to arrive if sent.	People come to the web site rather than the CD-ROM being sent.
Many CD-ROMs may need to be looked at to find the required information.	Hyperlinks can lead the individual to related sites and material may be located in a short period of time.

Activity

Using the table headings below, identify the advantages and disadvantages of information being held on a CD-ROM and on the Internet.

	Advantages	Disadvantages
CD-ROMs		
The Internet		

Questions

1 What are the advantages of using web-authoring software to create web pages?

2 What are the advantages of using a word processor to create web pages?

3 How is the Internet a dynamic source of data?

4 What are the advantages to a company in producing its catalogue on CD-ROM rather than on the Internet?

5 What are the advantages of using the Internet rather than a CD-ROM to search for information?

Indexes and keyword searches

One of the most useful features included with any book is the index. The index is a list of keywords that appear in the book and the pages on which they appear. It is possible to look at the index, find the keyword, turn to the page and find the entry. Web sites contain linked pages and many web sites do not contain an index. To find what you want requires patience and a lot of luck. Indexes are created to speed up searches. This is how many search engines work. However, a search engine on the Internet will not contain details of every page that exists, whereas an index on a CD-ROM will have all details of all pages contained within it.

There are three main ways of finding information on the Internet:

- typing a web address and going directly to the page (or using an appropriate link)
- using a web directory
- using a search engine.

Typing a web address

If you know the address you can type it into the browser and go directly to the page. If you are on a linked or related page there may be a hyperlink to click that will take you to a relevant page. Some sites run 'rings'. These are links to sites that have a similar content.

Using a web directory

A web directory is similar to an online 'Yellow Pages' – it has categories and headings and each entry has been placed in that category or under that heading. A web directory is likely to have fewer pages available than a search engine but the relevance of each entry will be very high.

Using a search engine

The web uses keyword searches to locate information. The Internet contains vast numbers of web sites and so, to effectively find information, search engines and keywords should be used. A keyword is a word searched for in a search command. Keywords are not searched in any particular order.

Search engines contain databases that include details of the web sites that have been listed and the keywords related to each page within the sites. These databases are being continually updated as new sites appear on the Internet. Through the use of a search engine and keywords the search engine will find a list of sites matching the keywords.

The search engine searches each web page, and a list of the keywords is built up. Pages are given points – the number of other pages linking to a page and the relevance of the keywords to the search, increase the number of points. Keyword searches can be single words, more than one word, phrases or exclusions. To narrow down searches, parameter queries can be used. Operators such as AND, NOT and OR can also be used to narrow searches. Some examples are given in Figure 11.3.

Figure 11.3 Examples of searches

Search	Meaning
OCR	Searches just for OCR
OCR AND ICT	Searches for the words OCR and ICT anywhere on the page
'OCR ICT'	Searches for the words OCR and ICT together as a phrase
OCR ICT NOT GCSE	Searches for pages containing OCR and ICT but not the word GCSE.

It is possible to use search criteria when searching both CD-ROMs and the Internet.

Questions

1 A CD-ROM is a static information source. Identify **two** other static information sources.

2 Explain how a CD-ROM, once it has been installed on a computer, can be a dynamic data source.

3 Describe **two** advantages of using a CD-ROM instead of a web site for researching information.

4 Describe **two** advantages of using a web site instead of a CD-ROM for researching information.

5 Describe the differences between a web directory service and a search facility.

6 Describe how a user could reduce the number of their search results.

Filtering access

Filtering is the restriction of the information that is available. Completely free access to any information means that there are no restrictions on what you can see. However, there will always be restrictions on what you can see – some may be deliberately filtered, and some may be filtered accidentally.

Different browsers can view different web pages – for example, some browsers cannot see frames and so any information contained in frames is filtered from these browsers . Some people, who do not like Microsoft, have created web sites that cannot be viewed by Microsoft browsers – another example of filtering.

There is also legal filtering – some information and pictures are illegal and the service provider will remove them – that is, filter them. This occurs more with newsgroups than with Internet sites, although

Internet server providers (ISPs) will remove sites from their servers if they are illegal.

Software can also filter sites – it is possible to remove advertisements, pop-up windows and even graphics from sites to speed up the delivery of the content.

The most common form of filtering is that of stopping individuals from accessing web sites which contain inappropriate content. These sites can be pornographic, violent, dangerous or incite people to inappropriate (for example, racist) behaviour.

Filtering systems can work by looking at the web title, searching for excluded words on the page or by the use of lists.

There are two types of lists – open and closed. An open list allows access to everything except what is on the list – it contains the excluded sites. A closed list allows access to everything on the list but nothing else. (This is known as the walled-garden approach.)

Intelligent filtering means the assigning of a points system to words, captions and page information. When a certain level of points is reached, the page is banned.

hint In your exam you will be asked to provide examples. The examples you give **must** be relevant to the context of the question being asked in the examination. If the question is about a garden centre, give an example to do with garden centres.

Question

Why is Internet access sometimes filtered in schools?

End of Chapter 11 tests

Test 1

A company currently uses CD-ROMs sent to all their customers to advertise their books. They are considering advertising the books on the Internet.

1 Compare using a web site with using CD-ROMs for the purpose of advertising the books. [6]

2 The company has decided to develop a web site to advertise the books. Evaluate the use of a word processor for this task. [6]

3 Describe **three** benefits of advertising the books on the Internet. [6]

Test 2

A report is to be presented to the board of directors of a large supermarket chain.

1 A member of staff could use the Internet or a CD-ROM to perform the research for this report. Explain the advantages of using the Internet rather than a CD-ROM for this task. [8]

2 The report will be published on the Internet in two versions – one for the management of the supermarket and the other for the customers. Explain why two reports are published. [6]

3 Explain the use of a keyword search for the supermarket's web site, for example would typing in the word 'supermarket' be useful? [4]

12 | Databases

Objectives

Your objectives for this chapter are to:

◎ identify tables, records, fields, primary keys and foreign keys, and define relationships between entities

◎ identify the characteristics of data in first normal form, second normal form and third normal form

◎ describe the advantages of normalisation

◎ describe the components of a data dictionary

◎ explain the use and design considerations of tailored data-entry screens, reports and queries for meeting user requirements

◎ describe different types of queries and explain when they might be used

◎ compare a spreadsheet to a database management system as a means of storing and handling data.

Keep these objectives in mind as you work through the chapter.

Tables, records, fields and keys

Databases involve a large amount of terminology and it is essential that the key terms are understood before progressing to the later sections of this chapter.

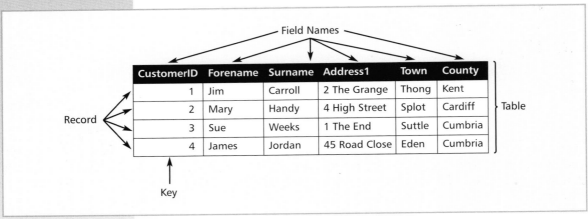

Figure 12.1 Key terms of a database

CustomerID	Forename	Surname	Address1	Town	County
1	Jim	Carroll	2 The Grange	Thong	Kent
2	Mary	Handy	4 High Street	Splot	Cardiff
3	Sue	Weeks	1 The End	Suttle	Cumbria
4	James	Jordan	45 Road Close	Eden	Cumbria

Table

Tables contain data about 'things', for example, students, orders, purchases, customers, suppliers, and so on. A table is a data structure made up of rows and columns that contains data about the items.

A table is a very specific and regulated item within a database. It is also known as a relation. The following must be met for the data structure to be called a table:

● The table must have a unique name.

● Each field/column must have a unique name.

- Each record/row must be unique.
- Each data item within a field must contain only a single data item.

The order of the records within the table does not matter. The order of the fields does not matter.

Record

A record is a single row within a table. It is a collection of data about a single item or a single event. For example, a record might be about an individual – a customer, an order that has been placed, an item in stock or an appointment.

Records are made up of fields and can contain different data types. In a table, each record must be unique.

Field

A field is an individual data item within a record. Each field within a record should have a unique name. A field should only contain a single data item.

Fields have individual data types and can have their own validation.

Records are rows in database tables that contain all the data about one individual or object that the record describes.

Fields are individual lines in a database record. The equivalent in the practical database of an attribute in the theoretical database.

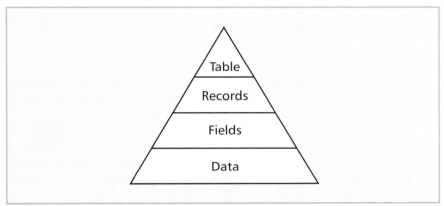

Figure 12.2 A table is made up of records, records are made up of fields and fields are made up of data

Keys

There are several different keys that can be applied to a table. The most important key is the primary key. The primary key is a field in the table that allows each record to be uniquely identified. Every value of the primary key must be unique.

The **key field** uniquely identifies a record.

Forename	Surname
Jim	Smith
John	Adams
Jim	Smith
Jan	Carroll
Mary	High

Wrong
Neither of these fields is suitable as a primary key as there are duplicate values.

ID	Forename	Surname
1	Jim	Smith
2	John	Adams
3	Jim	Smith
4	Jan	Carroll
5	Mary	High

Correct
ID can be the primary key as it has a unique value in each record.

Figure 12.3 The primary key is a field in the table that allows each record to be uniquely identified

Primary key

The primary key can be of two types:

- simple
- compound/composite.

A simple primary key is one made up of a single field only – like ID in Figure 12.3. A compound primary key is one that combines more than one field to make a unique value.

In Figure 12.4, a student can only be in one place at a time. Therefore, combining the student name, date and period gives a unique value. These three fields could be combined to make a composite primary key.

Student	Date	Period	Present
H Top	12/12/2004	1	Y
S Small	12/12/2004	1	Y
P Andres	12/12/2004	1	N
H Top	12/12/2004	2	Y

Figure 12.4 Three fields can be combined to form a composite primary key

Secondary key

A secondary key is a field that is identified as being suitable for indexing the data. It is used to sort the data in a different order to the primary key. A table can have many secondary keys identified.

Foreign key

A foreign key is used to link tables together. A foreign key is a primary key in one table that is linked to a field in another table. The data types of the fields that are linked must be the same.

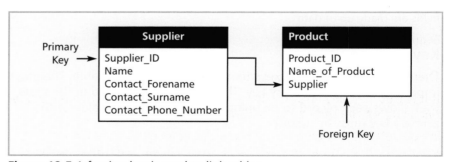

Figure 12.5 A foreign key is used to link tables

Questions

1 Identify the **four** requirements of a table.
2 What is the difference between a field and record?
3 Identify **three** properties of a field.
4 What is the role of the primary key?
5 Describe the difference between a simple primary key and a composite/compound primary key.

6 What is the role of a secondary key?

7 Using an example, describe how a foreign key works.

Relationships between entities

Entities are difficult to define. Peter Chen, who introduced the entity relationship model in 1977, defined an entity as 'a thing which can be distinctly identified'! The idea of an entity is central to understanding entity relationship models. There are some general observations we can make about entities that can help.

- The world is made up of entities.
- Entities can be classified into entity types:
  - For example, we can identify EMPLOYEE as an entity and instances of the entity EMPLOYEE would be individual employees.
  - It may help to view the entity as the table and the entity type as a record.
- Each entity of the same type has a set of properties that can be applied to the entity type:
  - For example, the entity EMPLOYEE has a salary and a department where they work. This applies to every entity type.
- Entities can be linked to each other by means of a relationship.

There are three types of relationship that can be identified as existing between entities:

Relationship	Symbol used
One – One	——┼———┼——
One – Many	——┼———<
Many – Many	>——<

Figure 12.6 Relationships between entities

One–one relationship

If it is true that any instance of the entity X can be associated with only one instance of entity Y then the relationship is one-one.

When determining one-one relationships you need to consider the time scale and not be concerned with historical values (see Figure 12.7).

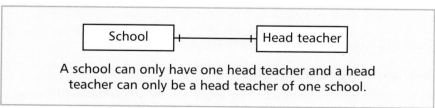

A school can only have one head teacher and a head teacher can only be a head teacher of one school.

Figure 12.7 A one–one relationship

Historically, a school is likely to have had many head teachers and a head teacher may have held a post as a head teacher at a previous school. It is therefore easier to discount what may have happened historically when considering relationships.

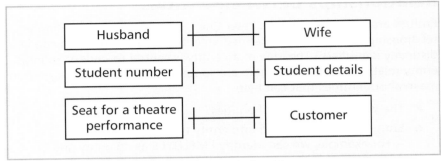

Figure 12.8 Other examples of one–one relationships

In database design it is uncommon to find a one-one relationship. If there is a one-one relationship then it is likely (but not always so) that the tables would be combined.

One–many relationship

This is the most common type of relationship between entities. A single instance of an entity can be associated with many instances of another entity. Within the relationship, it is true that many instances of an entity are associated with only a single instance of another entity.

When looking at entities and relationships, it is necessary to look in detail at the situation as the relationship between similar entities could be different in different situations.

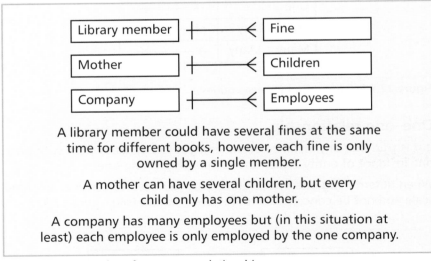

A library member could have several fines at the same time for different books, however, each fine is only owned by a single member.

A mother can have several children, but every child only has one mother.

A company has many employees but (in this situation at least) each employee is only employed by the one company.

Figure 12.9 Examples of one–many relationships

Many–many relationship

In this case, many instances of an entity can be associated with many instances of another entity (see Figure 12.10).

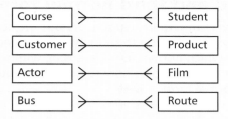

A student in a school takes many courses. A course has many students registered on it.

A customer can purchase many products and a product can be purchased by many customers.

An actor has been in many films and a film has many actors.

A bus has many different routes that it travels on. A route has many different buses that do the same route.

Figure 12.10 Examples of many–many relationships

Many–many relationships break the rules of normalisation. There should be no many–many relationships in a normalised database. If you have a many–many relationship a link entity needs to be added. This is an entity that sits between the two current entities and has a one–many relationship with each.

Each course has many students registered on it and a student can attend many courses and is in many registration books.

A customer can place many orders and a product can appear in many orders.

An actor can be a cast member of many films and a film has many cast members.

A bus goes on many trips but for each trip there will only be one bus doing it.

Many trips will cover the same route (at different times) and one route will appear in many different trips.

Figure 12.11 Link entities are added to many–many relationships

Questions

1 Describe the degree of the relationship between:
   a) person to birth certificate
   b) film to academy award
   c) car to owner
   d) teacher to school
   and explain your reasoning.
2 Resolve the following many–many relationships:
   a) additives to plants
   b) books to authors
   c) library member to books
   and explain your reasoning.
3 Describe the characteristics of an entity.
4 Describe the **three** types of relationship.

185

First, second and third normal form

The examination will not require you to carry out the actual process of normalisation. It will require you to know the rules of normalisation and be able to identify which normal form data is in, with reasons. This section does not, therefore, cover how to normalise data but what to look for in each normal form.

Normalisation

Normalisation is the process of defining a data model.

Normalisation is a process that data undergoes in order to reduce redundancy and inconsistency, and to make it easier to use and maintain. There are specific rules attached to each normal form.

Before a table gets to first normal form it is in unnormalised form – UNF or 0NF.

First normal form (1NF)

The **first normal form** is the first stage of normalising a data model. It involves ensuring that all data items are atomic and that there are no repeating fields.

A table is in 1NF if every data value in a field is atomic (that is, the data value cannot be broken down any further) and each record does not contain repeating data.

Name
Jim Smith

Wrong
Two data items

Forename	Surname
Jim	Smith

Correct
Single data item

Figure 12.12 Atomic means that the data cannot be broken down any further

As defined earlier, a table has its own set of characteristics:

- Each row must be uniquely identifiable.
- Each field name must be unique

For each row to be uniquely identifiable, it needs a primary key. When showing a table with data in it, the primary key is identified by putting an * next to the field name.

All the field names used in a table must be unique – they cannot be copied.

StudentID *	Forename	Surname	Class	Test	Test	Test
1	John	White	11IT	A	B	A
2	Adam	Green	10DT	C	C	B
3	Lorna	Red	11Mu	B	D	E

Figure 12.13

The table in Figure 12.13 cannot be in 1NF because the last three field names are the same.

To be in 1NF there must be no repeating data in a record. What constitutes repeating data?

As you can see, the data in the test fields is repeated. This also causes problems – what happens if there are more than three tests, for example?

The table needs redrawing to meet the criteria for 1NF.

Checks for 1NF:

- Does the table have a primary key?
- Is each field name unique?
- Are there any repeating fields in a single record?
- Is all the data within a field atomic?

ID*	StudentID	Forename	Surname	Class	Test
1	1	John	White	11IT	A
2	1	John	White	11IT	B
3	1	John	White	11IT	A
4	2	Adam	Green	10DT	C
5	2	Adam	Green	10DT	C
6	2	Adam	Green	10DT	B
7	3	Lorna	Red	11Mu	B
8	3	Lorna	Red	11Mu	D
9	3	Lorna	Red	11Mu	E

Figure 12.14 The table in 1NF

Second normal form (2NF)

A table is in 2NF if it is 1NF and all its non-key attributes are dependent on the entire primary key. (Or to give it the technical definition, every non-key attribute is fully dependent on the primary key.)

2NF is based on functional dependence. A data item Y is functionally dependent on data item Z if, once you know the value of Z there is only one possible value for Y at a given time (see Figure 12.15).

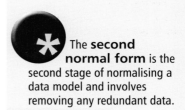

The **second normal form** is the second stage of normalising a data model and involves removing any redundant data.

OrderNo*	CustomerID	Product	Quanitity	Date
1	Jones Toys	A4 Pad	5	18/05/2005
2	Adams Hats	Blue Pen	20	20/05/2005
3	Mike's Stereos	A5 Pad	12	20/05/2005
4	Paint R Us	Carbon Paper	8	21/05/2005

Figure 12.15

In Figure 12.15, the OrderNo is the primary key. If the OrderNo is known then you can find out the customer who placed the order, what they ordered, how many and when. By knowing the one field value, it is possible to work out the value of all the others.

If the table only has a single key as a primary key then the table is already in 2NF.

In Figure 12.16 suppliers supply parts to a company. Each city is given a delivery value based on how long it takes goods to arrive. Each item of stock is only supplied by one company. There is a compound primary key of SupplierID and StockNumber.

SupplierID*	Delivery	City	StockNumber*	Quantity
A10	10	London	P1232	1254
B10	15	Paris	H4365	5476
C10	20	Berlin	J4587	2546
C10	20	Berlin	J4586	6453

Figure 12.16

Functional dependence:

- The delivery is only dependent on the SupplierID.
- The city where the supplier is, is only dependent on the SupplierID.
- The stock they supply is only dependent on the SupplierID.

However, the quantity of each part supplied is dependent on both who the supplier is and what part has been supplied.

This means that the table in Figure 12.16 is not in 2NF – not every non-key field is dependent on the entire primary key – in fact the only non-key field to be dependent on the entire primary key is quantity.

To be in 2NF the table would need to be broken down (see Figure 12.17):

SupplierID*	Delivery	City
A10	10	London
B10	15	Paris
C10	20	Berlin

SupplierID*	StockNumber*	Quantity
A10	P1232	1254
B10	H4365	5476
C10	J4587	2546
C10	J4586	6453

Figure 12.17

Now, every non-key field is entirely dependent on the primary key.

Checks for 2NF:

- Is the table in 1NF?
- Does it have a single primary key (that is, is it already in 2NF)?
- Can all of the non-key fields be found out by using the entire primary key?

Third normal form

The **third normal form** is the third stage of normalisation and involves ensuring that every attribute of an entity that is not part of the primary key is wholly dependent on that key.

A table is in third normal form if it is in 2NF and there is no functional dependency between non-key items. (Or to give it the technical definition, every non-key attribute is non-transitively dependent on the primary key.) In simple terms, the question: 'Are any of the non-key fields dependent on any other non-key fields?' can be asked. If the answer is no, then the table is in 3NF.

Take the following tables in Figure 12.18 which we have already confirmed are in 2NF:

a)

SupplierID*	Delivery	City
A10	10	London
B10	15	Paris
C10	20	Berlin

b)

SupplierID*	StockNumber*	Quantity
A10	P1232	1254
B10	H4365	5476
C10	J4587	2546
C10	J4586	6453

Figure 12.18 a) Supplier table, b) Stock table

There is a supplier table (a) and a stock table (b).

The stock table is in 3NF – all non-key fields (in this case, just quantity) are fully dependent on the primary key.

The supplier table is not in 3NF. The city is determined by the primary key and the delivery is determined by the primary key.

However, if we know the city, we can also determine the delivery. This makes the delivery determined by the city as well as the primary key – hence the table is not in 3NF.

To turn it into 3NF we need to remove the dependency:

SupplierID*	City
A10	London
B10	Paris
C10	Berlin

City*	Delivery
London	10
Paris	15
Berlin	20

SupplierID*	StockNumber*	Quantity
A10	P1232	1254
B10	H4365	5476
C10	J4587	2546
C10	J4586	6453

Figure 12.19

All non-key items are now fully dependent on the primary key. All tables are now in 3NF.

Checks for 3NF:

- Is the table in 2NF (and also therefore in 1NF)?
- Are all non-key items fully dependent on the primary key?

Correct notation for table structures

When writing data structures there is a notation that is universally understood and should be used.

The table name should be in capitals and the attributes (field names) in brackets separated by a comma. The primary key is underlined and foreign keys are overlined.

For example:

SUPPLIER (<u>SupplierID</u>, City)

CITY (<u>City</u>, Delivery)

STOCK (<u>SupplierID</u>, <u>StockNumber</u>, Quantity)

Questions

1 Describe first normal form.

2 Explain why the data structure in the following table is not in first normal form.

Student Name	Year	Classes	Games	Games
Fred Smith	11	11ICT 10Ma2	Football	Rugby
Sonia Banks	11	11MA4, 11Mu	Netball	Lacrosse
Maggie Stuart	10	11En1, 11Ma1	Hockey	Rugby

3 Describe second normal form.

4 Explain why the data structure in the following table is not in second normal form.

Seat Number*	Performance	Date*	Time*	Customer Forename	Customer Surname
A1	We Will Rock You	27/12/2004	2.30	John	May
B1	We Will Rock You	27/12/2004	2.30	Fred	Deacon
C1	We Will Rock You	27/12/2004	2.30	Brian	Taylor
A1	We Will Rock You	27/12/2004	7.30	Roger	Mercury

(The primary key is a compound key – Seat Number, Date and Time)

5 Describe third normal form.

6 Explain why the data structure in the following table is not in third normal form.

ID*	Forename	Surname	House Name/Number	Town	County	Postcode
1	John	Davies	18 Bright Road	Nottingham	Notts	NG8 5EP
2	Alice	Hall	24 Halls Avenue	Nottingham	Notts	NG8 5ET
3	Joan	Stevenson	19 Walbrook Close	Nottingham	Notts	NG8 5EZ

7 Explain why it is an advantage to have a standard notation for tables.

Advantages of normalisation

The normalisation process gives many advantages to the database that emerges at the end.

The final tables will have no redundant data within them as normalisation removes redundant data from tables. The process also removes duplicate data. This saves on storage space and makes the data consistent. If you are holding multiple copies of the data and only update one of them, they are out of sync, and it may not then be possible to tell that they are duplicates. If this happens the data has lost consistency and it has lost integrity – how do you now know which data is the right data?

A normalised data structure is easier to maintain. If the data is not duplicated then an update on a single piece of data will mean that any process that uses the data can be relied upon.

The data that is stored at the end of the process is stored in an efficient structure. This means that, as every data item is atomic, it is possible to combine the data in any desired format. If multiple data items were stored in a single field and only part of the field was required, a lot of programming would have to be done to extract the item required.

The database structure is very flexible. This means that if the requirements of the organisation using the data alter, it should be possible to adapt the database without a major redesign of the structure.

The advantages of normalisation can be summarised:

- removes redundancy
- increases consistency
- increases integrity
- easier maintenance
- flexibility for future expansion.

Components of a data dictionary

The data dictionary is often described as a database about a database. It contains metadata. Different database packages will contain slightly different information in the data dictionary. The list in Figure 12.20 is the basic data that would be expected in them all.

Figure 12.20 Basic data dictionary

Data	Description
Table Name	The name of the table – a unique name for each table in the database.
Field Name	Each field is identified.
Field Data Type	The data type allocated to each field – text/string/date/Boolean, etc.
Field Length	The number of characters allocated for the contents of the field.
Field Default Value	If a field has a default value that automatically appears on the creation of a new record.
Field Validation	Any validation applied to the field.
Table Security	Who has access to write, update, edit, or delete values to and from the table?
Keys	Primary keys are identified.
Indexes	Any field which is indexed.
Relationships	Relationships between tables are identified – one–one, etc.

Tailoring data-entry screens, reports and queries

As with many applications, the general interface provided may not be user friendly enough for an average user to complete the required tasks. In databases this is more of an issue than in other applications.

When designing and creating any feature that is going to be used or seen by the end user, it is this user who is one of the prime considerations – their ability and the task that they will have to complete.

Design considerations for forms

The interface for a standard database is aimed at the developer not the user. The implication is that the developer will then use the tools available to build an appropriate interface for the user. This is done through the use of forms. These forms can be created:

- within the application
- using web-based forms
- using third-party programs such as a programming language to access and manipulate the data.

When designing and creating forms, there are several elements that need to be taken into consideration.

Consistency

If there are several forms, then the user will expect buttons to be in the same place, font and font size. If a date is to be entered in several places then the format it is entered in must be the same every time – dd/mm/yyyy, for example.

If the data being entered into the computer form comes from a paper form then there needs to be consistency between them – they need to look the same. This will help the user and speed up the data entry.

The interface should also be consistent with other applications. Menus, labels, interface actions should correspond with the user's idea of what will happen and their previous experience. This will assist the usability and reduce the time it takes the user to learn how to use the interface.

Relevance

The interface should not ask for redundant material. It should require the minimum of input and user actions. The information provided on screen should not be excessive – it should be concise and useful.

Every task should require the minimum number of key strokes to complete. This will aid memory and make learning easier.

Supportiveness

There needs to be a balance between too little and too much information being given to the user. The user does not want redundant information but they need enough to feel supported in the task. There needs to be feedback – visual, and perhaps audible, to confirm their actions.

Visual and audible cues

The user needs some reassurance that what they are doing is correct or has been accepted by the system. This can be done through visual cues – messages, green lights and expected response. If they have made a mistake, error messages should be displayed informing the user of the error and how to solve it, or perhaps the use of the colour red. There could also be audible cues – for example, beeps.

Figure 12.21 Error message

Memory and learning

The user must be able to remember what they have done. It is unlikely that the user will use the system only once, so the interface needs to be designed in such a way to enable the user to remember. This is linked to naturalness – the interface must appear appropriate for completing the task and reflect the user's knowledge and understanding. If the user can relate to items within the design, this will assist with memory and the use of the interface.

General considerations

The interface needs to accommodate differences in user requirements. Novice and expert users alike need to be able to use the system.

The use of white space needs to be considered. This is the amount of empty space on a form – too much and it looks bare, too little and it is difficult to read and absorb details.

Also important is the use of colour – too bright and it can hurt the eyes! Colour can be used to trigger memory – using different colours for different screens, for example. Colour blindness needs to be taken into account when choosing colours to use for backgrounds, fonts and highlighting areas.

Validation can be used in the shape of drop-down boxes, check boxes, and so on, to support the user in their data entry.

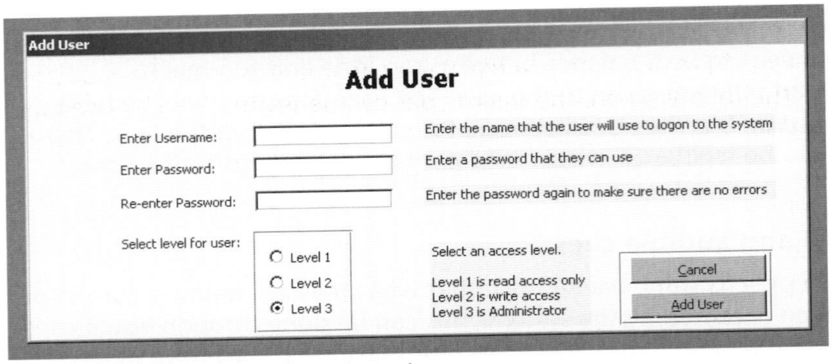

Figure 12.22 Validation drop-down box

The main design considerations discussed above regarding forms also underpin the design of queries and reports.

Design considerations for queries

When designing a query the output is the most important factor. What information is required from the query? This in turn leads to the fields and calculations required to generate the information required.

The query itself should not be the final document that the user sees. The query should be the underlying data structure used by a report.

Design considerations for queries should also take into account where the information is going to come from – a form or dialogue box perhaps, and these should have relevant considerations. The error messages that are to be displayed if something goes wrong must be taken into account, as should how the query will be run – for example, a shortcut key, command line, button, icon or menu option.

For more information on queries, see page 195.

Design considerations for reports

The report should be 'fit for purpose'. It should contain the required information and be presented in such a way that it can be easily understood. This may mean textually, numerically or graphically.

There should be headings to inform the end user of the purpose and content of the report. There should be a consistent use of font, font size and colour. There should be enough white space to make it readable but not so much that it seems to have been used just to fill the page.

Not all design considerations apply in all situations. You need to take into account the user and the purpose and some design considerations will not be appropriate.

> ## Questions
> 1 Describe **three** design considerations that should be taken into account when designing a form.
> 2 Explain how the end user should be taken into account when designing a form.
> 3 Identify the **two** most important design considerations for a query.
> 4 What are the similarities between the design considerations for a report and for a form?
> 5 Identify **two** design considerations for a form and, for each one, explain how it affects the usability of the form.

Types of queries

The ability of databases to run queries is what makes them particularly useful. The following are the main types of queries that can be used in a database:

- Select queries
- Parameter queries
- Complex queries
- Action queries
- Cross-tab queries.

Select queries

These return data from one or more tables and display the results in a results table. The select query can be used to group or count the number of records found.

A select query can be used to select fields from various tables and return all the values that match. In Figure 12.23, a database has two tables – Product and Supplier. A supplier supplies many different products. The user of the database might want a report that only shows the product name, the supplier name, contact surname and phone number.

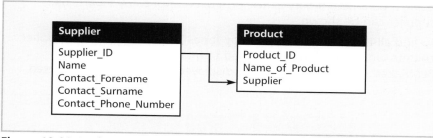

Figure 12.23 A select query

A select query can be used to deliver the required information. It takes the required information from all relevant tables and presents them as a single table to the end user (Figure 12.24).

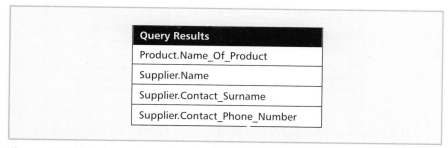

Figure 12.24 A select query table with different fields coming from different tables

Parameter queries

A parameter query is a type of select query. However, records are only displayed if a field within a record matches a given value.

The parameter is the value that is used by the query to select records. Figure 12.25 shows a selection of records from the Product table. Each product has a supplier. Some suppliers supply more than one product.

Product_ID	Name_Of_Product	Supplier
1	Red Pens	Jones The PenMaker
2	HB Pencil	Pencils 4 All
3	Lined A4	The PaperMaker
4	Blue Pens	Jones The PenMaker
5	Purple Pens	Jones The PenMaker
6	Plain A4	The PaperMaker
7	A4 Book Cover	The Paper Place
8	Green Pens	Jones The PenMaker
9	Spiral Notebook	The PaperMaker
10	Propelling Pencil	Pencils 4 All

Figure 12.25 Selection of records from the Product table

Using a parameter query all the products supplied by a particular supplier can be shown.

To find all the products supplied by Jones The PenMaker, the Supplier column would need to be searched to match the text 'Jones The PenMaker'. The other fields to be displayed also need to be selected.

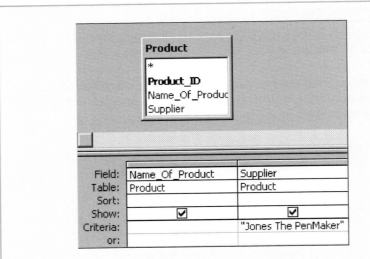

The results of the query will display two fields and four records:

Name_Of_Product	Supplier
Red Pens	Jones The PenMaker
Blue Pens	Jones The PenMaker
Purple Pens	Jones The PenMaker
Green Pens	Jones The PenMaker

Figure 12.26 Parameter query to find products for Jones the PenMaker

In Figure 12.26, the parameter has been 'hard-coded'. This means that the query cannot be changed – whenever it is run it will always and only search for Jones The PenMaker. There may be occasions where the user would want to search for different suppliers. It would not be efficient to have separate queries for every supplier – not every supplier would be known when the database was being designed.

Parameter queries can be created that ask the user for the value to search for. These are known as dynamic parameter queries. A dialog box can be created which takes a value from the user and uses that value in the query (Figure 12.27).

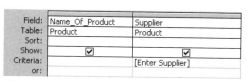
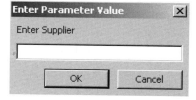

Figure 12.27 Dynamic parameter query

The parameter value in the query asks a question. The user enters a value in the dialog box and this value is then used. This makes the query more useful than hard-coding the value.

Complex queries

So far, the queries have only searched using one parameter value. A complex query is a parameter query that searches using more than one parameter value.

Figure 12.28 Complex query

The query in Figure 12.28 searches for all contacts at Jones The PenMaker called Smith.

You can have as many parameters as you like in a query.

The parameters can be joined together in three ways:

- AND
- OR
- NOT.

AND

AND will include all records found from both queries: only records containing Jones The Penmaker as the Supplier Name AND a contact called Smith will be found.

OR

OR will find records that match one or the other or both searches:

searching for Jones The Penmaker OR contact surname of Smith will find contacts called Smith who do not work for Jones The Penmaker and it will find every contact for Jones The Penmaker whether or not they are called Smith.

NOT

NOT query is an inverse query: searching for products NOT supplied by Jones The Penmaker requires a search to be done for products supplied by Jones The Penmaker and then these records are removed. What is left answers the question.

Complex parameter queries can be represented using a Venn diagram (Figure 12.29).

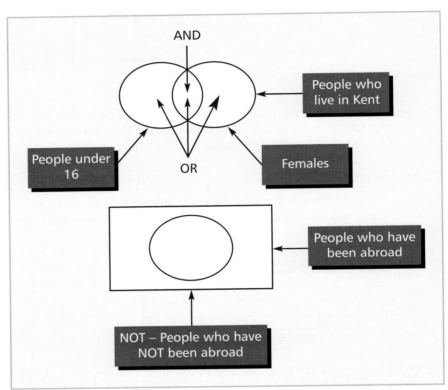

Figure 12.29 Complex parameter queries can be represented using a Venn diagram

Action queries

An action query is a type of select query that modifies the data source. There are different types of action query, the main ones being:

- Delete query – deletes records from a table. For example, if a product was no longer supplied its record would be deleted.
- Update query – changes values within existing records. For example, if a supplier contact changed.
- Append query – adds a new record to the table. For example, if a new product was released.
- Make table – creates a new table. This might be used when archiving the data.

Cross-tab queries

Cross-tab queries summarise large quantities of data and perform calculations on the data. They organise the data in a spreadsheet-like format.

In Figure 12.30, samples of the tables have been given. A table of items lists all the items sold by a company. The order table shows orders placed.

a) Item table:

ItemCode	Item	Type	Subtype
673	2B	Pens/markers	Pencils
102310	2B – (Pack of 12)	Pens/markers	Pencils
677	2H	Pens/markers	Pencils
102366	2B Pencils – (Pack of 12)	Pens/markers	Pencils
50	51626A 500 Black 500 InkJet Compatible	Toner cartridges	Ink Jet Cartridge
1618	A4 Feint Ruled Pad Mgn/Hole Punched	Pens/markers	Pads
101458	Asst Cols – (Pack of 8)	Pens/markers	Highlighter
101424	Asst Cols – Highlighter (Pack of 4)	Pens/markers	Highlighter
261	Asst Cols – Highlighter	Pens/markers	Highlighter
272	Asst Cols – Highlighter	Pens/markers	Highlighter
102361	B – (Pack of 12)	Pens/markers	Pencils
102222	B – Pencil	Pens/markers	Pencils
4324	Ball Pen Dudley Choice Black	Pens/markers	Pens
4327	Ball Pen Dudley Choice Blue	Pens/markers	Pens
3497	Battery Procell IND MN1500	Misc	Misc

b) Order table:

OrderNo	Product	Customer	Date	Quantity
10201	50	5400	23/12/2002	1
10196	50	5400	22/12/2002	9
10155	50	5400	14/12/2002	1
10224	50	5400	30/12/2002	13
10067	261	1427	08/12/2002	14
10269	272	6305	07/01/2003	3
10229	272	6305	01/01/2003	13
10256	272	6305	05/01/2003	12
10241	272	6305	03/01/2003	3
10221	610	1310	29/12/2002	5
10202	610	1310	23/12/2002	13
10197	610	1310	23/12/2002	1
10250	610	1310	05/01/2003	6

Figure 12.30 a) Item table, **b)** Order table

A cross table can be created to show the number of each type of item that has been sold. Part of the query results are shown in Figure 12.30.

Type	Clips	Erasers	Highlighter	Ink Jet Cartridge
Fastenings etc	368			
Misc				
Office equipment		3		
Paper				
Pens/markers			302	
Tone cartridges				71

Figure 12.31 Cross table

The cross-tab query collates and summarises data.

Questions

1 Describe what is meant by a select query.
2 Give an example of a parameter query.
3 Identify **two** different types of parameter query and give an example of each.
4 What is the difference between a static and a dynamic parameter query?
5 What are the advantages to the end user of a dynamic parameter query?
6 What is a cross-tab query?

Comparing a spreadsheet to a database

Typically, spreadsheets are used for calculations and databases are used for sorting and searching. However, with more recent software the lines between the two applications have become blurred.

It is possible to perform calculations using either a database or a spreadsheet. Databases allow for calculations to be made in tables, queries, forms and reports. Integrating these with the scripting language adds additional functionality when it comes to mathematical calculations.

Spreadsheet packages can store data – the row and column layout is very similar to a table. Columns can be given field names and data stored. Basic database search functions exist within spreadsheet packages and data can be sorted.

As this blurring between the two types of package has occurred, it has become more difficult to select which type of package to use in which situation. There are, however, some general guidelines, which although not completely accurate, do demonstrate differences between the applications.

Databases are designed to store data, run queries on the data and present the results from the queries in an acceptable output to the end user (reports). They have tools and wizards built into the application designed to assist specifically with this purpose. The programming code used to write the application has been optimised for data handling. This means that it has been written with this specific purpose in mind and performs this action better and faster than general-purpose code. An analogy is racing cars – an old mini will be able to get round a race track but a specially designed and built racing car will perform much better.

Relationships can be created easily in databases and through features like cascade update and cascade delete, the integrity and consistency of the data can be maintained. Creating relationships in spreadsheets is achieved through cell references and is difficult to maintain.

Spreadsheets are designed to perform calculations on data. They have wizards and tools built into the application to assist in this purpose. Their codes are optimised for calculations rather than sorting and searching.

Questions

1 Describe **three** features of a spreadsheet that make it suitable for performing calculations.
2 Describe **three** features of a database that make it suitable for sorting and searching data.
3 Describe **three** criteria that could be used to decide whether a spreadsheet or a database was the most appropriate application to use.
4 Explain the difference between a spreadsheet and a database.

End of Chapter 12 tests

Test 1

A small corner shop runs a newspaper round. Until now, the details about the newspaper round have been stored manually. The shop wants to computerise its records.

The shop will require a database.

1 Describe the following database terms:

   i)   table
   ii)   record
   iii) field.   [6]

2 The first designs for the data structure included the following. Explain, giving reasons, why the following is not in first normal form (1NF).

   CUSTOMER (Customer name, customer address, newspaper, newspaper, newspaper, delivery round)   [5]

3 The following entities have been established:

   i)   Customer
   ii)   Newspaper
   iii) Round
   iv)   Delivery person
   v)   Order.

Draw out the entity relationship diagram for the tables and explain the degree of the relationship between each entity. [8]

4 Describe **two** advantages of normalisation. [4]

5 Explain **three** considerations the designer must take into account when creating the user interface for the database. [6]

6 Describe **two** types of queries that could be used in the database. For each type of query, give an example showing how the shop might use it. [6]

Test 2

An estate agent currently stores all the data about the business on paper. She wants to computerise her systems and has employed a database expert to assist her.

1 From the following database design, identify the primary and foreign keys.

CUSTOMER (CustomerID, Forename, Surname)
PROPERTY (PropertyID, Address, Price, Seller)
SELLER (Forename, Surname, SellerID, Address, Phone)
OFFER (CustomerID, PropertyID, Price, Date, Accepted) [6]

2 Identify the characteristics of data in second normal form (2NF). [2]

3 Explain, giving reasons, why the following is not in second normal form. This is an attendance table showing whether an employee arrived to work on time or late and whether there was a reason.

ATTENDANCE (EmployeeID, OfficeID, Date, Attendance, TrafficCondition, Reason) [4]

4 Identify **three** components of the data dictionary for the estate agent's database and, for each component, explain how it would be used in the creation of the database. [6]

5 Describe **three** tools that could be used to tailor the user interface for the estate agent and explain how each tool could make the interface suitable for the novice estate agent. [6]

6 Describe how the estate agent could make use of a cross-tab query. [2]

7 The estate agent could have used a spreadsheet or a database. Compare the two applications as a means for storing, sorting, searching and reporting. [6]

Common applications

Objectives

Your objectives for this chapter are to:

◎ identify basic tasks for which standard/generic applications software can be used

◎ describe the characteristics of common applications software

◎ analyse the needs of different users of applications software

◎ explain the need for a consistent house style

◎ explain the need for different file types

◎ compare custom-written with off-the-shelf software

◎ describe how system interfaces can be tailored to meet the needs of the user.

Keep these objectives in mind as you work through the chapter.

In this chapter, you will consider two different types of software applications. One type is standard/generic applications. These are packages such as word-processing or spreadsheet applications that can be used for many different tasks. The other type is applications that have one main purpose, for example route-finders or stock-control software.

Basic tasks for which standard/generic applications can be used

Standard or generic applications are general-purpose software packages that are used for every-day purposes. This term is used to refer to all common applications packages such as:

● word processors
● databases
● desktop publishers
● spreadsheets
● presentation software.

All the above are called general-purpose applications, because they can be used for lots of tasks and not just one specific task.

Word processors

These are used to create, edit, format, store and print text-based documents. These documents include letters, memos, theses and reports. Mail merge procedures can also be completed using word processing software.

Databases

These are used for handling data, for example, sorting and searching. The data can be split into tables and relationships created between the tables to allow the data to be combined in a useful manner. The data can be sorted by different methods and by using different fields – one field, or more than one, as required.

✳ A **word processor** allows the entry, editing and formatting of text to create a range of documents.

Databases are organised collections of one or more tables containing related data records.

Desktop publishers (DTP)

DTP can be used to produce flyers, brochures, business cards, posters and invitations. It can also be used to create newspapers, covers for books and to typeset books. Any task that requires a large number of graphics or complex layouts is suitable for a DTP package. DTP enables an inexperienced user to create professional-looking publications.

Spreadsheets

These display and process data. They are capable of performing a wide range of calculations and so are generally used to process numerical data. A spreadsheet package can also handle text. They are used to create graphs, to use 'what if…?' calculations, and for goal seeking, forecasting (including trend lines, for example, trends in sales figures) and data-pattern analysis. Any task that involves the manipulation of numbers is suitable for a spreadsheet.

Presentation software

Presentation software can create OHTs or slideshows. It can be used for kiosk applications or presentations for speeches. It can run without intervention on a timer or with user intervention.

Activity

Identify some tasks for which the following software could be used:

a) a graphics package

b) a web-authoring package.

The characteristics of common applications

There are many common applications that are used in business, commerce and education. The features of each of these are generally specific to the task for which they are used.

Booking systems

There are many different things that can be booked – rail tickets, theatre tickets, cinema, doctor's appointments, and so on. There are three main ways of booking:

- telephone
- Internet
- in person or by mail/fax.

The information a booking system requires is an event, a customer and a date and time. Booking systems via the Internet are becoming more popular. The combination of email, which can be used to notify individuals of events, with direct links to booking systems and the ability of the online systems to retain settings, means that mail shots can be tailored to individual preferences.

The booking system must allow the user to:

- select a time and date
- select an event
- specify the number of tickets – for adults, children, etc.

Desktop publisher programs are used for page layouts that combine text and graphics to create a variety of publications.

Spreadsheets display and process data in a table of rows and columns and are generally used to process numerical data.

Presentation software creates OHTs or slideshows for presentations.

- check the availability of tickets for the date/seating/number of tickets required
- check the price of the selected booking
- go backwards and forwards within the booking procedure to change options if required
- make a payment and receive confirmation of the booking (via email or a booking number).

School administration systems

These are systems used within schools and colleges to assist in administration. Administration can be related to students or staff, with three distinct features being utilised. These are:

- the use of a database to hold records
- a facility to record student marks
- an attendance monitoring facility.

Database system

This feature should allow the user to:

- store personal details about students such as next of kin, doctor, mode of transport to school
- have a unique identification number – a UPN (Unique Pupil Number) that follows a student through their school career.

Recording marks

This feature should allow the user to:

- record marks against subjects for each student
- store historical data about the student
- prepare reports based on student results.

Attendance

This feature should allow the user to:

- record attendance, absence and type of absence for a student
- summarise attendance
- produce lists of outstanding absences
- produce required averages of attendance for the purpose of school documentation.

Diary systems

These are systems that can represent a physical diary on the computer. They include calendars and can break each day down into segments. Each segment can then be booked. The computer-based diary has all the functionality of a paper-based diary and more. Usually diary systems are connected with time management systems or integrated into personal organiser systems – systems that attempt to duplicate the functionality of the Filofax™ by including contact details, notes pages and journals. Diary systems have many different levels of use. They can be used at a very simple level for just recording day-to-day activities, or they can be used and shared to arrange and invite people to meetings and to give reminders. They can be used in a business setting or on an individual basis.

The system must enable the user to:

- search, book, edit or delete appointments for a time slot or for the whole day
- give reminders about appointments and recurring events
- send out invitations to meetings if connected to an email system
- allocate appointments to categories
- allow themselves and (if required) other users to access the diary using different access levels.

Route-finders

These are pieces of software that allow the user to enter a variety of information about the start and destination of a journey and the software will then plot a route between the two. This can be requested and printed out prior to the journey and from an organisation's web site, or through the use of in-car navigation systems. With an in-car system, it is possible to change the route mid-journey – if during a journey the driver becomes aware that a road coming up is blocked, the route can be changed to avoid this road. Some new systems can automatically receive the traffic information and change the route accordingly without direct driver-input.

Software

The system must enable the user to:

- specify start and destination locations
- specify places and roads they want to pass through or avoid (perhaps to avoid a motorway)
- specify the type of journey – scenic, fastest or cheapest
- save/print out the route in a number of formats, for example, as text or a map.

In-car navigation systems

- The same information as for the software above is required.
- The system then directs you road-by-road, confirming your location with a global positioning system and adjusting its directions accordingly.

Questions

1 What are the advantages and disadvantages of booking via the Internet as opposed to in person/by mail?

2 Compare the use, advantages and disadvantages of a computer-based diary with a manual one.

3 Compare the use of a software-based route-finder with using a map.

Stock control

This is a system that records how much of each item is in stock, when orders are due and how much stock is required on certain days. If necessary it can order stock and update the stock records when the stock is delivered. It therefore needs to have links to suppliers. Many organisations have moved over to JIT (Just In Time) ordering. If a lot of stock is being held, then that stock needs to have been paid for and it is not producing profit until it is sold. JIT ordering works on the principle of keeping the stock that is held to a minimum and, through the use of ICT and logistics (transportation systems), the aim is to have the materials delivered either on the day they are required, or, at the very earliest, the day before.

There are two main users of stock control – shops and manufacturers.

Shops try to keep their shelves stocked but they do not want a surplus – particularly if the goods are perishable. Stock-control systems for shops need to know about special offers and other events that may increase sales.

The manufacturing stock-control systems need to know all the components that are required to create a product. They need to be linked into the ordering system so that they can see how much stock they require to meet demand. They also, as with the shops, need to be linked to the sales information so that they can identify trends and prepare for surges in sales, for example, for Christmas and forthcoming promotions.

The system must enable the user to:

- produce a list of all stock items and the suppliers
- produce a list of all components for the item if the stock is manufactured
- know the minimum and maximum stock levels
- work out how much to order
- know the delivery times for stock items that have been ordered
- have links to the orders database
- update the stock records when deliveries are received
- link with the budgeting system
- store previous sales figures
- predict stock requirements based on previous sales
- have manual override on items being ordered.

Customer records/accounts

Any company that deals with customers, needs to keep records about them. The records need to include contact details and ordering details. Invoicing and accounts need to be accurate so that they can be audited. Computer systems for storing records and accounts are commonly used and essential to the running of a business. If customer details or invoices are incorrect, customers will lose confidence and go elsewhere. The Data Protection Act (1998) has implications with regard to storing customer information and how that information is used. The system must enable the user to:

- store contact details of customers
- have a unique ID for each customer
- store orders giving each a unique number
- store orders against customers details
- generate invoices/credit notes for orders

- store customer payments against the customer details
- produce customer statements and outstanding invoices
- handle discounts and returns.

Multimedia training systems/self-paced teaching systems

Multimedia is the use of still images, animation, video, text and sound. Training is the imparting of knowledge and skills to achieve a designated task. A multimedia training system is the overall package where the multimedia and the training come together – the multimedia being the method used to deliver the training. Self-paced teaching systems are systems that use multimedia training but it is the trainee who decides the pace of the training. These use multimedia training as its method of delivery.

Multimedia training systems

These systems should have the following features:

- the use of video clips to demonstrate a feature
- the use of images and text to give additional explanation
- the provision of step-by-step features.

Self-paced teaching systems

These systems should have the following features:

- questions at a suitable level for the user
- a positive approach to learning
- screens as simple as possible
- the user able to move from one question to the next based on their responses
- the teacher able to intervene at any time
- each student teaches the system his or her voice (though note that mistakes are easier to make with an audio input)
- the teacher able to view a student's progress
- statistical information available to everyone
- help screens available for people who are stuck
- easy to move on to next stage.

Both systems

Features of both systems include:

- the ability to go backwards and forwards and redo sections if necessary
- the use of different methods of learning – text, video, images, sound
- tests and instant feedback for the student
- an uncritical, sympathetic on-screen 'teacher'.

Different users of applications software

Different users need different things from the software they use. For example a secretary, a translator and a scientific author will have very different requirements.

A **secretary** will need a wide range of fonts, a spelling- and grammar-checking facility and templates. S/he will require functions that are commonly used to be easily available, as s/he will be working with many different people and many documents. The secretary is likely to need to keep copies of all letters and to send out mailings using the mail merge facility.

A **translator** will take a document from one language and convert it to another language. The translator will need a language specific dictionary and a facility to insert specialist characters.

A **scientific author** will need a technical dictionary and thesaurus, automatic section numbering and indexing, specialist clip art, the facility to import and export, and the automatic facility to format work into a report style.

These are only three examples of different users of generic software. There are many more.

House style

House style or corporate image refers to a company or organisation's standard method of presenting its documents and other communications. The public will become familiar with a company or organisation's house style and will recognise it immediately.

Logos are part of a company or organisation's house style. Many logos are immediately recognisable and help the public to relate to a company or organisation.

A house style uses templates and macros, which are set up to make the use of the style easier. Headed paper can be used (the style may include the setting of the top page margin). The company or organisation's colour scheme may also be utilised on any documents produced. Other features that would be defined by a company's house style include the fonts to be used, the different paragraph styles, the layout of documents and any graphics that can be used.

House style is a set of rules followed on all documents sent out by a company or organisation to maintain a consistent appearance.

209

Through the use of a house style, it is less likely that important information will be omitted as templates will be used to include much of this information.

To get a professional, consistent style and colour scheme a team of designers will usually have to be employed. It is important, therefore, that all staff are made aware of the house style and that it is used by everyone in the company, in order to reap the benefits of this expenditure.

Using a house style can allow several documents from different teams to be integrated into a final document or presentation. Different people can work on different parts of the same document and use the same style and templates.

File types

Different software providers create their own methods of storing files from their applications. Different applications from the same provider will also store the files in different formats. This is because different file types are suited to different applications – for example, doc is word processing, xls is spreadsheet and mdb is database (Microsoft extensions).

Another reason for having different file types is that within the operating system a file type is allocated to a particular program – this is usually done automatically on installation. This enables the operating system to know which program to start when a user wishes to open a file.

Knowing the file extension or the type of file can help the user when searching for files. For example, to search for a letter saved in a Microsoft word processing application a search can be performed to find all the doc files.

Converting files

If data is saved in one application but the user needs to use it in a different application then the data will need to be converted. The applications may be completely different – for example, a word processing document and a spreadsheet – or they may be the same application, but different versions of it, for example Word 97 and Word 2002. Files can also be converted across different computer systems, for example, PC to Mac.

Some file types are universally recognised:

- txt and rtf (rich text format) – for converting text files
- CSV (comma separated variable) and TSV (tab separated variable) – for converting spreadsheets or tables of data
- DBF and CSV – for converting databases.

If these file types are used to save a file then it is easier to convert the data.

There are two standard procedures for converting files from one format to another.

> To take an example, a file saved in Package A needs to be read in Package B.

Option 1: Package A can save the file in Package B's format.

Procedure:

- Open the file in Package A (Open).
- Save as or export to the Package B format (Convert).
- Open in Package B and save (Save).

Option 2: Package A cannot save to Package B's format.

In this case the file should be saved to a third format – one that Package A can export to and Package B can import from.

Procedure:

- Open the file in Package A (Open).
- Save as or export to the third party format (Convert).
- Open the file in Package B (Import).
- Convert to the format required by Package B (Convert).
- Save in the new format (Save).

Questions

1 Identify the specific word processing tools required by a secretary and a scientific author.

2 Why are there so many different file types?

3 How can a file from one software package be converted so it can be read by another software package?

Custom-written versus off-the-shelf software

There are two main ways that software can be obtained by the end user. (There are more but for the OCR AS level ICT specification you only need to be concerned with custom-written software and off-the-shelf software.)

Custom-written software

Custom-written software is when the software has been written to meet the specified needs of an end user – usually a company. The software is developed by a software provider working with the user to determine the requirements of the software design. The software provider then builds the software to meet these requirements, and then implements and tests it.

The advantage of custom-written software is that it meets the requirements of the user exactly. The user will specify the functions of the software and the software will be developed to incorporate those functions. Off-the-shelf software has many features that may not be required by the user. This is known as 'bloat ware' - many of the functions of the software are not required and may never be used by the user. These functions increase the memory footprint (the amount of hard drive space taken up by the software). With custom-written software there are no extraneous functions as the software has been written to meet the specific requirements of a company.

Custom-written software is written for a specific purpose for a specific end user.

Once custom-written software has been developed, installed and paid for then the user owns the software. This means that the user can sell the software to other companies, which may cover the cost of development. However, the initial cost of the development may be very high.

Specialist back-up and support will be available from the software provider who developed the software. This back-up may involve correcting bugs, training users or assisting in extending the functionality of the program. There will, however, not be the wider support community usually available with off-the-shelf software, such as books, discussion groups, etc.

One of the disadvantages of having software custom-written is the time factor. It takes a long time to analyse, design, develop, test and implement a new piece of software. It may be that during the time taken to develop a piece of software, the requirements of the user may change.

If there are mistakes in the code then it may take some time to find and fix these mistakes. Following implementation, when the software has 'gone live', problems may occur when the software is being used in a live environment for the first time.

Off-the-shelf software

Off-the-shelf software is a term used to define any software that can be purchased, installed and used immediately. One of the main advantages of off-the-shelf software is that it is generally cheaper than having software specifically written. The cost is a one-off purchase price.

Also, as off-the-shelf software has a large number of users the software is likely to have been tested by many people and a lot of the bugs will have already been removed. It must be remembered that a piece of software can never be fully tested but the more testing that has been carried out, the less likely it is that problems will occur.

Another advantage is that if off-the-shelf software is purchased then a choice of software manufacturers is available. For example, word processing software is available from Microsoft, Corel or Lotus and many other software manufacturers. The software is immediately available and it can be installed and used almost immediately.

One of the most important advantages is in the support available. Lots of people will be using the software; this means there will be books, discussion groups, qualifications, web sites and trainers who can assist the users. There will be bug fixes and patches released by the manufacturer and it will be possible to upgrade the software at a minimal cost.

There are disadvantages to purchasing off-the-shelf software. Among these is the fact that, as the software has not been written to a specific set of requirements, there will be many features and functions that are not needed by the user that have been included in the price of the software. The software is also likely to have a large memory footprint. It may not fully meet the needs of the user and so compromises need to be made.

In addition, the cost of the software is for a license to use the software. The ownership of the software stays with the software manufacturer who developed it.

Off-the-shelf software can be bought, installed and used immediately.

Comparison of custom-written software and off-the-shelf software

Figure 13.1 Comparison of the main features of custom-written software and off-the-shelf software

Feature	Custom-written	Off-the-shelf
Cost	Need to hire a company or person to write the software, expensive (many thousands of pounds). You do own the software at the end and can sell it on to recoup some of this cost.	Either a one-off cost or a yearly rental cost. May be talking thousands of pounds plus additional costs for each workstation it is used on.
Support	Only likely to get support from the people who have written the software – problems may arise if they choose not to support it or go out of business.	Discussion groups, online help, books and training courses.
Purpose	Will fit the purpose precisely and should do exactly what was requested. May be some problems if the analysis was wrong. If it was not specified however, it will not be there.	May have to be altered and edited to fit the purpose. May never meet the purpose precisely. Will have many additional features that may or may not be used. Better to have them there and never use them than to want them and not to have them?
Testing	Will only have been tested by a few people and there may be many bugs. Correcting them will take time.	Will have been tested by many individuals. Bug fixes should be released regularly by the company.
Availability	Will take time (perhaps a few months) to complete the analysis, etc.	Immediately available.
Choice	There is a choice as to who to get to write the software. As the design will be specified, users will have a lot of say.	Choice between the packages available (but none may be an exact fit).
Upgrade	New printers and drivers for peripherals may not be supported and major upgrades might not be possible. If the software does not use a recognised file format, it may not be possible to upgrade.	Likely to use a standard file format and the company is likely to release upgraded products. Support for new peripherals and operating systems should be standard.
New staff	Will not be familiar with the new software.	May well be familiar with the new software.
Footprint	Small footprint.	Large footprint.

Questions

1 What is meant by custom-written software?
2 What is meant by off-the-shelf software?
3 What are the advantages of custom-written software over off-the-shelf software?
4 What are the advantages of off-the-shelf software over custom-written software?

Tailoring system interfaces to meet the needs of the user

An interface assists the user to complete a task. An interface makes it easy for the user to enter data and navigate around the different options. Generic packages, for example, spreadsheets and databases, can be customised to help the user enter data, select options, and so on.

Buttons, forms, menus and macros

An interface can be tailored to meet the user's needs through the use of buttons, forms, menus and macros.

Buttons

Buttons can be used to take the user to a specified page or to run a selected action/command. A macro can be run through the user selecting a button. For example, a command button can be added to the interface of a database to run a search, or to sort or edit data. A button can also display pictures or text.

Forms

These can be used to assist in the entry of data. A form can give the user help and guidance as to what data should be input. Instructions to the user and error messages can be included on forms. It is also possible to include some validation when forms are being used in a system interface. A form may include drop-down boxes for data selection, option boxes and fill-in boxes, which can automatically assist a user.

An example of an automatic fill-in box might be when a postcode is entered and the street name and town automatically appear. The user would then simply have to input the house number. This is a very common facility in business today.

Menus

Menus enable a user to select actions. There are three main types of menu that can be used:

- full-screen
- pop-up
- pull-down.

Each type of menu gives the user choices of actions that are available (options not available are usually greyed out and the user will not be able to select them).

Macros

It is macros that enable buttons, forms and menus to operate. A macro will be associated with each of these features and will enable the action selected by the user to occur.

Benefits and problems

There are benefits and problems with customising a user interface.

The benefits include the simplification of data entry for the user. This should lead to fewer mistakes. Through the use of forms, buttons, menus and macros the time taken to enter data can also be shortened and users become more productive. The data entered can also be validated on entry. The complex interface is simplified for the benefit of the user.

The main problem with customising a user interface is the level of technical knowledge required to create and test the interface. If changes are required, for example to meet the evolving needs of the business or organisation, then this may take time. If the software on which the interface is built is upgraded then there is no guarantee that the interface will still perform as required. If a problem occurs with the interface or an option is not available on the button or menu then the user will not be able to complete the tasks.

When a user interface is being customised, there are some design aspects that should be considered:

- A consistent layout should be used which should follow the house style or corporate image.
- The colours used should be carefully selected; they should not clash and should be easy to read by the user.
- The font, style and size should be carefully selected; the style of the text should be clear and the size of the font easy to read.
- Graphics and animation should be selected to meet the needs of the user. Any graphic selected should be fit for the purpose with the number of graphics used kept to a minimum.
- Any text used should be useful and clear. This should provide help and assistance to the user using simple and natural language.
- The information on the screen should flow in a logical order.
- The interface should be easy to learn and use. This will minimise the training required and the number of instructions that have to be remembered by the user.
- Clearly marked exits should be included in simple and natural language.
- Commonly used functions should be given a short-cut/button/menu option.

Questions

1 Identify **three** different controls that can be used to customise the user interface.
2 What are the disadvantages of customising a user interface?
3 What are the benefits of using buttons and forms to customise a user interface?

hint In your exam you will be asked to provide examples. The examples you give **must** be relevant to the context of the question being asked in the examination. If the question is about a specified business, give an example to do with that business.

End of Chapter 13 tests

Test 1

A company has recently introduced a telephone ordering system.

1 Describe **three** design considerations that should be taken into account when designing data-entry screens to input customer orders. [6]

2 The data-entry screens are to follow the company house style. Explain what is meant by house style. [4]

3 The ordering system is to use custom-written software. Describe **two** advantages to the company of having the software custom-written. [4]

4 A stock control system is to be linked to the telephone ordering system. Describe the characteristics of a stock control system. [6]

Test 2

A company specialising in antique books is updating its systems.

1 The company logo is saved using a graphics package. Describe how this logo could be transferred to a word-processing package without using Cut/Copy and Paste. [2]

2 Explain why it is important to have the company logo on every document produced by the company. [4]

3 The manager is to use an electronic diary. Describe the characteristics of electronic diaries. [6]

4 The company is to update the database it currently uses. Describe **three** advantages and **one** disadvantage to the company of purchasing an off-the-shelf software package. [8]

Coursework

Objectives

Your objectives for this chapter are to:

◎ understand the different types of tasks

◎ know what evidence needs to be supplied to get marks.

Keep these objectives in mind as you work through the chapter.

The coursework is worth 40% of the AS award and is marked out of a total of 120. The coursework is structured and it is essential that you attempt all of the tasks and all of the elements within each task. There will be a range of tasks, but it is likely that there will always be one spreadsheet and one database task.

Design

A design should be completed either by hand or using a different piece of software from the one that will be used to create the final work.

A design could be for a web page or document – this will require the layout to be given. Designs can also cover spreadsheets and databases where the layout of the screens – input and output – as well as the data structures themselves, might be required.

There will always be information given in the question, and this must be included in the design. It might be information to be included on a web page, questions that need to be asked, or a data-capture form that is currently used that needs computerising. If you miss out even a single piece of information, you will lose marks. Read the task carefully and check that you have included all the required information.

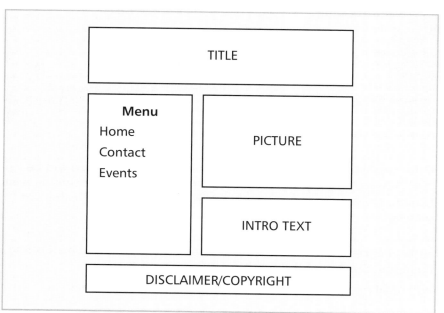

Figure 14.1 Example of a student's design and design specification

Where any user interface or presentation to a user is concerned, such as a slide presentation, web page or input form, then you might be asked to give a design specification.

A design specification is information about the design. It covers formatting aspects such as the colour, style and size of the font to be used. If you are required to create a design and a design specification, the best thing to do is to create the design on a sheet of A4. Stick the sheet of A4 into the middle of a sheet of A3 and then, on the space surrounding the page, write the design specification.

It is always worth looking further into the task to see whether you are going to have to create your design. If you make your design too complicated and difficult you may not be able to create it and will lose marks later on. A most useful hint when designing is Keep It Simple (KIS).

Create

This is the development – the creation of the spreadsheet, database, web page or presentation. The only evidence that the moderator has about your creative process is what you print out and submit. You may have created a fantastic system but if you do not provide useful printouts, you will not get marks.

There are usually two types of evidence required – the underlying evidence and the user interface.

Underlying evidence

The underlying evidence includes formulae in spreadsheets:

		A	B
	1		
	2		
	3	Quotation	
	4		
	5	Customer Name:	
	6	Customer Address:	
	7		
	8		
	9		
	10	Type of Paving Block	Clay Brick
	11	Type of Base	Concrete
	12		
	13	Length of Driveway	8
	14	Width of Driveway	8
	15		
	16	Area of Driveway	=B14*B13
	17	Number of Blocks Required	=(B16+(B16*5%))/(VLOOKUP(B10;J10:K17;2))
	18	Total Cost of Paving Blocks	=VLOOKUP(B10;J10:L17;3)*B17
	19	Amount of Sand Required	=B16/20

Figure 14.2 Formulae in spreadsheets

Make sure you widen the columns so that the entire formula can be seen. You may be required to annotate the formula. This means, in plain English, say what is happening. This can be a hand-written comment such as:

In Figure 14.2, the formula in Cell B16 is taking two values, the length entered in cell B13 and the width entered into cell B14 and multiplying them together to get the area.

With mail merge it may be necessary to show the field codes:

Field codes are the underlying codes that supply the data from the data source to the mail-merged letter.

In web pages you may be required to show site maps, directory structures and even the code used to create the pages.

Databases require the most evidence. In tables you need to provide the data structure and validation. The forms may need to be shown in design view. Forms and reports might be based on queries. These will need to be shown and you will need to annotate them – tell the moderator how they work.

Figure 14.3 Field codes

User interface

The evidence required for the user interface is a screenshot or printout of the actual interface that has been designed. This might be a form in a database, the cells where data is to be entered in a spreadsheet or spaces in a word-processed document. The user interface is what the end user will see of the application.

Testing

There are two parts to testing: the test plan and then actually doing the testing.

In some tasks the two sections will be linked. You will need to create a test plan and then run the tests.

Test plans should cover three main areas:

- Valid data – the normal data that the system should work with.
- Invalid data – incorrect data. The system should pick this up and generate an error message.
- Extreme data – boundary data (data on the edge of tolerance).

If, in a spreadsheet, you had a cell that should only accept numbers between 1 and 20, there are up to five tests that could be performed on the cell:

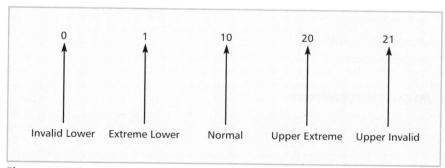

Figure 14.4 Five tests that can be performed on cells

Two of the tests will produce error messages.

With spreadsheets and databases you need to test that the data-entry system works:

- Does it only allow the correct values to be entered?
- Do queries produce the right results?
- Do lookups return the correct values?
- Do the formulas work?

All of these features can generate tests. Make sure that you carry out different tests, not just the same one several times; for example, five tests with normal data on the same cell, will not be an effective test.

When testing – if you are given a test table in the task – use it. Make sure you follow the instructions for testing. You will be asked for a certain number of valid/invalid tests, make sure you have enough of each.

When producing the output of the tests, you need to make sure that the test number on the test plan matches the number of the output – the two need to go together.

When you present the results of testing, make sure that the data value that was input can be seen.

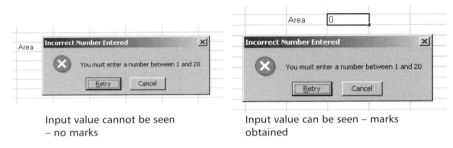

Input value cannot be seen – no marks

Input value can be seen – marks obtained

Figure 14.5 Input value visibility

The testing of web pages and presentations is slightly more complex. You have the standard tests to make sure that it works – do the buttons/hyperlinks go to the correct place? Does the code work? You also have to test in different situations. Web pages and presentations are likely to be used on different computers to the ones they were developed on. This gives rise to tests to do with:

- processing power
- operating systems
- software (different browsers and different versions of the same browser)
- monitor size
- graphics card
- resolution.

Documentation

There are two types of documentation – full user documentation and help sheets.

All the documentation that you will create will be for a specific purpose and a specific audience. You must bear these two points in mind at all times. Is the documentation that you are creating 'fit for purpose'?

Full user documentation

This contains surrounding elements that make up all user documentation:

- title page
- contents page – this should be automatically generated by the software

- introduction/purpose
- the guide itself (help sheets on individual aspects)
- troubleshooting
- gossary
- index.

The documentation should have page numbers and be presented appropriately for the audience.

The troubleshooting, glossary and index sometimes cause problems and are dealt with separately below.

Troubleshooting

The troubleshooting section contains likely problems and their solutions, specifically related to the applications being used. If you were writing user documentation on how to fill in a data-capture form online, you would not include problems such as – 'the computer won't switch on', 'I can't print it because there is no paper in the printer'. The problems and solutions must be related to the data-capture form, for example, 'I cannot write the date in the date of birth field', 'it won't accept brackets in the number field', 'it won't automatically look up my address from my postcode', and so on.

Glossary

The glossary must be related to the task and to the audience. A glossary is like a dictionary – it contains definitions of terms that the user of the guide may not understand. There is a glossary at the end of this book.

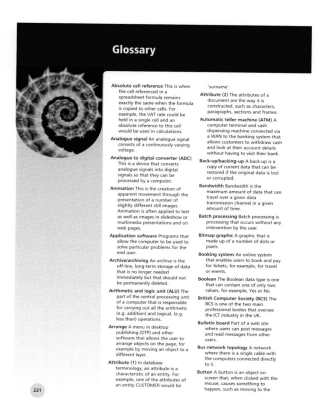

Figure 14.6 A glossary

Index

The index is a quick way of finding out on which page certain words or subjects appear.

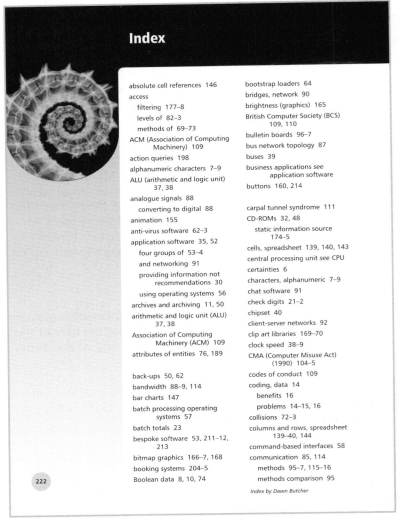

Figure 14.7 An Index

Help sheets

Help sheets need to have text and pictures, such as screenshots. You need to begin by considering how the application is to be opened and where the file is located.

The rest of the help sheet should focus on giving instructions. One problem with help sheets is that with images and text the layout can get moved around and nothing ends up where you want it to be! This means you can spend more time moving images around than on the content.

One way around this is to create a table with two columns. On one side you put the text and the other has the pictures. This ensures that the pictures do not move (Figure 14.7).

Whether you are providing help sheets or full documentation, once you have completed it, spell-check it and reread what you have written. Pass it over to a friend and ask them to try using it. Finally, check back against the task – has everything necessary been covered?

General

There are some general rules that you should follow that will help you in getting good marks in coursework.

Read through the whole of the task before you start and look to see if anything you are doing at the beginning is going to be used later on – this is particularly likely with regard to design and creation, test plans and the results of testing.

Figure 14.8 Creation of a help sheet

To add a new customer in Access:	
With the customer form on the screen Choose the Insert Menu and New Record	File Edit Vie... Insert Format Records Tools New Record Ctrl++ Object... Hyperlink... Ctrl+K Tab Forename Surname Rogers Address 1 123 Address 2 Dusty Bin Town Granada Postcode GR4 5NJ
This brings up a blank record	Forename Surname Address 1 Address 2 Town Postcode

When designing, read the task and mark any important pieces of data that you are going to need to include.

Look at the number of marks available – this will give you an indication of how much work is going to be required. If possible, if you are asked for five tests or to enter 10 records, do a few more just to be on the safe side.

Spell-check everything and check it through. Sometimes the spell-checker will not pick up a spelling mistake – you may have misspelt the word but accidentally used another word that has been spelt correctly! It does not take too long to re-read your work and correct the mistakes but it could cost you valuable marks if you do not.

Use the correct software – just because you happen to like a particular piece of software does not mean it is appropriate for the task. Listen to the guidance that your teacher gives you about software selection.

You must attempt all the tasks and all parts of all the tasks. If you are having problems, think about a workaround – it will not get you marks but will allow you to move on to the rest of the task. For example, if in a spreadsheet there is a formula that is difficult and you cannot do it, just type in the answer expected by hand. At least the rest of the spreadsheet will work and you can move on to the later parts of the task.

Think about the presentation of your work – cover sheets for each task with your name, candidate number, centre name and centre number are very helpful. Good organisation of the work makes it easier to find marking points.

Make sure that you do not submit your work in ring binders or plastic folders – cardboard folders are the best with your details on the front cover. Place your name, candidate number and centre on each sheet if possible.

Finally, don't panic. You have plenty of time to learn the skills and complete the work.

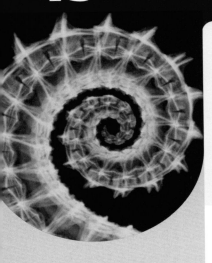

Objectives

Your objectives for this chapter are to:

◎ understand how to learn the material

◎ be familiar with the examination papers

◎ know how to cope with examination questions.

Keep these objectives in mind as you work through the chapter.

The examination papers

There are three modules making up the AS award. The grade you are awarded depends on your mark for the structured tasks and your two examination results being combined (the technical phrase for this is aggregation). You can take your time over completing the structured tasks but you will have just one and a half hours to do yourself justice in each of the two written papers. You need to be aware that most candidates will obtain a range of grades within the three modules they take. (Note: you stop being a student and change into a candidate when you enter for the examination.) The examination board (OCR) state this clearly in the syllabus:

'In practice, most candidates will show uneven profiles across the attainments listed, with strengths in some areas compensating in the award process for weaknesses or omissions elsewhere.'

So do not worry if you obtain a lower grade in one or two modules. The essential point to bear in mind is that the examiners looking at your paper will have a set of acceptable answers, called 'marking points', and you need to provide sufficient evidence in your answers to be awarded the allocated marks from these. You need to focus on hitting the requisite number of marking points in each of your answers.

General points

Here are some general points for you to bear in mind in examinations:

Handwriting

Make it neat. If the examiner cannot read your handwriting you are likely to lose marks. Only use black or blue ink. Other colours cause confusion and some are difficult to read.

Essay questions

Answers must be in continuous prose. Do not use bullet points. You will limit your marks if you do.

Doodling

This gives a bad impression. If you have time to spare, spend it going back over your paper to add more detail.

Crossing out your answers

Use a single line through what you want to erase (not Tippex™); do not obliterate it because you could still get some marks if it is actually correct and you have not written a new answer.

Think carefully before you cross out a large section of text – is it really wrong or are you starting to panic and not think clearly?

Marks for written content

There are 4 marks awarded for the quality of the English in your answers. These marks will be awarded for the questions requiring essay-type answers. Make sure, therefore, that you use punctuation and capital letters where necessary and that you spell the technical terms correctly, especially those that are given in the question.

The examination for 2512

This will probably be your first examination in AS level ICT. You will not have a previous grade to worry you, but it will still be a trial. The paper will look similar to some of the GCSE papers you will have taken. Do not be fooled into expecting the AS paper to be as easy.

This paper has between 10 and 15 questions for you to answer to the best of your ability. Questions use a context to help you write suitable answers. The paper covers a lot of material and some candidates do not perform very well when they take it. You need to prepare thoroughly to avoid this – using this book is a good start!

Reasons for poor performance are:

● The shock of an AS paper. You need to realise that AS is harder than GCSE, which you may have found to be easy.

● Candidates are not prepared. Too many written answers show that the candidate does not know enough about the topic in the question. You will not have this problem, will you?

● Failing to answer adequately. Some answers require a higher level of response, not just a list of points. Later we will discuss the types of questions set.

Planning revision

The break down of marks given below will help you to revise.

The following rough percentages/marks are designed to give you a general idea of the weighting of each syllabus component and the amount of revising time required:

511: 22% (19 marks)
512: 12% (10 marks)
513: 12% (10 marks)
514: 10% (9 marks)
515: 22% (19 marks)
516: 22% (19 marks)

This shows which sections have more marks and to which you should allocate more time. It is worth pointing out that about 7 marks is the difference from one grade to the next. You only need to make a couple of mistakes in two sections of questions and you could drop down a grade. So, do be careful.

Answering the questions

The question paper has lines for you to write your answers. There will be approximately two lines for each mark in a section. You may find that you can write a good answer, in your view, in half the space. If this is so, do not worry. If you need more room then use a blank page and tell the examiner where it can be found. The papers are designed to allow plenty of space for your answers but do not feel that you have to fill all the lines, as some candidates do, usually by repeating an answer they have already given.

This paper requires a lot of technical knowledge in the six areas set out in Chapters 1 to 6 of this book.

If you need to plan your answer then please do use a list of points, a diagram or any other device.

BUT do not use:

● the margin labelled 'For Examiner Use'
● (as we have said above) any colour of ink other than blue or black. This is important and worth repeating!

With up to 15 short questions you will be asked questions on very different points. Do not assume that one question leads into the next. In this module, all the questions are separate. A difficult consideration is: just how much detail do you need to go into in your answers? Do think about this and match your response to the marks allocated. A two-paragraph essay for 2 marks is not sensible, is it? If you do this sort of thing you will leave yourself short of time at the end.

When you have finished a question, look carefully through your answer while it is fresh in your mind. Ask yourself these questions:

● Does the answer make sense as you read it?
● Have you repeated an answer?
● Can you understand what you have written – is it what you meant to write?
● Have you identified an item and then described or explained it when asked to do so?
● Have you provided enough marking points for the marks available?
● Can your handwriting be read?

Now move on to the next question.

Activity

Be prepared!

a) Obtain a copy of the syllabus for the module 2512 online at www.ocr.org.uk and find ICT A/AS level. Highlight the topics that you don't understand. Ask for help. If necessary, you can use the forum at http://www.ocrict.org/forum/index.php. Note that this site is not part of OCR.

b) Look at past papers and identify which topics have appeared over the past two years; this will indicate what might be used this year. Find an essay question and plan an answer. Compare your answer with others in your group.

The examination for 2514

This module builds on your knowledge of 2512 and explores practical applications using generic software. The first thing to note is the word 'generic'. You must not use brand names in your answers because OCR does not permit these. This is to make the examinations fair for all candidates. Brand names include terms such as 'Internet Explorer' (a web browser) and 'Zip file' (a compressed file). The module has only four sections, which have been covered in detail in chapters 7 to 13.

Examiners find that some candidates do not have a detailed knowledge of the subject, so be prepared. Know which application is the most appropriate for a given task and be prepared to give reasons why.

For example, if you are asked why a word processor was used to create a report rather than a text editor:

Answer: This was because the author needed a spell checker to ensure the words were correctly spelt. A facility for enhancing the font was also essential. This made the document more readable and highlighted key words. Bullet points could also be used for clarity of layout.

The syllabus sets out in each section what you need to know. Be aware of the open and closed lists and make sure you know what type of application would be used where and why. The questions you answer must be based on these sections.

You are likely to take this paper at the end of your first year by which time you will have gained in confidence as well as knowledge and understanding. (Well, we hope you will.) You may have a result for 2512, or you may be taking 2512 and 2514 together. If you have taken 2512, you may well be concerned that this result was lower than you expected. Now is the time to ensure that you are fully prepared for this second paper, in order to gain the best result possible. This paper has only 4 to 6 questions and you need to make sure that you provide the level of detail required in your answers. If you can produce good detailed answers then you will obtain a better grade. So, there is every incentive for you to work just that bit harder.

Planning revision

The following rough percentages/marks are designed to give you a general idea of the weighting of each component and the amount of revising time required:

531: 30% (26 marks)
532: 37% (32 marks)
533: 16% (14 marks)
534: 17% (14 marks)

Answering the questions

This paper uses a scenario to help you focus your answers. An example scenario could be a chain of garages. This organisation would need to hold records, keep financial accounts, produce typeset materials, and send messages. There is therefore plenty of scope for setting questions. You must provide answers that use the context; writing about how a school secretary would use a word processor, instead of a member of the garage's administration staff, will earn no marks. Using the context gives you a better idea of what you could write; picture a person carrying out the tasks asked about in the question and the reasons why a particular item could prove beneficial to them.

Again be careful in your answers to ensure:

- you are not repeating yourself
- you have described or explained when appropriate
- that there is enough material to achieve the allocated marks
- you write clearly.

Developing an understanding of the required material

Before you can be successful in an examination you must understand the theory – or those topics set out in the syllabus. There are various ways of doing this, which we will look at now.

Making notes

Some students find it difficult, or feel it is pointless, to make notes in their lessons. Please avoid this attitude. The act of writing notes helps your brain to remember the points your teacher or the textbook is making. Try to find useful models for difficult topics. For example, use lists with points and explanations in a table. Use diagrams if they help you understand. Drawing a similar diagram in the examination may also be a useful prompt to help you answer a question.

Looking over notes

Now that you have some notes you must use them. I would suggest:

- the night after the lesson to make sure you understand them
- when friends ask you questions
- when revising.

Asking questions in lessons

This is a personal matter. Some students like to hide in a class to avoid being asked questions. Don't be shy; ask if you do not understand. In this way, you will gain confidence in providing answers. Examiners appreciate a candidate who exhibits confidence in their answers. It takes time and effort to become confident in a topic but the effort is worthwhile. However, there is also the converse problem of being over confident and going over-the-top in your answers.

Try explaining queries to friends

This is a great way of making sure you know the topics. You will have to think of different ways of answering if your friend does not understand. If you do not know the answer, then it is better to find out now rather than in the examination room.

Practice writing answers to questions and have them checked against the marking scheme

Activity

Collect a group of friends. Take your copy of the syllabus for the module 2512 and work through section 5.1.2, making sure that everyone knows what is meant by each section. For example, can you all 'describe common storage devices, indicating typical uses'?

Highlight the topics that you don't understand. Ask for help. If necessary use the forum at http://www.ocrict.org/forum/index.php Note that this site is not part of OCR.

Repeat this for each section of the syllabus under 5.1.x.

Work through 2514 in the same way when you have sat 2512.

How you react to examination papers

This is something that needs careful consideration before you, the candidate, go into the examination. Some candidates cope easily with examinations while others can't cope at all, and many fall between these extremes. The better you are prepared the more likely you are to be in the first group. Take your time in the examination room. The questions have been tested to ensure that most candidates will have sufficient time to complete all of the paper in the time allowed. Read the paper through first, and plan how you will answer each question. Do not worry that you have not been taught a particular scenario, look for the understanding required in each question, and then picture your answer. Try not to leave any questions unanswered.

You must read the question carefully and make sure that you really understand what the question is asking. You may have been told to read it twice. Recognise, from your knowledge and recall, what is being asked from the syllabus. Use your knowledge and the structure of the marks allocated to put together a set of information that you think will meet the needs of the question. This is the mental work necessary for the basis of your answer. You now have the task of setting this out clearly in words. Some candidates find this quite difficult so make sure you have plenty of practice.

One common error is to rephrase the same answer and imagine it is a second response. Examiners recognise this and will not award marks. You need to give different answers to earn more than one marking point.

Types of examination questions and how to answer them

Comparing the two papers, 2512 may use a context for a question to help you answer it, 2514 will definitely do so. 2512 will ask a number of short questions with the longer answers at the end of the paper. 2514 will bring these in at an earlier stage. You will therefore need to practise answering short and long questions and to recognise where each is required.

Looking at past papers you will see that the questions all include a keyword such as 'identify' or 'describe'. You must recognise these and respond correctly. These words determine what you are required to do to be awarded the allocated marks.

The keywords used are shown below:

State or identify

Here, you have to write a single word or phrase.

Example:

A database package holds data in fields. For example, names would be stored as text.

State **three** data types, other than text, commonly used in databases. [3]

The answer should be three from: Boolean, numeric, date, memo, object (such as a photograph or sound).

Note how the word 'three' is in bold font to make sure you are aware of how many answers are required. In this type of question you could include one extra, if you wish, to be on the safe side. Do not however include a long list. The marker will only go down three or four items and the correct ones might be at the end of your list and not be awarded marks.

Three words from this list is all that is required. Other correct answers are possible and you would gain marks for these.

Give

The candidate has to provide the examiner with more information than a single word statement.

Example:

The owner of a shop is worried about unauthorised users accessing his computer database if he goes online.

Give **two** examples of illegal actions using ICT. [2]

Your answers should include two phrases from:

- illegal use of data
- copying data
- hacking into restricted files
- intercepting credit card details.

Here you need to use a phrase. A single word such as 'hacking' – seen too frequently – will not be given marks. Make sure you provide enough detail; 'hacking into confidential data' is a much better answer and will be awarded marks.

Describe

This is moving to a higher level of difficulty. These answers offer you the chance to earn more marks, usually two but sometimes more. You need to provide an answer that matches the question asked, using the given context. Remember, a good description might earn extra marks in some questions. Take your time in thinking about these questions and preparing what you will write.

Example 1:

Spreadsheets are used for modelling situations. Describe the features of spreadsheet applications that enable them to be used just for modelling. [2]

Your answers should include a description such as, 'how variables can be changed [1] and the application automatically re-calculates values [1]'. Other features, such as formatting column widths, will not earn marks, as they do not relate specifically to modelling.

Example 2:

A word processing package is used by both an engineering manager and an office secretary. The manager uses it to produce engineering reports, the secretary for letters.

(a) Describe **two** features of the word-processing package that would be important to the manager but not necessarily to the secretary. [4]

(b) Describe **two** features of the word-processing package that would be important to the secretary but not necessarily to the manager. [4]

The answers to part (a) should include any two of:

- thesaurus
- special symbols
- technical dictionary
- page numbering
- auto-format for subheadings.

For part (b) the answers could include any two of:

- mail merge
- standard letter templates
- images.

You would be awarded marks for stating what the feature was, for example, thesaurus, and for describing what it was used for, for example, looking up synonyms of words.

There is a range of possible answers here – try to work out some more.

Explain

This type of question usually requires you to provide both advantages and disadvantages to show each aspect in the context and to provide reasons for these being valid. There are questions that ask for just one side (for example, just the advantages of a system) so be very careful as you read the questions. Your answers must be continuous prose. Using a list will only score low marks. Lists are fine for planning the structure of a short essay but are not at the same high level as prose. Do not be deceived into thinking that, because the marking schemes are listed points, that your answers must be the same.

Example 1:

The branch of a video rental shop has at least two electronic tills, including a processor and file storage, linked to a local file server in the shop. Whenever prices change or offers occur, updates are made on the local server, which then sends data to the tills. Only the manager of the shop is allowed to update the prices, not the sales assistants. Every few minutes the tills send data to the local server giving details of the sales.

Explain the advantages and disadvantages of each electronic till having its own processor and backing store. [4]

Answers should include:

Advantages:

- faster access to data
- individual record at each till in event of failure.

Disadvantages:

- more expensive hardware
- the server would not always have totally up-to-date data.

You should provide both sides of the situation. Note that you must not just state quicker, cheaper or easier. These statements must be qualified, for example: 'It is quicker to access data using an intelligent till.' You must also use different points in the advantages and disadvantages. Repeating the same point will earn no further marks. And remember, you need to use continuous prose for your answer.

Example 2:

Explain the advantages and disadvantages of wizards in applications [4].

Advantage: easier (no marks so far) for a novice user to (1) quickly produce a result (1).

Disadvantage: The end result may not be (1) exactly what the user required (1).

There are a number of other possible answers. Try to build up a list.

A similar question might be worded as:

Explain the advantages to the company of operatives using wizards to create database reports. [4]

To be more effective in these higher-level questions, first identify the item you will use and then write its description and, if required, the reason why it is appropriate.

Discuss

This is an explanation that requires you to reach a conclusion.

Example:

Many readers of newspapers have access to the Internet. This allows them to read a wide range of online newspapers and magazines. Discuss the increasing availability of online newspapers and magazines. [8]

The answers expected include a discussion of both the advantages and disadvantages. Items for discussion are:

- up-to-date news
- global news, not just national news
- less chance of bias, e.g. no state control of media
- legal considerations
- less capital tied up in printing
- variety of reading
- greater access to marketplace
- copyright of images/texts harder to police
- multimedia and other HTML features
- cannot be read as easily on the move
- effects on newsagent
- customised newspapers.

End your discussion with a **concluding** statement that gives your own view.

The list above is not exclusive – there is other information that would be accepted as part of the answer. Note the emphasis on the last point – reaching a conclusion. This can be for or against the point made in the question depending on your evidence. It would be silly to write that something is a good idea if all of the items you have identified and explained are negative ones.

Do make sure that you include a specific conclusion at the end of the answer: 'In conclusion…', 'Overall…', 'On balance…'.

Compare

Here you will need to write about two ways of dealing with a situation. You will need to identify the good and bad features of the alternatives and to describe them.

Example:

Compare the use of a spreadsheet and a database application for holding data on customers for a garage. [6]

Your answer will need to identify a feature/item and give an explanation of how each application would cope. One method you can use to help you is a writing frame as shown here:

Item/feature	Spreadsheet	Database
Searching for a customer	Can use a filter	Can use parametric queries
Sorting records	Can sort only a single column or all the columns	Can only sort all of the columns
Create a file for mail merge of selected customers	Need to ensure comparability with program being used – may need to export to CS format	Can use built-in features and mail merge from within database
Create a report on selected customers	May need to export the data to create a functional report	Can create and store reports internally
Carry out and save queries	Can carry out a query but cannot store queries	Query is a built-in feature

Figure 15.1 A writing frame

You then need to write your answer in continuous prose. Make sure it is clear that you have compared the two applications. Use words such as: 'whereas', 'and', 'but'.

Activity

Look through past papers and find questions using compare/explain as keywords. Produce writing frames to structure your answer.

Now write your answers in continuous prose. Do a number of these type of questions because they are where you can gain a number of marks.

How to practise answering questions

You really must spend time working on questions.

At the end of a topic

Here you will have the opportunity to find out what you have learned in the topic. Your teachers may well give you tests at this point.

Before school tests

It makes sense to do well in school tests. Your applications for further education are based on the outcomes of these tests. It is another opportunity to measure your knowledge and understanding under examination conditions.

According to your revision plan

You will draw up a schedule for revision! Then over this period you should answer questions to ensure you know the style to use and the subject matter.

hint Draw up a schedule for revision.

Past papers

Use them. They are the best guide to the style of question to be set. Your centre will have copies. They are not available online. Do be aware that each examination board uses the same subject material in their syllabuses but expect different marking points in the answers to their AS examinations. That is why you need specialist books like this one.

hint Use past papers as a guide.

Identify likely topics

You should have built up a table of the topics in questions over the past few years and looked for a pattern. The syllabus uses letters of the alphabet as code to identify each section.

By answering lots of questions and having them marked according to the marking scheme you will learn just how much you need to write. In a 'compare' [6] question you could write comparing four items/features rather than the three required for the 6 marks. This might give you the opportunity to have an extra attempt to be awarded marks. Do not write five or six features because you are now producing a list and only the first three at most would be considered. Using only one extra answer is good style and accepted by markers. You must ensure that it is a different answer.

In the examination

This is the end point that all your preparation has been leading up to; you really do need to be prepared. You then stand much more chance of giving answers that will be awarded marks. There are some techniques that you could use in the examination room that might help you do the best you can.

Focus on the question you are answering

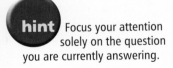

hint Focus your attention solely on the question you are currently answering.

Forget the last question and the next section. Concentrate on reading the current question and structuring the best answer you can to match the key word and the marking scheme. Some candidates go wrong in a question and this disturbs their concentration for several more questions. Try to focus and forget!

One mark per minute

If a question is worth two marks then do not spend more than two minutes writing an answer. Sometimes the essay answers from a candidate go too far and are too long. This means that later answers are rushed and marks are lost because of the time wasted.

Find a relax point

During the examination you will need to give your brain, back and eyes a brief rest. Look at the clock or at a point some distance away and just relax for 30 seconds or so. Do not look around the room as this will distract others and may cause a nuisance (it will also interrupt your thought processes). Take two different pens to the examination with different shapes to help rest your hand as you write for a sustained period.

Don't cross too much out

Be organised in what you want to erase. Use a single line and then calmly write a second answer. Sometimes markers see third attempts with previous answers crossed out with lots of ink. This is a sign that the candidate is losing control. Stay cool.

Always read carefully what you have written

Yes, read it through. Is it exactly what you need to say? The words used and their order can make a difference so take care. You need every mark.

Just a bit extra

Just add one more example in your response if it is appropriate. Just take that bit of extra time to think about your answer before you start to write. Take care reading your answer.

Last few words

Remember that examiners really would like to give you the marks, but they need to see that you can write a clear answer to the question set. Examiners are nice people, but they cannot read your mind! As you write your answers think about what the examiners will read from your response.

Finally, in the words of Douglas Adams and many teachers: 'Don't Panic'.

hint Take a break and relax for 30 seconds or so.

hint Cross out with a single line.

hint 'Don't Panic'.

Glossary

Absolute cell reference This is when the cell referenced in a spreadsheet formula remains exactly the same when the formula is copied to other cells. For example, the VAT rate could be held in a single cell and an absolute reference to this cell would be used in calculations.

Analogue signal An analogue signal consists of a continuously varying voltage.

Analogue to digital converter (ADC) This is a device that converts analogue signals into digital signals so that they can be processed by a computer.

Animation This is the creation of apparent movement through the presentation of a number of slightly different still images. Animation is often applied to text as well as images in slideshow or multimedia presentations and on web pages.

Application software Programs that allow the computer to be used to solve particular problems for the end user.

Archive/archiving An archive is the off-line, long-term storage of data that is no longer needed immediately but that should not be permanently deleted.

Arithmetic and logic unit (ALU) The part of the central processing unit of a computer that is responsible for carrying out all the arithmetic (e.g. addition) and logical, (e.g. less than) operations.

Arrange A menu in desktop publishing (DTP) and other software that allows the user to arrange objects on the page, for example by moving an object to a different layer.

Attribute (1) In database terminology, an attribute is a characteristic of an entity. For example, one of the attributes of an entity CUSTOMER would be 'surname'.

Attribute (2) The attributes of a document are the way it is constructed, such as characters, paragraphs, sections and frames.

Automatic teller machine (ATM) A computer terminal and cash dispensing machine connected via a WAN to the banking system that allows customers to withdraw cash and look at their account details without having to visit their bank.

Back-up/backing-up A back-up is a copy of current data that can be restored if the original data is lost or corrupted.

Bandwidth Bandwidth is the maximum amount of data that can travel over a given data transmission channel in a given amount of time.

Batch processing Batch processing is processing that occurs without any intervention by the user.

Bitmap graphic A graphic that is made up of a number of dots or pixels.

Booking system An online system that enables users to book and pay for tickets, for example, for travel or events.

Boolean The Boolean data type is one that can contain one of only two values, for example, Yes or No.

British Computer Society (BCS) The BCS is one of the two main professional bodies that oversee the ICT industry in the UK.

Bulletin board Part of a web site where users can post messages and read messages from other users.

Bus network topology A network where there is a single cable with the computers connected directly to it.

Button A button is an object on-screen that, when clicked with the mouse, causes something to happen, such as moving to the next slide in a presentation.

By-product of processing The by-product of processing is using the result of processing (calculation, sorting, searching, comparison, etc) for something the process was not originally intended for.

Carpel tunnel syndrome Pressure on the median nerve in the wrist that is caused by repeated wrist movements such as typing.

Cartography Drawing of maps.

CD-ROM An optical storage medium that can hold about 700Mb of data.

Cell A single addressable location on a spreadsheet that can contain a label, data or formula. The address of the cell is given by the labels of the column and row it is in, e.g. B3 is in column B and row 3.

Central processing unit (CPU) Sometimes called the brains of the computer, the CPU performs the core processing functions.

Character A character may be a letter, digit, punctuation mark or other symbol.

Check digit A check digit is calculated using a set of numbers and then added to the end of them. It is used as a validation method to detect errors in data entry and transmission.

Chipset A group of microchips that actually control the flow of information on the computer. They are the controllers for the memory, cache, hard drive, keyboard, etc. These groups of chips direct traffic along the bus and can allow devices to talk to each other without having to go through the CPU.

Clip art/Clip art gallery Libraries of pre-drawn pictures that can be copied and edited. They may be distributed with applications software, purchased on CD-ROM or downloaded from the Internet.

Code of conduct A set of principles that are drawn up by an organisation to lay down standards in a workplace.

Coding of data This is taking original data and storing it in a different representation to standardise and organise it, for example, a postcode.

Column A vertical group of cells in a spreadsheet.

Command-based user interface A user interface where the user has to type commands into the computer to carry out tasks.

Complex query A query that searches on more than one criterion using the operators AND and OR.

Compression software Software that reduces the size of a file to reduce the amount of storage space it occupies and to reduce the time it takes to transmit.

Computer Misuse Act (1990) An act that makes unauthorised access to, and modification of, computer material, i.e. hacking, illegal.

Configuration file The config file is used to personalise settings, for example having a particular set of icons on a toolbar.

Consumables Materials used in a computer system, which are used up and must be replenished. This includes paper and ink/toner cartridges.

Control unit The control unit controls the functioning of the CPU and data flow.

Copyright Designs and Patents Act (1988) An act that makes it illegal to steal or create unauthorised copies of software and to reproduce manuals, books, CD-ROMs and music.

Cross-tab query A cross-tab query calculates a sum, average, count, or other type of total for data that is grouped by two types of information – one down the left side of the datasheet and another across the top.

Custom-written software Also known as tailor-made or bespoke software, this is software that is specially written for an organisation for a specific purpose.

Data Data is the raw facts and figures before they have been processed. Data itself has no meaning.

Data dictionary A data dictionary contains details of all the entities and attributes in a system. This will include the name of each as well as the data type, format or length and any validation required.

Data handling Using a computer to process data by sorting, searching, calculating, etc.

Data Protection Act (DPA) (1998) An act designed to regulate and safeguard data held by organisations about private individuals.

Data source Where data comes from.

Data type This is the type of data that can be located such as a field in a database. Examples include integer and Boolean.

Database/Database management system (DBMS) A database is an organised collection of one or more tables containing related records. Programs that are used to create and manipulate databases are called database management systems.

Data-entry form An on-screen form that is used to enter data into a computer. The form will contain spaces where the user types the data.

Date/time A data type that holds dates or times in a variety of formats.

Deep-vein thrombosis (DVT) A condition where blood clots form, usually in the legs, due to sitting in one position for an extended period of time.

Desktop publisher (DTP) A program used for page layout that combines text and graphics to create a variety of publications.

Diary system A program that allows the user to keep an electronic diary, often with facilities to set alarms and to schedule meetings.

Digital camera A camera that stores the images taken in digital format on a memory stick, rather than on film.

Digital signal A signal that consists of only two states, on and off (0 and 1).

Digitiser A device that converts an analogue to a digital signal.

Distributed processing This is where different parts of the processing are carried out by different computers, connected together. Once completed, they are combined to achieve the specified goal.

Double entry This is a method of verification where the same data is entered twice. The data is only accepted if both versions match.

Driver A piece of software that allows a peripheral device to communicate with a computer and its operating system. It contains specific commands needed by the peripheral device.

Duplicate data Data that is repeated within database tables. It increases the storage space required and causes problems when the data is updated.

DVD An optical-storage device, similar to a CD-ROM, but that has a storage capacity of 4.7Gb or more.

Dynamic information source/data Data that is obtained from sources such as the World Wide Web that can be constantly updated.

Electronic Communications Act (2000) An act that is designed to facilitate e-commerce and recognise digital signatures as well as setting up a register of cryptography service providers.

Email The sending and receiving of messages through computer communications.

Entity In database terminology, an entity is the name given to anything you can store data about, for example CUSTOMER, SUPPLIER or ORDER.

Ergonomic design This is equipment that is designed so that people can interact with it in a healthy, comfortable and efficient way.

Expert system A computer program that is made up of a set of rules that analyse information about a specific type of problem.

Export To output a file with a different file type so that it can be opened by a different program.

Eye-typer An input device that fits on to the muscles around the eye so that a pointer on the screen can be moved by moving the eye.

Fax A means of transmitting text and graphic documents over the telephone network.

Feedback Feedback occurs when the output of a system is fed back to the input. In a central heating system, the thermostat measures the temperature of the room. If it is too cold, the heating is switched on. This raises the temperature, which is measured, and when it gets too high the heating is switched off and so on. This feedback loop allows a constant temperature to be maintained.

Field An individual line in a database record. The equivalent in the practical database of an attribute in the theoretical database.

File The most important data structure used for storing data on mass storage devices such as a hard disk.

File access/organisation This is how the data in the file is organised and, therefore, how it can be accessed.

File type Files can have many different file types depending on the type of data they contain and the software used to create them. The file type is given as a three letter extension to the file name, separated by a full stop, e.g. .doc, .bmp.

Fill A command in graphic software that allows an enclosed area to be filled with a particular colour or pattern.

Filter A tool for selecting items that meet a specific criterion in a spreadsheet or database.

First normal form (1NF) The first stage of normalising a data model. This involves ensuring that all data items are atomic (contain only a single item of data) and that there are no repeating fields.

Fixed-length record A record where the number of characters that it can contain is specified.

Flat-file database A database that consists of a single table.

Flip This is a graphic tool that transforms an object into its mirror image, either horizontally or vertically.

Floppy disk A small portable magnetic storage medium that has a storage capacity of 1.44Mb.

Footer Text that appears on a document in the bottom margin of a page.

Foot-mouse A mouse that is controlled using the foot.

Footnote A note commenting on a point in a document, printed at the bottom of the page.

Forecasting Predicting future events based on current data.

Foreign key A field in one table that is also the primary key in another and that is used to link the tables in a relational database.

Form A type of user interface where the user types in data in spaces provided on the screen – see Data-entry form.

Form control Buttons provided on a form to allow the user to move to the next record, or to the previous one, for example.

Formula A mathematical expression entered into a spreadsheet cell, whose value is automatically calculated and entered in the cell. Examples are 3*A1, D3+D4.

Frame An area of the screen that can contain text or graphics and that can be positioned and resized independently.

Function A pre-defined formula in a spreadsheet that can be entered in a cell to carry out a specific calculation. Examples are SUM(A1:E1), AVERAGE(A1:E1), MAX(A1:E1)

Generic/standard applications software Software that is provided for a range of tasks rather than one specific task, for example word processing or spreadsheet software.

Global Positioning System (GPS) A device that uses satellites to determine the exact geographical location of the device.

Grammar checker A piece of software that checks the grammar of text by comparing it with a set of rules.

Graphical user interface (GUI) A user interface that uses pictures or icons rather than text for the user to interact with the computer.

Graphics package A software package designed to manipulate images. This may be either a painting package for bitmap graphics or a drawing package for vector graphics.

Graphics tablet An input device where the user draws with a stylus on a flat surface, as if they were drawing on paper, and the drawing is reproduced on the monitor.

Group(ing) Combining objects on screen so that they can be manipulated as one.

Hard disk A large capacity magnetic storage device that is the main storage facility for software and data in a computer.

Hardware The parts of the computer that you can touch, such as monitor, keyboard and processor.

Hashing algorithm Hashing is a set of rules that allows the address of a record to be calculated from a key field so that each record can be accessed directly.

Header Text that appears on a document in the top margin of a page.

Hierarchical database A hierarchical database is one where the data is held in a tree structure.

Hotspot An area on a screen display that responds to a mouse click. This may be a piece of text or a graphic that will take the user to another page or screen.

House style This is a set of rules that must be followed for all documents sent out by an organisation so that they maintain a consistent appearance.

Hypertext A word or phrase that, when clicked on with the mouse, takes the user to another part of the document or another document altogether, such as a web page.

Image library A library of ready-to-use images such as photographs that can be copied into documents or presentations.

Import To bring in and open a file that is not in the usual file type for the software being used.

Index A separate file that contains the locations of all the records in a database file.

Indexed sequential file A file that is organised sequentially (in order) but that also has an index to certain points in the file.

Indirect source When data is used for a purpose different from that for which it was originally collected, or when the people/companies collecting the data are different from those using it.

Information The result of taking data and processing it. This involves giving the data meaning.

Input The data that is put into the system.

Integer The Integer data type contains whole numbers with NO decimal places.

Interactive A presentation, for example, that provides buttons and/or hotspots so that the user can make choices about their path through it.

Internet A network of computers that spans the whole world.

Joystick An input device that controls the position of the cursor on the screen by moving a stick.

Key field The field that uniquely identifies a record.

Keyboard An input device that consists of a set of keys for all the letters of the alphabet as well as numbers and symbols, plus keys that carry out specific functions such as delete.

Keyword search A search based on words that have been picked out as representative of the meaning of a document or web page.

Knowledge Knowledge is the use and application of information.

Layering This is where frames or objects appear in different layers in a document. The objects can be overlapped and the relative positions of the layers can be changed.

Length check This is a validation rule that checks that the number of characters entered is correct.

Levels of access Levels of access are required to ensure that information remains confidential. Access to files can be restricted to certain people and what they can do with the file can also be restricted.

Linker A linker puts together the modules that make up a program to create a single executable program.

Loader A loader takes a program from disk and places it in memory so that it can be run.

Local area network (LAN) A network that is within a locally defined area, that uses high-speed connections, that can have direct connections between computers, uses cables that are owned by the company and is able to share local peripherals.

Loudspeaker A device that enables music and other sounds to be output from a computer.

Machine cycle The four steps carried out by the CPU for each machine language instruction: fetch – decode – execute – store.

Macro A set of stored commands that can be replayed by pressing a combination of keys or by clicking a button.

Magnetic storage media Data is written and read with an electromagnet.

Mail merge Combining information from a spreadsheet or database with a standard document to allow the user to create and send a personalised version of the same document to many different people or organisations (recipients).

Manual check Manual comparison of data on paper with the entry typed into the computer.

Master document/slide The features that will appear on every page of a document or every slide can be set up on the master document/slide. This can include background and text colours, positions of frames and the font styles and sizes.

Memory stick A solid state device with a storage capacity in excess of 1Gb, available in a variety of formats.

Menu A list of options from which the user can select.

Merge field The fields in a database or spreadsheet that will be used in a mail merged document. The fieldnames are used as placeholders in the document.

Microphone A device to allow sound such as voice or music to be input into a computer.

Mode of navigation The method of moving around a presentation, such as hotspots, buttons and hypertext.

Modelling Creating a computer model of a real-world situation so that variables can be changed to answer 'what if?' questions.

Monitor A device that takes signals from a computer and displays them on screen.

Motherboard The main printed circuit board in a computer that carries the system buses. It is equipped with sockets to which all processors, memory modules, plug-in cards, daughterboards, or peripheral devices are connected.

Mouse A pointing device that can be used to select items. It has buttons on top to make selections and a sensor underneath to allow the pointer to move on screen.

Multimedia A presentation that includes different types of media including text, graphics, sound and video.

Multimedia publishing package A software package that is specifically designed to create multimedia presentations.

Multimedia training system A training package that uses the elements of multimedia to provide instruction.

Multi-tasking operating system An operating system that involves the processor carrying out several tasks at the same time, or appearing to do so.

Multi-user operating system This system allows more than one user to access it at the same time.

Natural language interface This interface allows the user to use their own language to communicate with the computer.

Negative This is a facility in graphics software that coverts a picture to its negative, so white areas become black and black areas become white, like the negative that is produced when a film is developed.

Normalisation This is the process of refining a data model.

Numeric keypad A set of keys, either at one end of a normal keyboard or separate, that consist of number keys and operators such as +, –, / and *.

Optical Character Recognition (OCR) OCR software converts the characters in an image into text for use with word processing programs.

Off-the-shelf software package A software package for a specific purpose that can be bought in a shop, for example a route finder package.

Optical Mark Reader (OMR) A hardware device that can read marks made on paper. This is used for multiple choice tests and national lottery tickets.

Online banking A system that allows customers to access their bank account and carry out transactions using the Internet.

Operating system The software that is responsible for allocating system resources such as memory, processor time and disk space.

Optical storage media Storage where data is written and read using a laser.

Orientation This can be portrait or landscape. Portrait has the shorter edge of the paper at the top; landscape has the longer edge at the top.

Original source Data that has been collected by the person using it and used for the original intended purpose.

Output The results of processing data.

Overhead projector transparency (OHT) A sheet of acetate that has information written or printed on it that can be projected onto a screen using an overhead projector.

Packets A basic unit of data transmitted across a network, that is, a collection of data bits that travels as a single unit.

Page format The way that a page in a document is set out. This will include the size of margins, the positioning of page numbers, etc.

Paragraph A sentence or related sentences between two blank lines in a document.

Parameter query A query where the user can select or enter the item to be searched for.

Password A security device consisting of a set of letters and numbers known only to the user (or should be) that when used with a user ID allows the user to access a computer system.

Patch Code released to update or repair software.

Plotter An output device that transfers a drawing from the computer onto paper by moving a set of pens.

Port A connector on a computer for the attachment of a peripheral device such as a printer or keyboard.

Presence check A validation check that checks whether a required data item has been entered.

Presentation A set of slides that can be presented to an audience on a large monitor or projected onto a screen.

Presentation software Software designed to create slide presentations.

Primary key A field that makes each record uniquely identifiable.

Printer Printers produce hard-copy output (output on paper).

Probabilities The likelihood of events occurring.

Processing Processing is performing some action on data. This might be sorting, searching, saving or editing.

Professional body A formal group that is set up to oversee a particular area of industry.

Programming language Software that can be used to create tailor-made software.

Protocol A set of rules that allows communication between computers.

Puff-suck switch An input device that allows the user to control the computer by blowing through a tube.

Random-access file A file where an individual record can be accessed directly.

Random-access memory (RAM) The working memory of a computer.

Range check A validation rule that checks whether the data input is between the values set.

Real This data type contains numbers that will have decimals.

Real-time operating system An operating system that has been developed for real-time applications.

Record A row in a database table that contains all the data about one individual or object that the record describes.

Referential integrity This ensures that it is not possible to enter a reference in a database to a link that does not exist.

Regulation of Investigatory Powers Act (2000) An act that relates to the monitoring of communications (telephone calls, emails, post, etc.).

Relation(ship) The links between tables in a relational database.

Relational database A database that consists of a number of related tables.

Relative cell reference This is when the cell referenced in a spreadsheet formula changes when the formula is copied to other cells. The cell referenced is relative to the cell that contains the formula.

Repetitive strain injury (RSI) Chronic pain experienced in the arms, shoulders or back due to repetitive actions.

Ring network topology A network where the computers are connected together to form a circle or ring.

Rotate A tool in graphics software that allows an image to be turned through a selected angle about a point.

Route finder An off-the-shelf software package that allows the user to enter the starting point and destination of a road journey. The program then provides a detailed route based on chosen parameters.

Row A horizontal group of cells in a spreadsheet.

Rules A set of procedures that must be followed.

Scanner An input device that converts information on paper into a form the computer can use.

Search engine A remotely accessible program that lets the user do keyword searches for information on the Internet.

Searching The process of looking for information that matches certain criteria.

Second normal form (2NF) The second stage of normalising a data model. This involves removing any redundant data.

Secondary memory A means of storing large amounts of data outside the computer's primary memory, for example on a hard disk.

Section A section is a portion of a document in which page-formatting options can be set.

Self-documenting systems A system where all the necessary documentation is included within the system.

Self-paced teaching systems A system that allows a learner to interact with it and learn at their own pace.

Semantics The meaning of the sentence. The words and relationship of the words within the sentence give a meaning.

Sensor A device that responds to a physical property, such as temperature, by producing an electrical signal that can be processed.

Sequential file/access A serial file that is sorted.

Serial file/access Records are stored one after another with no regard to the order.

Shade A tool in graphics software that allows the application of shading to an object.

Sharpen A tool in graphics software that can provide greater definition to an image.

Simple query A query based on a single criterion.

Single-user operating system An operating system that allows only one person to use it at one time.

Slide transition How presentation software moves from slide to slide.

Slideshow software Software designed to create slideshow presentations.

Soften A tool in graphics software that reduces the definition of an image.

Software The programming code that makes a computer work.

Sorting Putting data into a pre-defined order, such as alphabetical or numerical.

Spell checker Software that checks the spelling of words by comparing them with a stored dictionary.

Spreadsheet An application consisting of a table of rows and columns. Cells can contain labels, data or formulae that enable automatic calculations to be carried out.

Star network topology A network where each computer has its own connection to a central point, usually a hub or switch.

Static information source/data Information that is provided in a form that cannot be easily changed, for example on CD-ROM.

Stock control An application that allows the tracking of goods in stock.

Storage Devices that are used to hold data and programs, such as a hard disk.

Style sheet Style sheets are used to set out the layout of documents. They can also be referred to as master documents.

Supervisor mode A level of access that enables monitoring and management of a system.

Supplementary user documentation Documentation other than user documentation that is provided with hardware or software, for example, warranty, licence, product key.

Syntax/syntactic The rules of the sentence. Each sentence or item of information has rules to follow – the rules make up the syntax.

Table A table is a collection of related records in a database.

Tape drive A magnetic storage device that stores data on a tape rather than a disk.

TCP/IP A protocol that allows computers to communicate both on the Internet and on LANs.

Teleconferencing This is where there is real-time interaction between people without video, for example chat rooms.

Teleworking This is where employees work from home and communicate with their company by computer.

Template A template is a standard document with pre-set layouts and formats.

Test data A set of data that is devised to test all aspects of a system. This will include normal, extreme and abnormal or erroneous data.

Test plan A numbered list of all the tests that will be carried out on a system together with the data to be used and the expected results.

Testing The process of checking that a system works as intended by carrying out the test plan.

Text/string A data type that can hold any alphanumeric character – this includes numbers, text and symbols.

Thesaurus A program that offers alternative words with a similar meaning.

Thesis (singular)/Theses (plural) A thorough presentation of an original point of view based on academic research, often as part of work for a degree.

Third normal form (3NF) The third stage of normalising a data model. This involves ensuring that every attribute of an entity that is not part of the primary key, is wholly dependent on that key.

Topology A description of how the physical devices in a network are connected together.

Touch screen A screen that allows the user to select items on the screen by actually touching them.

Trackerball A pointing device with the ball on the top, which the user moves to control the position of the pointer on screen.

Translation software/translator A program that translates source code written in a high-level language to a language that the computer can understand – the object code.

Type check A validation rule that checks that the data entered is of the correct type.

Ulnar neuritis Compression of the ulnar nerve in the elbow caused by leaning on the elbow for prolonged periods of time.

User documentation Documentation that explains how to use a piece of hardware or software.

User ID A unique identifier for a user that identifies who the user is to the system.

User interface The method by which a user communicates with the computer.

User mode Levels of access that allow different users to use the system as opposed to monitoring or managing it.

Utilities Small programs that assist with the maintenance and monitoring of a computer system and its use.

Validation This is a check carried out by the computer when data is entered to stop data that does not conform to pre-set rules being entered.

Variable A variable is a name associated with a particular memory location used to store data. Variables are used because they allow data to be stored, retrieved and manipulated without knowing in advance what that data will be.

Variable-length record A record where the length is automatically adjusted to fit the data being entered.

Vector graphic A graphic that is represented by objects or geometric shapes that can be moved around the screen and positioned.

Verification The process of ensuring that data entered into a computer matches the original paper version.

Video conferencing Conducting a meeting with people who are geographically remote through the use of video/sound equipment.

Web authoring software Software that provides tools to enable the creation of web pages without the need for detailed knowledge of a web programming language.

'What if?' The use of spreadsheets and modelling enables the user to change specific values, so that results are recalculated, to answer questions that start 'What if…?'

Wide area network (WAN) A network where the computers are geographically remote and are connected by equipment that is owned by a third party.

Wizard A wizard is a facility that assists the user in the production of a document. It offers a series of screens into which the information is inserted. When the wizard is closed the user is presented with the completed document containing the information in the pre-set format.

Word field Word fields can be used to add additional information to a mail merge document or to select specified recipients of the document. An example is ASK.

Word processor A generic application package that allows the entry, editing and formatting of text to create a range of documents.

Word wrap The facility within a word processor to automatically move a word onto the next line when it will not fit on the current line.

Workbook A set of linked worksheets in a spreadsheet package.

Worksheet A single sheet of rows and columns in a spreadsheet package.

World Wide Web The standards that allow the publishing of multimedia documents that can be read by anyone with access to the Internet.

Index

Index by Dawn Butcher